ELIAS CANETTI AND SOCIAL THEORY

Also Available from Bloomsbury

Contemporary Philosophy and Social Science: An Interdisciplinary Dialogue,
ed. Michiru Nagatsu and Attilia Ruzzene
The Primacy of Resistance: Power, Opposition and Becoming, Marco Checchi
The Ethics of Resistance: Tyranny of the Absolute, Drew M. Dalton

ELIAS CANETTI AND SOCIAL THEORY

The Bond of Creation

Andrea Mubi Brighenti

BLOOMSBURY ACADEMIC
LONDON • NEW YORK • OXFORD • NEW DELHI • SYDNEY

BLOOMSBURY ACADEMIC
Bloomsbury Publishing Plc
50 Bedford Square, London, WC1B 3DP, UK
1385 Broadway, New York, NY 10018, USA
29 Earlsfort Terrace, Dublin 2, Ireland

BLOOMSBURY, BLOOMSBURY ACADEMIC and the Diana logo are
trademarks of Bloomsbury Publishing Plc

First published in Great Britain 2023
This paperback edition published 2024

Series design by Charlotte Daniels
Cover image: Fig. 104. – Curves for equal breadth dn of the bands of flow.
U.S.A., 1905, Nov. 28, 8 a.m. Dynamic Meteorology and Hydrography (1910),
author: Vilhelm Bjerknes. Issue 88 of Carnegie Institution of Washington
publication (© Carnegie Institution of Washington, 1910)

A catalogue record for this book is available from the British Library.

A catalog record for this book is available from the Library of Congress.

ISBN: HB: 978-1-3503-4441-9
          PB: 978-1-3503-4440-2
          ePDF: 978-1-3503-4442-6
          eBook: 978-1-3503-4443-3

Typeset by Integra Software Services Pvt. Ltd.

To find out more about our authors and books visit www.bloomsbury.com
and sign up for our newsletters.

Al mio cucciolo Leonardo

CONTENTS

LIST OF FIGURES

ACKNOWLEDGEMENTS

I would like to acknowledge all the Canetti scholars who, over the years, shared their valuable works with me, particularly Johann P. Arnason, Christian Borch, Andrea Borsari, William C. Donahue, Roberto Farneti, Julian Preece and Hansjacob Werlen.

I also wish to express my gratitude to the colleagues and friends who read and commented on bits and drafts of this work *in statu nascendi*, including Alessandro Castelli, Nicholas DeMaria Harney, Carlo Brentari, Peter Chambers and Andreas Oberprantacher.

INTRODUCTION

Seize the century

Elias Canetti famously declared that, with his book *Crowds and Power* – published in 1960, after nearly thirty years in the making, since 'I made no attempt to simplify, to make things easy for myself'[1] – he had sought to 'seize the 20th century by the throat'.[2] Were Canetti able to write again today – had he, for instance, a chance to complete the planned, but never written second volume of *Crowds and Power* – would he similarly reclaim for himself the task of 'seizing the twenty-first century by the throat'?

Once we look comparatively at the twentieth and twenty-first centuries in an effort to 'seize them by the throat' – a forceful expression, whose aim and method also certainly call for clarification – their differences cannot appear but in an accentuated way: the twentieth century looks like a squarely monolithic century, dominated by the rise of mass society, late colonialism, industrialism, modernism, totalitarianism, technocracy, suburbanism, liberation wars and the dominance of fossil oil economy. By contrast, what we have seen so far of the twenty-first century speaks of global uncertainty, new competitions for geopolitical dominance, awful persistence of the colonial trauma, military occupations, irregular wars and terrorism, worldwide rise of populism and autocracy in various guises, unprecedented societal and economic inequality, illegibility of high financial economy markets and an embarrassing continuation of fossil fuel burning interlocking with hard-to-predict social–natural effects – including global climate change, mass animal extinction, Polar caps melting and ocean warming, antibiotic crisis, global pandemics and a generalized threat to the biosphere. Not to say that a whole host of even more ghostly phenomena related to advances in high-technological and biotechnological sectors, such as artificial intelligence, mass surveillance and genomic manipulation, also affect our present in depth.

The configurations of power in the twenty-first century thus appear much harder to grasp and pin down theoretically in any single, definitive way. This book suggests that, somewhat paradoxically, the alleged anti-modernism of Canetti makes him more *contemporary* than many contemporary social–political thinkers. Canetti stands out as a theorist who dared to stare straight into the eyes of the monster: he dared to face the disaster of his age, always with an attitude of resistance, and from a position of 'exteriority' (naturally, the term 'exteriority' will require a clarification). It is in this sense, this book suggests, that Canetti can be of help to meet the new epistemological and ethical–political requirements of our age. More pointedly, this book seeks to prove that Canetti's most fecund legacy can be retrieved in the context of a global renewal of social theory for the twenty-first century. Rather than a book *on* Canetti (which would be fatally doomed to reiterate the already-aired conclusions about an alleged 'lack of system and rigor' in the studied author), this book proposes a series of explorations *inspired by* a Canettian sensitivity.[3] What is proposed here is thus not so much a monograph on an author as much as, hopefully, the continuation of a gesture. Certainly, in a way, the book contains and presents a Canettian lexicon; however, it is not the one the broader public most often associates with his name. As will be shown below, rather than at crowds-and-power binomial, it is at more analytic phenomena such as commands, increase, resistance and commonality that the present book invites to turn attention to.

Even few scant biographic facts confirm the singularity of Canetti's position in the intellectual panorama of the twentieth century.[4] Born in 1905 in Ruse/Rousse/ Rustchuk/Rustschuk, then a small village in Bulgaria along the Danube, into a Sephardic community, raised multilingual in Germany, England, Switzerland and Austria, Canetti was a truly European intellectual – as well as, at the same time, a stern critic of European and, more widely, modern culture. He practised many types of writing, including the novel (*Die Blendung*, translated as *Auto-da-Fe* but perhaps better rendered as *The Blinding*), the satirical theatre piece (*Wedding, Comedy of Vanity, The Numbered*), the literary essay and literary criticism (collected in *The Conscience of Words*), the travelogue (*The Voices from Marrakesh*), the character sketch (*Earwitness*), the aphorism notebook (a long series of *Aufzeichnungen*, jottings or annotations), the autobiography (a monumental three-volume memoir, comprising *The Tongue Set Free, The Torch in the Ear* and *The Play of the Eyes*, largely consisting of youth recollections from the cultural atmosphere of pre-Anschluss Vienna, until about his literary debut at the end of 1935, and his mother's death in 1937) – not to mention more experimental writing such as the libretto for a *Monkey-Opera*. Canetti, it seems, could not stick to one genre, but was constantly pushed to explore new ones. As diverse as his choice of genres were his stylistic choices, ranging from the plain and calm clarity of the autobiographical account, to the expressionist linguistic outburst of the novel, and the thundering brevity of the aphorism. For his literary work, Canetti was awarded the Nobel Prize for Literature in 1981, preceded and followed by a number of other prestigious literary distinctions, including the Georg Büchner Prize, the Nelly Sachs Prize and the Franz Kafka Prize.

Certainly, Canetti was not what could be described as a nice personality. To the contrary, as a young man he exhibited a notoriously ambitious, short-tempered, intractable character.[5] Iris Murdoch, for instance, adapted him into the manipulative and cruel character Misha in her novel significantly titled *The Flight from the Enchanter*; and he seems to have inspired several more, rarely fine, novelistic characters. In the Hampstead artistic community, he was dubbed a 'guru,' or even a 'God-monster'.[6] As not uncommon among writers, Canetti had a strong persona, with egoist, self-centred, even obsessive traits, that in part derived from the relation to his mother as it impacted upon his attitude towards his wife and his several lovers.[7] It has recently been pointed out that, rather than a detached, ascetic scholar of power, Canetti was also someone practically interested in it.[8] However, over the years – and obviously, to the extent that his literary success was more firmly established – he became increasingly milder, more sober, perhaps more humane, more 'sentimental' vis-à-vis people and things, as well as more alone, and more open about his own weaknesses. Such change is perhaps anticipated in the passage from Kraus to Sonne as a reference point for humanness in the second and third volume of his autobiography. His Zurich period, from the mid-1970s, where he enjoyed a peaceful life with his second wife Hera, and when he became a father at 67, has been described as retreated, even secluded.[9] Following a kind of contradictory dual track, we see Canetti's latest production turn, on the one hand, more personal than ever – as in the 'English years' memoir, where his need to have an audience to enchant emerges in at times awkward ways[10] – yet on the other, increasingly spiritual and even impersonal,[11] possibly universal – devoted, in any case, to asserting the 'rapidity of the spirit' against the disasters of the century.

The importance of Canetti for the social and political sciences pivots mainly around *Crowds and Power* (1960), which has been called both 'an eccentric book' (Sontag 1981: 199) and 'an unsettling masterpiece' (Rutigliano 2007: 15).[12] *Crowds and Power* is the closest thing to an anthropology book Canetti ever wrote. Yet its approach is distinctive, in that the book appears to nourish itself mostly with ethnographic sources, and very little with the great anthropological theory of that time – such as Durkheim, Van Gennep, Lévi-Strauss, or the early Gregory Bateson and Margaret Mead. His only close personal acquaintance among social anthropologists seems to have been Franz Baermann Steiner, who had studied with Malinowski, Radcliffe-Brown and Evans-Pritchard.[13] Steiner and Canetti shared a passion for myths and folktales, but unfortunately Steiner died prematurely.[14] More significantly, *Crowds and Power* appeared just a few years before a new generation of anthropologists born in the 1920s – including scholars like Clifford Geertz, Victor Turner, Eric Wolf, Mary Douglas, Fredrik Barth and others – imprinted a strong innovation to mid-twentieth-century anthropology, applying symbolic, structuralist or Marxist lenses to their ethnographic materials. It has been noticed that the narrative developed by Canetti rhymes with an evolutionist perspective which structural anthropology had already effectively criticized before Canetti published his book (Robertson 2000). Just as the new generation of influential scholars largely ignored *Crowds and Power*, or perhaps even secretly despised it as the work of an amateur, there is little evidence that Canetti, on his turn, ever followed the works of the new leading voices in anthropology, even while planning (somehow reluctantly, as we know) a sequel volume of *Crowds and Power* to expand on the study of human metamorphosis.[15]

There is no doubt that *Crowds and Power* embodies Canetti's attempt to 'seize the century', as a passage from the autobiography, recalling the experience of participating in the workers' demonstration in Vienna that led to the burning of the Palace of Justice, details:

> During that brightly illuminated, dreadful day [15 July 1927], I gained the true picture of what, as a crowd, fills our century. I gained it so profoundly that I kept going back to contemplate it anew, both compulsively and willingly. I returned over and over and watched; and even today, I sense how hard it is for me to tear myself away, since I have managed to achieve only the tiniest portion of my goal: to understand what a crowd is.
>
> (*Mem* 490)

While Canetti was in touch with prominent intellectuals and authors of his time, such as Karl Kraus, Robert Musil, Hermann Broch, Theodor Adorno, Thomas Bernhard and many others, he remained an outsider to the academic world and never held any formal appointment or position. It is then not surprising that, despite a small number of committed supporters, *Crowds and Power* – which, as said above, Canetti himself regarded as his more accomplished contribution and his most intense long-term project ('my life's work') – was not received enthusiastically. Its anti-systematic attitude and its idiosyncratic use of sources and references made it unpalatable to academics. Perhaps, anthropologists regarded it more as the work of a literary author than a social scientist; maybe, political scientists could have placed it in the shelf of the realist tradition in the study of power, but at the time, the shelf was already squarely occupied by Hans Morgenthau (who was about the same age as Canetti, but was coming from Ashkenazi family, and had emigrated to the United States, rather than the UK). On their turn, sociologists could not cast their eyes on anything that was not thoroughly 'modern,' so that a lot of the materials covered by Canetti was a no-go zone to them – despite the fact that, admittedly, the study of crowds had been central to the definition of modern mass society, and so to speak, the very cradle of sociology.

As remarked by Johann Arnason (1996: 98), 'Canetti's interpretation of the crowd is set out in apparent isolation from the broader context of social theory, but its implications cannot be fully appreciated without reference to other perspectives.' Since the 1990s, Arnason pioneered an attempt to 'resituate' Canetti, recovering his work as a neglected sociological classic (Arnason and Roberts 2004). The attempt has been shared by a number of other social theorists – such as, in particular, John McClelland (1989), David Darby (2000), Michael Mack (2001), Robert Elbaz (2003), Enzo Rutigliano (2007), Christian Borch (2012) and Andrea Borsari (2018) – interestingly, again, scholars not belonging in any single tradition or school of thought. These authors have recognized that, in his relentless exploration, Canetti does provide inspiring insight into varied social phenomena such as grouping ('packs'), command, leadership, insanity, delusion, violence and resistance – and above all, if one may say so, the utterly unpredictable folly, the imaginativeness and stubbornness of human behaviour. If Canetti – as it has been observed during this revival of interest – has long been ignored by sociologists and political scientists, it was because, in the first place, he had ignored them. But even while – many years after all the scholars involved in those controversies have passed away – a more active reception of Canetti's thinking into sociology and social theory (and, to a lesser extent, political theory) has been going on for some time, an acceptance of him into the sociological canon has never been positively concluded – as his conspicuous absence in most reference and reading lists at undergraduate and graduate levels proves.[16]

The riddle of modernity

This book acknowledges that such situation is hardly surprising, but also encourages the reader to look at the positive aspect of the thing. Indeed, Canetti has remained a quintessentially provocative and stimulating *radical thinker*, who could have never been fully confined to the Procrustean bed of academic disciplines. Hence his enduring freshness, which this book hopes to celebrate. As seen above, as a nomadic intellectual *par excellence*, all his life through Canetti has remained largely deterritorialized from the institutional world of academia. Like other non-Zionist Jewish authors born a few years before him – such as Walter Benjamin (whom he admired) and Siegfried Kracauer – and like the teacher and original source of influence for that whole generation, Georg Simmel (who did not obtain any permanent position at the university until very late in his life), Canetti remained a-systematic, thoroughly transdisciplinary and ultimately largely unconstrained by scholarly 'manoeuvring.'[17]

Joussef Ishaghpour (1990) sums up Canetti's condition as that of an author 'not representative of any country, any school, any movement, nor any single genre of writing.'[18] The lack of representativeness – a mark that indeed is quite reminiscent of Simmel and Benjamin – made Canetti nearly the prototype of a 'private thinker,' as opposed to the archetype of the 'public professor.' Because of the diversity of his production – ranging, as seen, across the genres of novel, aphorism, essay, travelogue, theatre and autobiography – and because of his disregard towards the standard scientific lexicon, to try to cut down Canetti's oeuvre into disciplinary stockades is a rather sterile exercise, which defuses Canetti's insight, distorting his thought and failing to meet his most powerful challenge. Here, one is also invited to ask: Is not this very same *lack of representativeness* also the condition of social theory, i.e., an act of theorizing without a discipline that guarantees it?[19] And if so, is there not here a profound elective affinity between the writer (as *Dichter/Dichterin*) and the very conditions of knowability of social life?

This book submits that *Crowds and Power* is not, as it may appear at first sight, a psychology of crowds and how they helped German National Socialism, nor is it simply a treatise on the uniqueness of certain remote primitive societies and their legends. Rather, its design and ambition echoes some classics in anthropology of the generation preceding Canetti – most notably, Durkheim's *Elementary Forms* (1912). Fifty years before Canetti, the great Durkheim had studied from afar the totemic rituals of the Australian aboriginal peoples and, by doing so, had sought to advance, out of such materials, nothing short of *a general theory of society*. Canetti had a similarly ambitious scope in mind, but refrained from the attempt to build his vision into a cogent system as the Alsatian's. So, not only did he arrive too late to belong in the generation of the classics of anthropology, but his style of inquiry explicitly rejected the disciplinarization of knowledge that was anyway already well established by the time of his writing. He preferred to travel widely – wildly, at times – across the territories of anthropology, ethnology, psychology, psychopathology, philosophy, history, mythology and literature, interweaving facts from a variety of sources to build and support an original conceptual and imaginational scaffold. As a result, Canetti's ultimate goal goes in the opposite direction vis-à-vis Durkheim's, whose central objective resided in the institution and the institutionalization of a discipline endowed with a strict canonical methodology. This also provides the justification for the non-philological endeavour developed in this book, which, admittedly, the specialists of Canetti might not favour. The proposal here is to regard Canetti as a fundamentally 'incomplete' author, an open author who does not possess – and does not wish to possess – a complete system of thought. By their very nature, authors like these inherently authorize, if not encourage, more heterodox interpretations of their work: and the point lies precisely with finding which alternative test of interpretation one can substitute to that of 'fidelity'.[20]

Another crucial background cultural motif in Canetti, which this book invites the reader to reconsider, is a criticism of Freud – a controversial yet fashionable author in the Vienna of Canetti's youth. Later in life, Canetti admitted to have been 'deeply impressed' by Freud and preferred to direct his revulsion towards the *vulgate* of psychoanalysis; yet earlier on, in the 1920s, Freud stood to him as the last endorser of the tradition in crowd psychology originating from Tarde, Sighele and Le Bon, imported into Germany in the early years of the twentieth century (see Borch 2012). Canetti's main argument posits the crowd as a primary, independent phenomenon, countering the belief of crowd psychologists that crowds are always created by their leaders to serve their purposes. For Freud, however, the phenomenon of the 'group mind' is not grounded in some mysterious force of imitation or suggestion evoked in individuals by charismatic leaders; rather, it is made of investments of libido – ultimately, the desire to love and be loved, and the concurrent projection of desire through the psychic mechanism of 'identification.' Psychoanalytically, the leader is but the primeval father figure, against which the Oedipal ambivalence of sentiments is directed. Consequently, crowds appear to the originator of psychoanalysis ultimately as but one manifestation of the unconscious (Moscovici 1985) – with the understated clause that the unconscious can only be individual. Here, it becomes clear that what Canetti essentially rejects, even before the leader–followers hypothesis, is the individual-based vision of social reality that underpins the Freudian worldview. His, in other words, is not simply a rejection of the postulate of methodological individualism – for, after all, Durkheimian sociology had already offered an alternative to methodological individualism. More radically, it is a rejection of the modern (and, especially in the 1920s and 1930s, 'modernising') gaze onto the world.

If there was someone who, long before Bruno Latour (1991), believed that 'we have never been modern,' it was certainly Canetti. As remarked by Arnason, Canetti thought that modernity's cult of its own exceptionality and its presumption of superiority are largely unjustified. If modernity is a 'paradigm,' one must recognize, with René Thom, that 'paradigms always live above their means.'[21] Such attitude, it must be remarked, is very different from the anti-modernism of traditionalist and conservative thinkers. Shortly before Canetti, the subtle art of developing a displaced perspective on the present – one that interrogates it as a fossil, a ruin and a hieroglyph – was exercised by a Walter Benjamin, who was thirteen years his senior. Although the two never met, Benjamin can be regarded as a kindred spirit, in whose life the pivotal forces of the European century met and clashed, and who was able to introduce a sort of subversive *décalage* in the historical order so as to assert the power of an 'origin' – a 'truth,' as he named it – which was neither beginning nor evolution. For his part, Canetti writes in his aphorisms that truth is something that cannot be possessed, but is rather akin to a storm that washes lies away, and vanishes by this same stroke.[22] Such an affinity between Benjamin and Canetti, even in the absence of any direct contact between the two – yet certainly mediated by the strong impression that the figure of Karl Kraus had on both of them – will be probed and tested throughout this book.

Only deterritorialized authors can seek to produce a 'take from the outside' on their epoch. Perhaps, psychoanalysis initially produced a similar shock; but Canetti came of age at a moment when Freud's creature had been demoted into triviality: the 'Freudian slip' and the 'Oedipal complex' had already become jokes to spice up middle-class small chat. It is important to remark how Canetti's rejection of Freud does not lead him to embrace Jung. If Freud prescribed strict individual limits to the unconscious – so that each individual must, so to speak, carry its own cross – with the lure of the 'collective unconscious' Jungian psychology became suspiciously close to endorsing the existence of the 'racial Geist.' Jung's initial fascination with Nazism, and even more troubling, his subsequent quiescent silence about it, cast a long shadow over the possible uses and misuses of his 'Aryan psychology.' Sometimes, Canetti himself has been criticized for his alleged anti-historicity, his anti-modernism, his fixation on death and his dark vision of humankind.[23] But, this book suggests, in rejecting the modernizing vision, Canetti does not fall back into any temptation of irrationalism – as instantiated, for instance, by Jung's long-standing flirtation with occultism. Canetti knows well that the real issue lies not in positing the collective unconscious (only a necessary first step), but in asking the subsequent question: the unconscious of *which* collective? How is it that humans can *become* a collective at all?

Perhaps nowhere is the difference between Canetti and modern social theorists more visible than in the 1962 radio broadcasted exchange with Theodor Adorno. The crown prince of the Frankfurt school, Adorno was also on a crusade to chastise modernity by all means necessary. His line of attack was distinctly from within, seeking to prove that, ultimately, rationality is the worst enemy of itself, possessing as it does an intrinsic tendency to become totalitarian. Insofar as the requirements of rationality subject life to a stern domination (for sociologists, the Weberian 'cage'), as well as an ultimate, inescapable myth (the myth of the Enlightenment), rationality itself proves to be submitted to a 'negative dialectics.' Canetti, by contrast, wants to criticize modernity *from without*: understandably, this is a difficult position that runs the risk of stumbling into a series of paradoxes (How can someone living in the middle of modernity claim to have access to the non-modern experience? Is one not reinstating the myth of nature and the good savage?). For sure, whereas Adorno speaks the critical language of history and ideology, Canetti answers in a language that seems to reach out from a different epoch, if not a different planet.[24]

Adorno scorns archaism, sensing in it the danger of psychosocial regression – a regression that had already favoured the Nazi dictatorship. For orthodox Frankfurt scholars, all possible curative discourse must be historical – consequently, no room for confusions should be allowed between the primitive and the modern. Ultimately, this position turns into the well-known dichotomy between peoples *with* versus *without* history. During the radio exchange, Adorno, dubbing himself a 'pedantic epistemologist', stresses how crucial it is to distinguish reality from representation, so that for instance the 'invisible crowds' described in *Crowds and Power* can only belong to the sphere of representation, never to that of reality – to which Canetti politely concedes, but only to go suggesting that these invisible crowds were always very *effective* in the life of human groups and that, after all, even the moderns believe in the existence of 'crowds' of invisible bacilli – not to say that we are terrorized by the prospect of a catastrophic next pandemic of an invisible, invincible virus.

Canetti thus inevitably seems to open the door to animism, that illicit knowledge of the primitives – or perhaps, even worse, the barbarians. Adorno is worried by the risk of irrationality, and his allusions to controversial vitalist figures of the early twentieth century, such as the mystical and neo-pagan Ludwig Klages and the magical-Kabbalistic Oskar Goldberg, confirm this. It's as if he's prodding Canetti: You don't want to be in that company, do you? Yet, Canetti, insouciant about epistemological correctness (to echo the expression 'political-correctness'; and again, those who lack such skills are bound to appear 'barbarians'), perseveres with what we might call his 'adventures in the invisible', highlighting how it is precisely the 'archaic' element in crowds that makes them so compelling a phenomenon. The predicament in similar intellectual encounters is obvious: for modernist social theorists, even of critical bent, myths cannot but embody falsifying ideologies of sort, while for Canetti they convey some of the deepest insights into the human experience. So, what's in a myth?

Interestingly, it is precisely from the field of anthropology that, today, a vindication of Canetti may start seeing the light of the day. After functionalist, structuralist, systemic, symbolic, reflexive and postmodernist anthropologies, new threads in anthropological theory have led to programmes such as the 'ontological turn', associated with the names of Eduardo Viveiros de Castro, Martin Holbraad, Morten Axel Petersen, Philippe Descola and others. While the 'turn' terminology may sound trite (and has, of course, sparked heated debates inside anthropology itself), what is at stake, in extreme synthesis, is the attempt to re-establish some significant connections between philosophy and anthropology, in a way that necessarily differs from the twentieth-century tradition of philosophical anthropology (Scheler, Plessner, Gehlen). The distinction between the natural and the social, as well as the distinction between matter and imagination, the new 'ontological' anthropologists argue, should not be assumed a priori, but should be regarded as *the outcome* of a series of plural ways of 'world-making.' Accordingly, what becomes 'perspectival' is not simply culture, but world-making and, a fortiori, the world itself. Of course, looking for something deeper than culture can be tricky, insofar as ontology could itself be said to be a type of cultural production; but more interestingly, there is here a realization that the relations between humans and non-humans (i.e., all that is 'out there in the world' and is not 'us') can be arranged in a wide variety of modes. The ways in which 'personhood' manifests itself are related to such transfers, licit or illicit, across the line that simultaneously separates and connects the region of humans (i.e., humanity) to the rest of the world. From this perspective, Canetti can be said to be the last twentieth-century author in the tradition of philosophical anthropology and simultaneously the first in the twenty-first-century rethinking of social ontology.

Regardless of whether one decides to look at Canetti as a lone forerunner of the contemporary ontological preoccupations in anthropology or not, it is easily understandable why the social theorists who have approached him may have been disappointed by the predominance of the power-death trope in his portrayal of human nature – incidentally, a view that was certainly not rare among German-speaking authors in the 1920s and 1930s. Arguably, this is also why the social–scientific literature on Canetti seems equally arranged into two rather neatly delineated camps: those who thoroughly reject him (including, for instance, Axel Honneth – on the basis of some grave misunderstandings, as it will be argued) and those who just summarize him. The 'summarizers' may be sympathetic, but rarely can they be called discussants in a proper sense, since their texts are, by and large, simple recapitulations of Canetti's own claims, without any open commitment as to whether those claims are shareable or not, and at which ontological or epistemological level. Doubtlessly, Canetti's anthropology remains disputable: it fascinates and, at the same time, also repels – not thoroughly unlike the seducer-egomaniac Canettian persona in the literary circles: always controversial, never boring. His vision speaks of something inconvenient, which strikes a chord of truth, but which one deems too one-sided and exasperated (a bit like Kien, the obsessional and reclusive protagonist of *The Blinding*) to constitute the whole story. However, as I hope to show in what follows, *Crowds and Power* cannot be adequately understood without taking into account that it is *both* a study *and* a critique of the monodimensionality and obsessiveness of power. It represents, in Canetti's own words, an attempt 'to find the weak spot of power.' Ultimately, *Crowds and Power* issues an invitation to recognize and explore the endless richness – and even wildness – of metamorphosis.[25]

This move is, arguably, consistent with Canetti's stigmatization of 'the avoidance of the concrete' as one of the most sinister phenomena in intellectual history. So, while our author has been criticized for not having developed a complete theory, in fact, he was the first to claim that he had always deliberately remained on the verge of 'the conceptual', refraining from entering its terrain.[26] The imaginational and the visionary registers are deliberately opposed to the theoretical as a specific way of knowing: indeed, the concept (*Begriff*, connected to *begreifen*, 'to grasp') is a way of approaching reality that is already imbued with power. Not only does Canetti's stance embrace the positive significance of mythical thinking, it also requires that one should never sacrifice reality to the construction of a beautiful system of thought.[27] It has been observed that his argumentation proceeds through 'a polyphony of observations and accounts', 'devoid of the prolixity that so often beleaguers scientific treatises' (Werlen 2000: 180). This is why – if he'd ever even tried – he would have probably not found anything of his taste in the grand theorizing that dominated mid-twentieth-century structural sociology (*à la* Parsons, to mention one). The visual – and more amply, the sensorial, the embodied – is what interested Canetti the most. At some point, Deleuze suggests that Nietzsche is neither a perceptual philosopher (one for whom knowledge is based on the senses alone) nor a conceptual one (for whom knowledge is only rational), but rather an *affective* philosopher: even in the domain of thought, Nietzsche proceeds mainly through affects (recall, to mention one, his astute use of the image of the medical hammer as a tool for philosophizing). For how much Canetti disliked Nietzsche, there is a clear affinity here – for just like Nietzsche, Canetti, too, is definitely a thinker-through-affects.[28]

By his own admission, Canetti always wrote as a dramatist.[29] It is particularly important to keep in mind this when one turns to examine his theoretical production. The whole of his scholarly endeavour seems to be underpinned not only by an empiricist sensitivity, but also by a visionary stance, where reality always appears to some extent as *enactment*. An implicit invitation issued by *Crowds and Power* is thus to perform a 'reality test' of social theory – where reality appears to be consistently conceived of as effectiveness, or forcefulness [*Wirklichkeit*]. In this sense, one current debate in contemporary moral and political theory might also intersect Canetti's earlier elaborations. Indeed, moral and political theory seems in the process of turning away from the formal theories of justice *à la* Rawls, along with canonical, procedural definitions of democracy, realizing that the social life of abstract notions such as justice and fairness can only be appreciated in that constellation of practically immediate, cogent situations where practices and perceptions of injustice, feelings of shame, envy, hate, rage and so on are at play. Martha Nussbaum has, for instance, attended to the significance of *disgust*, repugnance and fear, while Axel Honneth has explored *disrespect* as a crucial pathology of recognition. For his part, Peter Sloterdijk has insisted on the political significance of *rage* for mass mobilization (in a way inspired by Canetti). More recently, Michael Goodhart has laid out a view of injustice as a 'deforming force' in social relations. Such a focus on the series of what, with Spinoza, we might call the 'sad passions' – those abating the *agendi potentia* – clearly signifies the desire of a number of contemporary theorists to get down from the philosophical heavens (and havens) of systematic, deductive theory.

Yet, Canetti's plea for the concrete should not even be mistaken for a simple 'humanistic cry' of sort – although certainly there are interesting similarities between him and Albert Camus, beginning with an attitude which, with Camus, could be called 'radicalism of the middle'. Canetti powerfully pointed to the existence of a hybrid ontology of social life, constantly cross-cutting the line between the human and the non-human. Working within a horizon of concreteness-as-immanence, he squarely placed the human being in the midst of an animate planet, where the number of forces active in social life cannot be predetermined in abstraction. The discussion with Adorno evoked above, concerning the 'invisible crowds', offers a small illustration; more generally, one could say that, long before Latour's social–theoretical challenge to spot the 'missing masses' of associative phenomena, Canetti had stressed the deep continuity of social life as something that cuts across the discontinuity between the living and the non-living, the animate and the inert, the subjective and the objective. Humans, animals and things do not form distinct domains of existence; rather, they are taken in a common becoming, via a series of intersections and mutual possessions – even when these end up producing visionary delusions. Perhaps, in this sense, the very notions of rhizome and assemblage elaborated by Deleuze and Guattari in the 1970s may be proven to have a Canettian inspiration to them. We return to these issues more extensively in Chapter 4.

Towards a Canetti-inspired epistemology

It has been observed that a negative anthropology is quite visible especially in Canetti's theatrical and narrative production, crowded as it is with unilateral and obsessional human characters without any possibility of redemption. Most commentators so far have focused on reviewing in depth Canetti's anthropological and political ground assumptions and their challenging, endless questions such as 'Are humans always necessarily imprisoned-empoisoned by power?' In this book, we prefer to venture into the exercise of furthering a number of Canettian suggestions (or 'gestures') as relevant for their 'epistemological' entailments. If one accepts to explore the Canettian challenge at the epistemological level, rather than at the anthropological or ontological one, one must still invent ways not to fall prey of 'pedantic' epistemologies à la Adorno. That is why, rather than resituating Canetti vis-à-vis current social theory, this book invites the reader to undertake the experiment of resituating social theory vis-à-vis the epistemological challenges suggested by the Canettian gaze. Although, clearly, it is not thoroughly possible to sever epistemology from the substantive anthropological and political ideas it produces, there is, this book suggests, a way to leave substantial hypotheses relatively in brackets and expand on the lessons that can be drawn from Canetti's *œuvre* in the study of the properly social domain of existence. In this sense, the following pages invite the reader to shift the question, from the classic, yet hopelessly unanswerable interrogation about human nature, towards a more scattered, diversified, but also significantly more precise detection of how social life actually works in practice – better, how it can be seen working once a basic lexicon to detect it has been defined and refined.

Here, we begin to notice that the anthropological, the political and the social domains may not always be aligned: certainly, humans have a social life, but they are not alone in having it, given that many animals have extremely sophisticated social interactions, patterns and even *cultures* (the same species of bird, we have learnt, sings differently in different regions). Not only that, but two additional advances are needed: first, social life is itself an inter-species phenomenon, whereby animals from different species are joint into a single dynamic (a 'bloc of becoming,' in Deleuze's parlance). Such 'species,' also, are not necessarily defined by the criteria of biology. A number of alternative epistemologies enter the stage at this juncture – consider, for instance, children, social outcasts, foreigners, sexual minorities as instantiating such 'species.' What has been called 'pseudospeciation' is the rule, rather than the exception, in social life: luckily, however, this fact does not necessarily lead to its frightening logical end point, namely the dehumanization of the other as irreconcilable enemy – and yet, almost as assuredly, differences are always problematic to handle. Second, not only species but also *objects* and, yes, *spirits* too (aggregated as 'non-human' entities) are integral part of social life: they are present, not as sheer representations or beliefs, but as veritable actors, forces and even more importantly, persons or 'subjects.' Images, in a way, – even those fleeting simulacra in the flood of digital images – are an eminent instance of such spirits who stay by us. Indeed, what are images, if not spirits and visions that, in their ghostly existence, constantly accompany and mediate social life? Are not images – along with viruses and CO_2 – the invisible crowds of the new century?

One of the main reasons why such approach may prove fruitful is that social life itself is precisely an imaginary-imageal production. The new scenario is, as one appreciates, itself rather crowded. In the next chapters, the reader will be progressively made familiar with the epistemological shifts Canetti has initiated and which can be continued today in pursuit of a theoretical renewal of the social science. These preliminary remarks, however, already bring us to the contents and structure of the present book. Its four chapters pivot each around one key term that, deriving from Canetti, can be helpful to enhance our knowledge of the present. As anticipated, the choice of the topics to tackle differs from the usual focus of Canetti's scholars on the crowds–power duet. Not that the duet is unimportant, but the approach offered here privileges a type of 'slant' examination of social phenomena spanning a variety of domains that include economy, politics, culture, religion, art and ecology. Commands, for instance, discussed in the first chapter, have a tortuous relation with politics and the law: chains of command are usually observed in structured organizations, such as the army – not by chance does the model of the army served Max Weber to describe the political State, just as it served Freud to describe the crowd. But in light of Canetti, the model of command familiar to social scientists, including linguists and philosophers of language, turns out to be too logocentric to be realistic. Similarly, increase, examined in the second chapter, looks like an economic notion, yet with fundamental connections to ecology, politics and even religion. The types of phenomena of resistance described in Chapter 3 have certainly a political import, but they are likewise deeply connected to art and the creative act. Finally, commonality, as elaborated in Chapter 4, is the one notion that most amply speaks of *the century* – and, a fortiori, of our possibility of bringing our 'monstrous' present to a *redde rationem*.

To begin with, Chapter 1 carries out a reconnaissance into how contemporary social, political and legal theory has neglected, discarded or misunderstood the logic of commands. It explores some features of commands that remain largely undertheorized in the scholarly literature, just as they are invisible – either camouflaged or denied – in social action. The return of strongmen and power politics, the rise of new authoritarian political models and the heightening of social tensions (for instance, with increasing physical confrontations between demonstrating citizens and the police forces across the world) reveal the urgency of studying commands today. Since the beginning, it will become apparent how Canetti allows us to unsettle the relationship we give for granted between commands, power and the law. Is a command an instantiation, or an exception, to the rule of law? Is it its product, or its foundational element? What sort of psychological item is a command – a proposition, an imperative, a 'suggestion'? From a Canetti-inspired perspective, commands cannot be reduced to linguistic entities, but must be considered in the more complex frame of a direct connection between subjects and objects as they become 'coupled' within a shared environment. Commands unfold in a space that is located ambiguously between the realm of the subjective and that of the objective, between passions and institutions. From a Canettian perspective, commands would not exist without memory, a memory which is the raw material of all morality (as suggested earlier by Nietzsche). It is in this sense that thinking through commands may enable researchers to reveal new aspects of both the 'hidden face' of power and the visible 'force of law'.

The second chapter tackles the notion of increase in its many contemporary usages. 'The myth of increase' is an expression employed by Canetti to describe an ancestral drive towards the formation of crowds. Since humans have existed, they have wanted to be *more* and they have pictured themselves as becoming-more. Before Canetti, in the late nineteenth-century Gabriel Tarde had argued that the 'natural tendency' of, for instance, economic curves is the upward direction, since the 'normal tendency' of the 'social thing' is always towards expansion. As well attested, economic growth has defined a central credo of the twentieth century. In the present time of economic turmoil and structural crisis, we are drawn back to analyse the basic myth of increase and its underlying assumptions. Is growth inevitable? Can humanity exist without growth? And, even more troubling, can it continue to exist *with* growth? The chapter elaborates on the contemporary faces of the old myth of increase and inspects what is at stake in each of them.

What stands against the forces of command and increase? It should not be forgotten that Canetti is, through and through, a writer of resistance. Resistance plays a unique role in social collectives, although our current imagination of it appears insufficient and inadequate. Too often, resistance is simply understood as a practice that stands *against change*. Consequently, the main characteristics ascribed to it are identified as refusal and rejection. Even when it is acknowledged that change can be imposed – so that resistance is actually resistance against imposition – the implicit premise remains that resistance pivots around an inertia *vis-à-vis* some active force that besieges its subjects from the outside. This way, resistance tends to be framed as a practice essentially based on negation, or as the negative term in a dialectic of power. By contrast, Canetti opens up a wholly different conception of resistance, which reveals its crucial links to transformation, creation and change. The inspiration for a new conception of resistance as transformation arises here, whereby the notion can be recast as an encompassing category of human life embodied in a plurality of social forms and locales. On this point, a comparison between Canetti and Foucault can be enlightening, especially given the apparent contrast between Foucault's theorization of modern power as 'positive power' and 'biopower' vis-à-vis Canetti's apparently archaic grounding of power in death and survival.

The final chapter moves towards an even broader notion that proves necessary in order to craft an alternative to the 'demonic' forces of command and increase. For Canetti, the crowd embodies the quintessential experience of human commonality. But, in a world that is increasingly mediated and remote-operated such as ours, in a world of global frictions and salvage capitalism, of unrestrained surveillance and spectacle, of wars and stay-home sanitary emergencies, which are the new ways of experiencing commonality? Is the tide of crowds rising again – and if so, which are the new crowds of the present, and how to recognize them? For instance, could digital data be regarded as crowds in a data-driven and increasingly algorhythmically underpinned society? Which are, more generally, the new forms of 'interiority' more likely to define, in the long run, the present century? Canetti recognized in crowds and packs those peculiar social manifolds capable of grounding the experience of commonality; now, casting a novel light upon these formations may help us to advance towards a better understanding of the possibilities and the promises – but also the costs and the threats – of a world-in-common.

At this point, it would be tempting to regard the first two chapters (commands and increase) as the *pars destruens* of the argument, vis-à-vis the second two (resistance and commonality) as its *pars construens*. But such a dualistic, Manichean view must itself be challenged. A more subtle interpretation of 'seizing the century' is indeed called forth. Commands, increase, resistance and commonality, this book suggests, share a deep 'homeopathic' and 'pharmacological' structure, and exhibit a number of 'cathectic' dynamics. Put simply, 'pharmacology' is the science of the interactions between qualities (a certain type of drug) quantities (its posology): typically, the same drug can have widely varying effects at different doses and in different situations. This is also where the place of homeopathy opens up: in homeopathy, the cure is of the same nature as the illness; and the chance to turn the illness into its own cure requires finding the right quantity, the right rhythm and the right approach – the right 'composition' – in the structure of one's intake of the pharmakon.[30]

For its part, the 'cathectic' designates all those uncanny, yet perhaps not so rare, situations where polar opposites seem to match, or even go great together. The sense we may give to the term *cathectic* here must be clearly distinguished from the way it is employed in psychoanalysis, where it has been somehow confusingly used to render Freud's term for the charges of libido [*Besetzung*]. In Christian theology, the *katéchon* is the messianic 'retainer', keeper or entertainer – one may also say, a 'restrainer' – that impedes the arrival of the last time, that is of Apocalypse. Simultaneously, the very presence of the retainer somehow inoculates the last time into historical temporality.[31] It is perhaps possible to say that, through the notion of *katéchon*, the Early Christians negotiated their relation to the pagan Roman Empire and paved the way towards an institutionalized Church within the Empire – what eventually became the Christendom.[32] Naturally, an inescapable double bind links the *katéchon* to the Antichrist: for the very act of restraining 'the lawless one' entails, on the part of the Church as institutionalized secular power, an act of encircling and containing him, of being interwoven with him. This is a struggle where the two fighters grapple with each other so firmly and tightly that they cannot be torn apart. A temporality emerges that should be called 'chronic', rather than chronological – a tensional, unresolved temporality fraught with schisms and recurrences. In this sense, the pharmacological and cathectic perspectives explain why Canetti could claim to be struggling against power even while, in his literary and theatrical production, mercilessly putting on stage a grotesquely deformed humanity, one-dimensionally flattened upon a specific obsession – survival – that uniquely shrinks the horizon of life and the possibilities of coexistence.

In conclusion, this book submits that sensitivity towards cathectic formations in social life may offer an important twist to the old Cusan trope of *coincidentia oppositorum*. In the cathectic configuration, the opposites cannot be said to coincide; rather, the space between them becomes *singular* – it becomes *critical*. The cathectic thus signals the coming about of singularities of thought that cannot be brought back into any system, into any theodicy. In Canetti, the cathectic structure recurs *passim*, perhaps most notably in his conceptualization of the couple of power and transformation. As noted above, the theorization of the latter element remains incomplete, just as another unfinished aphorism book project, the posthumously published *Book Against Death*. Interestingly, such project was also referred by Canetti himself as the *Book of the Dead*. Here is a perfect illustration of cathectic composition: in the semantic space between the two alternative titles ('against death'/'of the dead') lies the complexity of the question. Partly an anthropological exploration of how humans have dealt with their dead, partly an existential grasping of our frightening connection to mortality, partly visionary snapshots into other possible worlds where death, dying and the dead are treated in what appear as bizarre ways, Canetti's *Tod-Buch* endeavour ultimately aims at the production of a type of *vital truth* that is not simply a crusade against death, as sometimes portrayed (following a description the author himself at some point indulged to), but could be rather described as a pharmacological entertainment with the enemy, a cathectic exercise of the present – on the verge of modernity, but on the outer, uncanny side of it.

And ultimately, is not the same claim by Canetti to have *seized the century by the throat* conveying a similar pharmacological–cathectic insight? As seen above,

Canetti rejects the theoretical domain as too forceful – for concepts seek to *seize* reality – but then reclaims for himself the most forceful act of apprehension, namely *seizing* the century. This perhaps suggests that neither power nor the conceptual may *per se* be always inimical forces – what counts, rather, is the possibility of bringing power to a *redde rationem*, while preserving enlivening lines of resistance that point towards an outside of power, along with the capacity to flank concepts with the transformative potential of images. Acquaintance with pharmacological and cathectic phenomena, I suggest, could help fostering a more subtle art of quantities, and new ways of reasoning about power in society – perhaps, ultimately, a promising approach towards developing a more vital understanding of our century.

Chapter 1

COMMAND

Figure 1 Commands have stings.

Command and death

On 10 July 2015, Sandra Bland, a 28-year-old African American woman, was stopped in her car in the city of Prairie View, Texas, by then-State-Trooper Brian Encinia. The sequence that led to her arrest, starting from the pretextual traffic stop, has been recorded by the agent's body camera and has since become widely known.[1] Three days later, Sandra Bland was found hanged in a jail cell in Waller County, Texas. She had committed suicide. Encinia would later be discharged from the law enforcement for improper arrest. Tragic as this incident was, it has been obscured by the many more, and much more barbaric, killings of African Americans by the police (or even former police agents) in the United States that have followed. Yet Sandra Bland's story must still be regarded as a frightening illustration of what a command can do. The video of her arrest is a shocking view, not perhaps so much for the explicit violence it displays, but for the painful sensation of the ugly reality it reveals, an ugly reality all of us instinctively recognize, despite the fact that it also proves so difficult to name it (least, control it). Once we have gathered the courage needed to *watch* the video once again, we are forcefully put face to face with the tough reality of command – the horror of issuing them, and the hardship and humiliation of enduring, or resisting, them. One is stunned, in particular, by how commands can rapidly escalate in a ramping up of intensity: the orders imparted by the policeman sound repetitive and standardized, but an increasing amount of energy is poured into them, visibly putting not only the victim, but the perpetrator himself, under a terrible strain. The verbal 'order' reveals itself as a weapon that is no less lethal than the taser handled by the officer – so that, ultimately, all those imparted commands should be regarded as having played an essential role in Ms Bland's death.

The arrest of Sandra Bland is, literally, a mortifying sequence. One can't escape the feeling of something deadly looming over the whole situation. The scene generates a mix of hard-to-tame feelings in the viewer: indignation, anger, rage, fear, terror, frustration, pain and sadness. Certainly, the episode cannot be adequately understood without knowledge of the larger historical context in which it is inserted, beginning with the history of slavery, racism, race relations and the 'exceptional' place of African Americans in the United States. All these factors have been extensively analysed by the historical and sociological literature (Wilson 1987; Holt 2011; Rawls and Duck 2020). What remains out of focus, however, is a specific engagement with the interactional format of command as a peculiar mode of social existence. A healthy and energetic person, Sandra Bland was killed by some form of 'order' as if pierced by a poisoned arrow. How could such a fatal outcome occur? Command is a crucial type of interaction that has been left largely unattended by social theory. This chapter ventures into some features of commands that, being under-theorized and under-reported, have also tended to remain invisible in social reality. It is suggested that Canetti's work allows us to rethink the relationship between commands, power, law, bodies and technology in a perhaps less comforting, but more realistic way.

Commands appear tautological, self-referential, non-argumentative, to begin with. There is not much to say about them. Canetti himself remarks that the first impression of commands is that of a perfectly transparent, self-evident reality. Commands look flat, uninteresting from a cognitive point of view. In fact, these social objects may prove to be more opaque than usually assumed.[2] In general, as this book seeks to show, the Canettian gaze is always interested in retrieving the bodily and spatial foundations of power. No matter how disembodied, ubiquitous and 'hi-tech' power appears under modern conditions – if one inspects it closely, one is always able to unearth the concrete, immanent set up, which, *by prolongation,* gives rise to the more abstract configurations one is first presented with. That is why, as detailed below, from a Canetti-inspired perspective, commands cannot be subsumed under simply logical, linguistic or legal entities; rather, they must be considered in the material frame of a direct connection between subjects, bodies and artefacts operating jointly within a shared environment, and subject to shared affects. In this respect, the puzzling temporality of commands also needs to be attended more in depth, as we seek to do in what follows. In sum, commands take place in a time–space that is located ambiguously between the realm of the subjective and that of the objective, between passions and institutions. In each command, all these elements are finally joint 'in the flesh' as well as in an uncanny type of 'memory.'

This chapter submits that re-examining commands may let us attain a novel gaze into the force of law and the hidden face of power – as well as, more amply, the forces of imagination and the capacities to organize and cooperate with others. What exactly is a command? Where does its effectiveness descend from? Which special resources are needed to exercise command and, correspondingly, which are needed to obey, or disobey? What are the consequences of commands for individual psychology, social interaction and social life more generally? The hypothesis entertained in this chapter is that at stake here are not only the social structures classically examined by sociology: once the frontiers of contemporary social life are considered also as a technological accomplishment, the whole scenario appears as one where humans are increasingly surrounded by and imbricated with advanced technical artefacts that prolong command. For instance, one could say that digital algorithmic applications represent a current prolongation of classic commands: indeed, as detailed below, algorithms are inherently imperative-operation structures capable of performing a command chain across heterogeneous materials. In this sense, a reconsideration of the limits of commands across the threshold between the human and the non-human is called forth. Perhaps, we can speak of a special 'command-machine' composed of heterogeneous fragments pieced together by a singular arrangement or – to have it with Deleuze – brought together into a single 'bloc of becoming.' An attempt at clarifying the nature of such a 'bloc' is the leading motif in this chapter.

The invisibility of commands

Some of the most prominent social theorists of the second half of the twentieth century seem to have shifted their theoretical attention away from the blatant situation of command towards the more subtle ways in which social power is invisibly, fluidly and imperceptibly exercised. If we look, for instance, at Michel Foucault, Pierre Bourdieu or Niklas Luhmann, we notice that, despite the obvious differences between their theories, their work is largely devoted to uncover the hidden logic of structures infused in social life and functioning seamlessly throughout the social body. So, the metaphor of 'capillarity' in Foucault (1982) is meant to capture, through an almost physical–physiological image, the way in which power circulates as a mode of relation between humans. Similarly, Bourdieu's (1997) notion of 'symbolic violence' refers to an imperceptible form of power slowly accumulated inside the subjects through education and culture, leading to the formation of a 'primary habitus' guiding actors in their routines. In Luhmann (1990), one may consider the forms of 'distinction', 'differentiation' and 'codification' each social operation and each societal system is defined by, whereby a system can only work according to its own distinctions in virtue of its aspects of closure, self-determination and self-organization. For Luhmann, no two social systems can ever 'see' the same thing, and no single system can ever 'see' its own environment; complementarily, different systems can couple with each other thanks to unobtrusive coordination and mutual in-transparency. All of this makes the occurrence of eruptive and disruptive events, such as commands, logically impossible.

Another major thread of social theory in the past three decades has focused on what has been called the process of 'reflexive modernisation' (Beck, Bonss and Lau 2003). This has been described as a situation where traditional social institutions – including those guaranteeing the direct execution of orders – are put 'in flux', due to an 'erosion of several ascriptive patterns of collective life' (*ibid.*: 6). On this account, during the 1990s contemporary Western society has been increasingly characterized as 'post-traditional' (Giddens 1991), that is, supposedly capable of freeing the individual from the coercive practices and the unwanted affiliations of tradition. A 'liquid modernity' (Bauman 2000) has thus been evoked, which would place more responsibility upon individuals for their achievements, but also endow them with greater possibilities of avoiding those direct and personal contacts perceived as oppressive and intolerable. More recently, in the same vein, neoliberalism itself has been defined as a form of governance 'without command' (Supiot 2015), on the basis of the idea, outlined by the late Foucault (and already foreshadowed by Gramsci), that individuals in pursuit of 'performance' self-regulate without the need of being told what to do, allowing for a new form of social control through 'freedom' (Lianos 2001).

In all these theorizations, the experience of command – namely, the experience of giving and receiving overt and personal imperative orders – comes to play an increasingly marginal role, if one at all. One reason for this might be that, in the Western countries during the post–Second World War era, the experience of command has tended to become 'sectorised', in other words, restricted and confined within specific sectors of social life – for instance, within formalized organizations, such as the army and the police, or in rigidly hierarchical workplaces, especially those where 'low-skilled jobs' are found. Together with sectorization, the crucial assumption has taken hold that commands must be *structurally predisposed* – which means, I know from whom I can receive a command, and, above all, I know the limits beyond which I can refuse to obey: 'I know my rights'.[3] Mechanisms of structural predisposition are assumed to guarantee the social circumscription of commands, constraining them within specific purpose-oriented contexts and formats, and subjecting them to well-defined statutory limits. Such a process of structural predisposition is made possible essentially by institutionalization: as soon as social interaction becomes institutionalized, patterns of expectations, rules, obligations, logics, statutes, rights and a whole institutional logic, come to be established (Douglas 1986). Commands then reappear only at a second stage, to somehow re-actualize the already-prepared, dense network of epistemic and normative patterns which institutions have produced.

This point can be clarified by looking at the role assigned to commands in legal theory. In the early nineteenth century, the English jurist John Austin (1995[1832]) – close to the utilitarian philosophers – outlined what became known as the 'command theory of law.' This theory defines positive law as a specific type of command emanating from a 'political superior' and addressed to a 'political inferior.' Austin interpreted commands as an expression of a subjective 'desire,' accompanied by the menace of a negative sanction (what he termed 'an evil') in case the command is rejected. By doing so, he set a very pragmatic test to determine whether or not a command is issued: 'If you cannot or will not harm me, in case I comply not with your wish, the expression of your wish is not a command, although you utter your wish in imperative phrase' (*ibid.*: 21). Austin also distinguished between 'occasional or particular commands,' whose scope only spanned specific occasions, and general ones, i.e., commands establishing a regular rule of conduct – with only the latter to be counted as law proper.[4] Incidentally, this distinction is widely regarded as the weakest part of his analysis, given that the criterion of generality turns out to be a continuum rather difficult to break off and specify in concrete occurrences.

As Austin's definition came under increasing critique during the twentieth century, it may be interesting to notice how another type of command-like notion continued to haunt early-twentieth-century legal theory: such is the notion of exception. Whereas the Kantian jurisprudential dream culminated in the 'pure doctrine' [*Reine Rechtslehre*] of the Austrian Hans Kelsen (1934), where the legal system is completely self-referential and sealed off from any external influence, therefore admitting no exception whatsoever (in a way that anticipates very much Luhmann's analysis of social systems), a deeply contrasting view of the legal system was offered by the German jurist Carl Schmitt (1927). As known, Schmitt saw legal sovereignty as dependent upon a 'decision' capable of suspending the system in place. By suspending, or bracketing, the normal course of the legal arrangements, the sovereign decision, 'freed of all normative ties,' in effect installs a 'state of exception.' The point, for us, is not so much to reconstruct the logical paradoxes that ensue from founding the whole legal system upon a singularity that is not part of it,[5] but rather to unpack what, in the first place, constituted a decision for Schmitt. This is not easy to do because Schmitt himself never provided any clear definition. While decision clearly does not equate with command, the similarities between them are likewise not the result of mere chance. Indeed, decision and command seem to share a special temporality capable of disrupting the regular flow of legal interaction. Both command and decision suspend the 'normal' flow of time and unleash a 'chronic' temporal experience.[6] Also, both command and decision seem to embody some form of individual or singular will. In Schmitt, in particular, it is decision that enables law and the polity to find an ultimate unity: decision is the 'personal' production of a subject who is uncompromisingly 'sovereign.' As reconstructed by Schmitt, the decisionist tradition spanning from Hobbes to Donoso Cortés harbours such a dream of political unity, an anti-liberal dream at core, where the bourgeois order of modernity is regarded as an endless and fruitless public debate, incapable of ever rising to the unifying level of decision. As Schmitt effectively summarized, 'dictatorship is the opposite of discussion.' However, after having been one of his latest and purest supporters, Schmitt abandoned a purely decisionist theory, complementing it with an 'institutionalist' perspective.[7] In his infamous 1933 essay celebrating the Nazi Party, Schmitt claimed that the new political–legal unity of the state would be founded upon the trinity State–Movement–People [*Staat-Bewegung-Volk*], thus effectively fusing the power of the norm (the State), with the power of decision (the Movement-Party) and the power of social institutions and mores (the People, as described, for instance, from the perspective of a legal anthropology).

Such a doomed 'Schmittian outcome,' which transformed Schmitt himself from the conservative-Catholic critic of the Weimar constitution into the chief legal theorist [*Kronjurist*] of the Third Reich since 1933, appears less 'exceptional' if one remembers that, in the previous generation, Max Weber, the father of German sociology, incurred into a distinct but not entirely unrelated lapse towards the end of his life. Despite his acute awareness of the dangers of caesarism and demagogic leadership (which he had critically diagnosed in the different cases of Napoleon I, Napoleon III, Bismarck and the Bolsheviks), Weber had his own decisionist moment when invited, in December 1918, to serve as an advisor in the commission for the drafting of the Weimar constitution (adopted August 1919). In a historical context of civic unrest and political tensions, Weber publicly campaigned for a strong presidential plebiscitary system, where the Reich President would be directly elected by the people, rather than nominated by the Parliament, and would dispose of strong powers – thus effectively siding with an inherently authoritarian legal architecture.[8] The ultimate criterion of legitimacy, Weber made clear in his sociology, cannot rest but in consensual submission. The problem is, of course, that consent can be manipulated in multiple ways – by propaganda and ideology, as it would become clear soon after Weber, as well as by the deliberate production of misinformation and conspiracy-thinking, as it is common currency today – to the point of reducing the ensuing consent to farce. That consent could be but a 'fiction,' Weber himself was forced to admit: that notwithstanding, he considered that, more profoundly, Caesarism could be *legally* illegitimate (as it implies usurpation of power and manipulation of opinion), and yet still *sociologically* legitimate (as it cannot but be grounded in actual mass acclaim). In short, the German vicissitudes in the first half of the twentieth century remind us how the three notions of decision, charisma and caesarism evoke a form of command that can only with difficulty coexist with the rule of law liberally conceived.

Legal scholarship in the second half of the twentieth century is thus unsurprisingly marked by a thorough rejection of any form of 'command theory' and its avatars. Despite their difference, both positivist and naturalist theorists agreed on this stance. John Austin's model has been challenged in multiple ways, not only on the basis of H.L.A. Hart's (2012[1961]) direct criticism of it, but also in the light of other alternative legal–philosophical reflections, such as Lon L. Fuller's (1964).[9] In his celebrated analytical undertaking, *The Concept of Law* (whose composition spans the 1950s and is thus interestingly contemporary to Canetti's *Crowd and Power*), Hart claimed that the coercive aspect alone does not capture law's totality, which is to work through rules – of which he distinguished two types: primary (or imperative) and secondary (or constitutive). Hart also contested the idea that sanction (Austin's 'threat of evil') is necessary to law. Above all, he focused on who is entitled to deliver imperatives to whom. Taking the extreme example of the bank robber, Hart reasoned that, while we would accept the formulation 'the gunman ordered the clerk to hand over the money,' we would feel uneasy about saying 'the gunman gave an order to the clerk to hand it over,' for the latter expression would seemingly attribute some legitimacy to an order that is clearly nothing else but an extortion. Having served in the army during the Second World War, Hart was particularly sensitive to the question we have referred above as the 'structural predisposition' of command. In between the lines, it is clear that, for him, a command is something that belongs to a military-like organization, where it is exercised according to a precise and well-defined hierarchy, so that 'a command is primarily an appeal not to fear but to respect for authority' (*ibid.*: 20).

While Hart is widely regarded as having razed Austin's theory of law, it would perhaps be more fair to say that he elegantly sidestepped it. Indeed, by juxtaposing the bank robbery and the army, Hart implicitly removed any reference to the criterion of 'political superiority,' which Austin had posed, although not much developed. Where Austin evoked a political problem, Hart gave an organizational answer.[10] His description of the laws as consisting of 'general directions' not addressed to anybody, and simply 'indicating' a type of conduct, which particular citizens are able to recognize and willingly apply to themselves, in fact presupposes an already very much disciplined situation, where commands are substituted, whenever needed, with neuter 'demands for compliance,' conceived of as gentle reminders of the general structural predisposition where those rules belong. For Hart, law can only exist in a 'settled' social situation, where no major political contention exists. To fully remove the spectre of command from the law, Hart contested that law can entail whatsoever form of 'address,' pushing the point so far as suggesting that even laws of which citizens are not informed about can be legally valid: nobody has been addressed, and yet a valid norm has been created (*ibid.*: 22). This vision contrasts deeply with Lon Fuller's (1964) attempt to renew the tradition of jus-naturalism. If the idea of secret laws sounds repugnant to Fuller, the reason is that, in his view, the law is an essentially motivational endeavour, which can only be based on fair play. The public aspect of law means that the latter is necessarily cast in a state of heightened visibility, whence it is actually able to address the subjects bounded by it. Fuller thus contends that what constitutes the law are the features of purposiveness and commitment, rather than those of imposition and force, of even of sheer logic: what he outlines is a morality of *aspiration* that 'starts at the top of human achievement,' rather than a morality of duty starting at the bottom (*ibid.*: 5).

Emphasis has been laid by some of the main legal theorists of the twentieth century on the fact that law symbolizes, institutionalizes and creates new logical spaces of meaning for patterned social relations, rather than directly compel people to act in certain ways. In the elaboration of radical legal pluralism, for instance, law appears essentially as a way of symbolizing social relations and visualizing reciprocal commitments which actors conceive and contract (Macdonald 2002). But, if commands have been evicted *de jure* from the theory of law, the relationship between command and legal institutions remains a much more ambiguous one. In their ideal diagrams, command and the law form two distinct sociological machines: once one tries to compare them, their differences become apparent in terms of the completely different relation they entertain with symbolism. Whereas law is deeply symbolic, commands are, by contrast, non-symbolic at bottom. In this sense, rather than being foundational of law, as Austin believed, commands with their indexical force infiltrate the law, moving and disseminating through its interstices and gaps. This realization contributes to a better understanding of how commands bypass and escape the regulations and the limitations imposed upon them by the legal structural predispositions. Using a category by Derrida (1967), one could speak of command as an uncomfortable 'supplement' vis-à-vis the law: what persistently remains when you have taken away everything that should be there. With the Canadian legal theorist Roderick Macdonald (2005), one could say that commands are part and parcel of the *tacet* of law, namely, the constitutive blind spot that cannot be spelt out, but which still informs the kernel of our more developed symbolic capacities. As Macdonald writes, 'The more precise our idea of what law should look like, the less we are able to see either the tacit within formal texts or the implicit of informal law.' It is precisely in the zone of the tacit and *the invisible* that the locale of commands manifests itself. In this sense, commands unwittingly expose what Walter Benjamin (1921) once imaginatively referred to as that 'something rotten in the law' [*etwas morsches im Recht*].

Ultimately, our point is that, because of its very institutional architecture and its scale (more on this in Chapter 2), modern society is, by and large, a society of obedience, although moments of obedience may not be immediately visible and localizable. We don't often realize, for instance, that an interaction device so ubiquitous as the password is, in fact, but a command in disguise – as, however, the French expression *mot d'ordre* makes clear. The theoretical task then turns into tackling the various shapes command and obedience assume today, attending their relative degrees of visibility and invisibility. To reiterate, the point is that there is much more to commands than the mere *logic* of commands, i.e., the logic of imperatives and obligations: while the latter is an important and well-explored field, it is far from exhausting the actual social life of commands. Making the space of commands visible to the theoretical eye may prove important, especially because tragic episodes such as Sandra Bland's death offer painful reminders that commands are not as out-of-date or as negligible as the sociological literature of the 1990s and early 2000s has suggested. Commands represent an unpleasant reality that needs to be dug into more attentively. The interest here is not simply analytical: if the thesis of a 'primordialist' Canetti merits to be considered at all, it is also (at least in part) to the extent that the present in which we live itself exhibits accentuated 'primordialist' features. The waves of illiberal populism and caesarism that have rocked the political arena in the 2010s have been accompanied by an increasing number of eulogies of command. Veritable theodicies of command have been heard that have sought to justify the new commanders and their orders as essential to social stability – even when in fact it was those commanders who were gravely disrupting social stability. In politics no less than in society, ruthless strongmen are, above all, issuers of commands, as is most visible in the case of war. In sum, while the power of commands might have been so far underestimated by sociological and legal theory, the current historical context, marked as it is by a return of forceful styles of leadership and voluntarist political stances, makes a reconsideration of commands quite timely.

What a command can do

To several modern observers, as we have seen, commands have appeared as an inconvenience, or even a scandal in the midst of civilization: indeed, it is difficult to situate them between normality ad exceptionality, between civility and barbarism, between institutionalization and disruption. Institutionalized commands, for instance, are supposed to strengthen the functioning of the institution that hosts them, although, as a matter of fact, they may turn out to thwart the official aim underpinning the institution in question. Understanding 'what a command can do' thus calls for a general review of the imagination of the social relation. It appears apposite that, from a Canettian perspective, 'getting real about commands' is both a theoretical and an ethical imperative. His approach may help us unpack a number of presuppositions, in view of reconstructing a more accurate psycho-socio-political framework where commands may 'make sense'. Overcoming the marginalization and exceptionalization of commands, we are led to recognize that the latter are not an exception to social life – to the contrary, they manifest social life in full, and in one of its distinctive *intensive* states. A command, in other words, offers an instance of basic, yet complete social experience, one where the socii are brought together in an intensive region defined by peculiar thresholds of non-metric *distance*. Neither a demonic, inexplicable force, nor a just a flat, self-evident verbal occurrence, commands offer to us no less than an illustration of society *ex vivo*: the *potentia* of social life.

The remarkable achievement of commands becomes visible as soon as we turn to consider even summarily the experience of obedience. The latter is at the centre of Stanley Milgram's (1974) experiment in early 1960s, possibly the most renowned psychology experiment ever conducted (more precisely, a series of eighteen experimental conditions). Despite the fact that generations of social psychologists have launched themselves into the most sophisticated critiques of the experimental setup, the methodology and the interpretations of the obedience experiment, the psychodrama created by Milgram lives on to this date, and has turned into a sort of modern archetype – to the testimony that his genius has actually hit an exposed nerve in our cultural experience of power in interpersonal relations.[11] Already an impressive heap by the late 1980s, when Bauman (1989) drew on the Milgram experiment in his attempt to explain the Holocaust sociologically, criticisms of Milgram have by now reached a level of detail – scrutinizing into the most minute aspects of background materials, transcripts and the informal notes at the Milgram's Yale archive – that have almost turned into a kind of sophistry. It is as if, behind the pretence of methodology and conceptualization, the experts in the field have mostly retreated from facing the looming fundamental question – feigning, so to speak, not to know what obeying means.[12] In fact, the problem raised by Milgram remains central for understanding social relationships of allegiance to command, deference to authority figures and the moral accountability for undertaken actions. Even as a *Gedankenexperiment* – which was not – the obedience protocol is daunting enough. For sure, Milgram's was a deliberately malignant design, meant to probe the dark forces of social life.[13] A specifically 'malevolent authority' – an actor playing a scientist figure with ostentatious cold-blooded, non-argumentative, absolutely non-empathic countenance – was put on stage to check at which point would a subject break free form the spell of the authority's order.

Although not in a strictly physical sense, Milgram's experimental subjects were deliberately locked inside an evil situation.[14] The expert commanding them (the 'experimenter') did not have any explicit coercive power over the participants, and was not overtly menacing them – no sanctions were ever mentioned[15] – but was vested with *just* the kind of power Milgram referred to as 'authority'. In the course of the experiment, the commands issued by the experimenter were quickly overflowing the type of legitimation – only implicitly stipulated at the beginning of the meeting – deriving from the mandate of an 'ordinary' civic morality and legality. The problem is, precisely, that we do not yet know what 'ordinary' means. This way, Milgram's experiments highlight that both the legitimacy of command and the legitimacy to command can be presupposed in their procedural correctness, whereas any demonstration of legitimacy – along with the consequent possibility of subjecting command to limitations – can be trumped by the mere factuality of actual commands occurring *ex vivo*. The course of events takes over, deferring *sine die* the demand for legitimation, to the point of making it ultimately irrelevant: the mechanism that enacts or guarantees the 'structural predisposition' and the 'social circumscription' of commands ultimately proves frailer than the social force of commands.

The take-home lesson of the Milgram experiment has been effectively framed in terms of 'how easily could one turn into a perpetrator'.[16] But, if complicity in submission is the sinister phenomenon Milgram made undeniable, in fact, the experiment proves that such transformation into a perpetrator is *not at all* easy: it does happen, but at a very high cost. Almost everyone struggles. Although elements of fiction are quite apparent to a distanced external viewer, there is little doubt that, to the experimental subject ('teacher'), the situation appeared extremely realistic: without such a realism, it would be difficult to explain the terrible emotional strain produced in the subjects. In Chapter 4, we return to consider such power of fiction in social life. Even when willing to obey, being commanded is not a pleasant experience. In addition, a specifically increasing degree of strain is introduced into the experiment by the increasing divergence between what one was asked to do and what one wanted to do, or was available to. Milgram underlines the role of the initial pledge of support which the subjects had given to the experiment: they were eager to collaborate, mostly for idealistic motives (the advancement of science), and they entered a situation lacking clearly defined boundaries – as indeed are most situations of everyday life. It was the everyday morality of civil peace they brought into the experiment that proved wanting in coping with subsequent events. At the same time, some sort of inertia kicked in, which made it easier for them to remain in place rather than discontinue the process: subjects were seated, and breaking off would have required them to stand up, becoming more physically active and confrontational. Such a simple change of posture is more difficult to enact than it seems: to bring even an unpleasant meeting to a close, is not easy. Besides, since the punishments increased slowly, it was becoming more and more difficult for the subjects to 'draw the line' where they could assert their disengagement.

In synthesis, the terrible tension experienced by Milgram's subjects must be attributed to at least two causes: (a) they were increasingly more conscious they were inflicting harm to someone; (b) they were likewise becoming more and more conscious that – whether they liked it or not – they were being commanded, and that it was hard for them to ignore, evade or contest those orders. Importantly, however, their will was never crushed. Nietzsche first pointed out in this sense that the will of the commanded is never thoroughly abolished: rather, we may say that, in the command relation, two different wills are casted in a *status of enhanced visibility* by the fact of their coming together. Command and obedience thus appear dynamic, tensional relations. Nietzsche (1885: 342) pondered:

> To what extent resistance is present even in obedience; individual power is by no means surrendered. In the same way, there is in commanding an admission that the absolute power of the opponent has not been vanquished, incorporated, disintegrated. 'Obedience' and 'commanding' are forms of struggle.[17]

Naturally, the sociological problem lies in clarifying which sort of struggle we are presented with here. One might want to consider which were, for instance, the factors that could have led to some easing of the tensional state. Milgram did provide some windows to that effect – as usual, quite tricky ones: against the recalcitrance of the naïve subject, the authority figure then asserts that he is assuming 'full responsibility' for what is going on. In other words: Could an increase in submission ease the tension of being commanded? The question, for the subject, translates into a moral–practical one: 'Can I fully, if temporarily, abdicate myself and the responsibility for my own actions?' As recalled above, *per* Weber, 'legitimacy' is ultimately nothing but the acceptance to be commanded. If so, the more I consent, the more the authority becomes legitimate, even as it commands reprehensible acts. Milgram's experiments in this sense dramatically illustrate the Austinian problem of 'political superiority', which twentieth-century legal theorists had made virtually invisible. Here, however, the command–machine does not unfold between just two elements, but between three: Milgram's interest lies in exploring the social structure 'X orders Y to harm Z'. In the triadic structure, a whole composition of forces and resistances comes into play[18] – for, on the other side of the wall, the victim ('learner') is *also* issuing 'orders', by demanding to be freed. Potentially, the victim, too, can turn into a 'legitimate authority', forming an 'incipient group' with the subject – if one were just available to listen, and take part. The experimental subject is thus here not simply in a tension between the authority figure ('experimenter') and his own moral consciousness, *but also* in a tension between two commands from two sources, demanding opposite performances.

In order to advance a minimally satisfactory social–theoretical inquiry into commands, Milgram's outcomes must be reconstructed from scratch. In particular, we cannot assume that people are just used to obey, or that they have stronger or weaker character, making them easy preys or stubborn resisters. We also need to retrieve the origins of those dispositions and attitudes, and how they are then poured into action. This is what Canetti – whose work Milgram seems to have been unaware of – had sought to do just a few years before Milgram.

Deadly encounters, thorny issues

Above, we have remarked the flat, tautological appearance of commands. Such a seeming 'meaninglessness' of commands may in part explain why most authors in social, legal and political theory have either ignored them, or focused their attention to them in narrowly selective ways. In general, interpreters seem to have focused on either *the context* in which commands occur (social structures, institutions), or, alternatively, *the state of things* brought about by them (social order), rather than on the peculiar and specific experience entailed by them. Psychologists have, for their part, come closer to the crux of the matter, although, as will be elaborated in what follows, their interpretation likewise needs to be expanded to attain a full-blown social theory of commands. In the immanentist perspective developed by Canetti, a command is, intrinsically, a relation of power: it rises as power and perpetuates itself as power. However, it is not simply the case that command offers an *illustration* of power. The perspective should be reversed: it is power at large, even in its most sophisticated, distributed and disembodied actualizations, that remains at some level connected to command as to its root. The latter can be understood as the power's *hæcceitas*, its 'just-thisness'. From this perspective, the archetype of power, its clearest instant manifestation, can be found in 'survival', to be explored more in details in Chapter 2.

A brief outline of Canetti's take on commands, at this point, may be helpful to set the scene for further discussion (*MM* 357–93/*CP* 303–33). As already noticed, Canetti begins by inviting the reader to unpack the apparently un-theoretical nature of commands, excavating, so to speak, their deceiving surface. In the phenomenal platitude of command, a number of distinctions are introduced, meant to illuminate the less visible aspects of such an experience. While in Chapter 8 of

Crowds and Power these distinctions appear to be articulated as dichotomies, they are, I suggest, better appreciated as extremes of a single 'prolongation,' stages in a series or, if one prefers, discontinuous moments within a continuous medium. First, Canetti distinguishes command [*Befehl*] from language [*Sprache*]; second, he distinguishes command as 'flight command' [*Fluchtbefehl*] and 'death sentence' [*Todesurteil*], from domesticated command [*domestiziert Befehl*]; third he distinguishes, within each actually occurring command, impulse or momentum [*Antrieb*] and sting [*Stachel*]. Altogether, such features are characteristic of what we have proposed to call the 'command-machine.' As we are going to see, a command–machine works thanks to three main mechanisms: acceptance, domestication and recoil.

The hypothesis that command is 'older than speech' is functional to suggest that its concreteness is grounded in vital facts: an actual biological configuration founds the command relation. Predation in the animal domain already presents us with the basic layout of command. Existentially, command originally appears on the verge of an abyss: the abyss of death. The original command looks like a 'death sentence,' whereby the prey must flee for its life [*der tödliche Ernst der Flucht*]. At its inception, command is but a hunt weapon, an arrow [*Pfeil*], prompt to grow into a full-blown war weapon. Looking at the command relation 'geometrically,' we could say that command is vector, i.e. oriented movement: indeed, the flight vector is strictly correlated with the predator's stare [*Blick*], its semblance, its sound. An immediate *Gestalt* element must be evoked here: the sheer apparition of the predator, the slightest hint of an 'intention' on its part, unleashes the flight of the prey. Rather than symbolic, it is possible to infer, commands are of *indexical* nature: an 'extended finger' [*ausgestreckter Finger*] pointing in a given direction, capable of setting someone in motion along that same direction. The flight command, in its instant and absolute requirement, shows that the device of command does not rest on 'neocortical' cognitive elaboration: it does not require one to do anything specific, it does not even describe a course of action to be undertaken, nor represent a ideal state of things to be achieved – it 'merely' requires the recipient to follow the line indicated by the directionality of the threat. Anyone who has seen the police charging the crowd at a demonstration, for instance, knows very well what this vector element consists of.

The very presence of the predator constitutes a menace [*Drohung*], and every command emerges out of an atmosphere of threat. Such an atmosphere is premised upon a deep physiological and ontological difference between predator and prey: their bodies, their attitudes, their postures are non-symmetrical and non-interchangeable. *A priori*, they could not be more different, as concerns both their mode of being (vegetarian *vs* carnivore) and their strength (attacker *vs* attacked). The fact that the predatory relation is, chiefly, inter-specific – i.e., occurring between animals of different species – determines the fact that command always acts upon its recipient as an external force. The predator's command, as said, descends upon the prey as a death sentence: if the command is sentence, it is because the sentence is punishment [*Todesurteil*]. The 'execution' of command is, quite literally, an execution. Yet, a command does not exhaust itself in such visible, 'catastrophic' guise. In its double composition as impulse and sting, the command joins what is most proximal with what is most distal. Impulse and sting speak of different spatial as well as temporal registers: whereas the former refers to the immanent performance of command, to the fact of being issued and carried out in the here and now, the latter, by contrast, evokes the archaeological, latent storage of received commands. Such split temporality proves essential for the transformation of command from a straightforward and relatively direct biological relation into a sophisticated social pattern inscribable, and inscribed, in social structures. Such is, precisely, the achievement of domestication: as soon as command comes to be associated with food and nutrition, a new moral economy is formed, whereby command averts from its foundation in violence and death. The new foundation transposes command from exceptionality to everyday life: command leaves the context of chase and flight, and enters the field of an organizational economy that includes education, work, cooperation, etc.

On the basis of such a minimal reconstruction of the Canettian diagram, a preliminary synthesis can be attempted. First, commands are rooted in the direct and immediate action and reaction of bodies, long before any normative abstract or symbolic scheme intervenes. Action and reaction are 'affective' in their constitution, in a very Spinozist sense – in fact, an affect is an alteration in the inner relations that constitute a subject. Command prioritizes action over norms and general directives. This does not mean that commands can never be symbolized, but that their root remains pre-symbolic and embodied. Second, commands are directly branched upon the basic state of social life, which is a state of heterogeneity.[19] In a command, we can see heterogeneous elements of disparate nature woven together into a continuum, as these elements come to be entangled 'in depth' in the social process. Heterogeneity thus refers not simply to social diversity, but to deep diversity of agents (humans, animals, tools etc.): the use of the term 'machine' can be granted precisely in this sense of piecemeal composition of parts geared together. Below, we return to consider more in details the remarkable accomplishment of commands in establishing immediacy across heterogeneity. Now, it is more important to turn to the implications of the peculiar temporality of commands.

What Canetti calls momentum [*Antrieb*] is clearly correlated with the psychological 'tension' experienced by Milgram's subjects. The command's momentum reveals that psychological tension does not solely derive from an inner moral conflict in the individual psyche, as Milgram hypothesized, but precisely from the social intercourse itself as it is played out in live time. Such intercourse is the proper locus of analysis, and must be reconstructed in all its constituents. Whereas in Milgram the focus is exclusively on short-term compliance, Canetti places commands in the protracted temporality of a whole life: obedience in the here and now has for both parties consequences over wide distances, and in the very long run. What the social psychologist has overlooked are, in other words, the long-term 'mnestic' traces left by the experience of command.[20] In the early twentieth century, the German physiologist Richard Semon (1921) called 'engrams' what remains in a living creature *after* the cessation of stimulation, whereby 'a permanent record has been written or engraved on the irritable substance' of the organism. Mnestic traces, or 'mnemes,' as Semon also called them, correspond to the formations of an implicit, living memory. Rather than being localized in any specific part of the brain, or the nervous system alone, as psychologists believe, the 'memory' built by commands is, so to speak, written directly in the flesh: such is precisely the sense of the Canettian image of the sting, or thorn.[21] We should not think of anything necessarily dramatic: indeed, stings are often quite modest, like small wood chips that do not even make us bleed. Not much painful, they are in general less noticed than the impulse part of command, which, on the contrary, pierces the victim like an arrow. Nonetheless, the sting of command leaves deep, permanent marks. In the long run, the risk is one of psychic saturation: 'A man can become so completely riddled with them [stings] that he has no interest left for anything else and, except for them, can feel nothing' (*MM* 380/*CP* 322). One, who cannot set oneself free from the unbearable burden of the stings sunk in one's flesh, runs a serious risk of having one's mental health crumbling down. So, following a peculiar 'karst-like' temporality, the stings remain intact and unalterable, getting heaped in a slow process of accumulation that may last for years and decades, until a sudden tipping point is reached. At that point, a terrible psychological burden – whose subterranean origins may have not been suspected – is to be suddenly released.[22] So, the impulse and the sting work in a completely different temporal order, but still jointly.

A different entry point into the issue of obedience can be envisaged once we take the role of stings into due consideration – for the effectiveness of command never simply derives from the command's momentum alone: the sting is crucial to explain why humans obey so much. Canetti explains this fact on the account that, once under some else's order, one 'does not accuse himself, but the sting' for what is being perpetrated (an attitude we must fully consider as 'fetishism'). That is why, as soon as one receives a command, one wants to pass it on, just like a match to be passed on before one gets one's fingers burnt. Stings derive from commands that have taken grip; by contrast, disobeyed commands fail to their aim: their strength to leave stings is lost and they vanish without a trace. This way, stings are extremely important facilitators of obedience. By accepting certain orders, humans affiliate with 'an order,' which in turn justifies their deeds – especially if one does not inspect too closely what the order is about. By following an order, *one becomes an order*, and one can see *even less* what the order actually is: but essentially, one passes on one's stings. Significantly, in the military jargon a 'command' is not a verbal message, but the operational unit created to carry it out: a group of humans is *named after* the very practice of being ordered and executing orders. Command and obedience can thus be regarded as media, or 'elements,' of the social relation. From this perspective, the command–obedience relation indicates that something shared, a 'commons,' is indeed created between the commander and the commanded. The problem is that, just as it splits time, command also splits space: the persons effectively joined in the command relationship are taken apart by the very dynamic of command, by its frightening asymmetry, so that their capacity to empathize is damaged. In this light, recent research in the neuroscience seems to vindicate both Milgram and Canetti: it is experimentally proven that obeying orders reduces empathy (Caspar *et al.* 2020).

The image of the sting as an alien presence in someone's body expresses the idea that, despite the psychosomatic depth at which it operates, a command remains inescapably external to the person who receives it. The creation of stings is thus directly connected to hetero-directed action, and this in turn explains the perilous consequences of command. Once understood as more than a metaphor, the image of the sting raises fundamental questions about the ontological status of commands in social life. The sting of command is not an interpretation of a message, or at the very least it cannot be reduced to that; an alien body in my flesh, it acts upon me as something objective, something that exists independently of my conscience. The transition from the domain of the subjective to the domain of the objective is manifested here: at this juncture, passions become institutions. From the point of view of the recipient, command is both s/he who commands – in the immediacy of the moment of reception – and, later, at the sting stage, a befallen and irrefutable fact, something as concrete as a sound, a gesture, a signal, an artefact, a shape that enters my perceptual field (particularly, visual, aural and tactile). From the moment I start carrying it out, the command becomes more and more objective, less and less human, increasingly less a manifestation of a contingent will, and correspondingly more an objective reality of the external world. The crucial ambivalence in the command machine thus seems to consist of this: the command appears simultaneously as both a relationship among human beings and a relationship between human beings and non-human, external, objective and, a fortiori, institutional entities. Interestingly, the situation recalls the analysis of embodied practical sense developed by Pierre Bourdieu (1972). For Bourdieu, subjects are completely imbued with social structures. Absence of any perceived violence, absence of visible commands, along with the ease with which people cope with their world and, mostly, perform adequately in it, must be imputed to habitus – namely, the fact that 'the very structures of the world are present in the structures (or, to put it better, the cognitive schemes) that agents implement in order to understand it' (Bourdieu 2000: 152). The source of commands apparently separated from any personal will, manifests itself as 'the world itself,' – a socialized world with the semblance of 'natural order of things,' with all its impersonal albeit imperative requests.

From this vantage point, however, we should say that commands also coincide with a *shrinking* of the breadth of life, as described, for instance, by the psychiatrist Eugène Minkowski (1970[1933]) in the 1930s. In his exploration of the psychopathology of space, Minkowski pointed to the notion of 'distance' as key to the production of psychological ease. Minkowski correlated 'positive distance' with the 'fullness of life' or, as he also called it, the 'organopsychic solidarity' of the living thing with its environment.[23] There is a fundamental phenomenological difference, Minkowski argued, between the 'clarity of visual space,' where the fullness of life unfolds, and the 'black night' where an intimacy of contact occurs. Humans are porous to the 'black light,' whereby the individual finds itself immersed in a 'soaking' milieu: in the dark, we do not know the boundaries of our own body, just as when we 'float' in a sound, or a music. Whereas the visual space preserves the positive distance, in black space phenomena not only penetrate one another, they also penetrate the subject and mix with it. The fullness of life seems to coincide with positive distance understood as a 'breadth' or latitude where phenomena, people and events can be located, and hosted in a respectful way. This is why positive distance proves essential for psychological wellbeing – on the contrary, whenever it is compromised, phenomena become cluttered and can no longer be disentangled. Psychotic states, Minkowski suggested, are characterized by an unwanted shrinking of positive distance: a contraction and undue agglomeration of facts that are normally set apart occurs, that threatens the individual's space of ease. In the psychotic mind, everything becomes connected, but also short-circuited, knotted, conflated, impossible to be spaced out. That does not mean that the 'black light' must be in itself negative in any absolute sense: everything that relates to intimate participation in the world also requires to some extent the permeable condition of the black light – despite the fact that such a condition is not properly 'subjective', but rather environmental, or, as we may also say, fully social.

In Canetti's *Memoirs*, the phenomenon of the shrinking of life is literarily rendered with the juxtaposition of the characters of Kraus and Sonne: whereas Sonne is the representative of an encompassing human commonality (we return to the topic in Chapter 4), Kraus's thundering accusations 'had the full force of *commands*' [*die volle Kraft von* Befehlen] (*Aug* 210/*Mem* 698). In his just crusade against injustice and corruption, Kraus turned into a sulphuric prosecutor, single-mindedly fixated on its targets, disdainful of any possible compromise, emotionally shut out of any commonality with the enemy – that is, with the accused. It does not surprise, in this sense, that command can generate a mental state of persecution: command is haunting us because it is not satisfied with what it is – it *wants to grow*. In Chapter 2, the consequences of a variety of increase phenomena are examined; but since now it is clear that, in line with the specifically animistic stance advanced by Canettian social theory, command has expansionist aims: in wanting to expand, it is unlikely to leave one alone. Ismaël el Iraki, a survivor of the 2015 Bataclan terrorist massacre in Paris, has powerfully captured such terrible truth: 'One of the things I discovered through this is PTSD [post-traumatic stress disorder] is an infectious disease given to you by those who exact violence on you.' We notice that the horrible 'directness' of a terrorist attack – as of any other act of war, along with other forms of even lesser violence – bears the same structure as command – for, after all, command itself is but a form of violence, functioning as an infectious disease: once one is infected, even if one does not succumb right away, a long process of recovery and liberation is still called forth.

What is needed to produce a truthful and enduring liberation from long-time accumulated stings, is the crowd. For Canetti, only the crowd can free individuals from the stings they carry deposited inside them. In Chapter 4, we return more extensively on the problem of how commonality manifests itself; for now, suffice to consider that, whereas commands establish the thinnest possible commonality between humans, the crowd embodies the largest and deepest. Importantly, every crowd comes into existence not simply through the progressive increase of the number of people convened in a place; rather, a special moment that 'materialises' (or, actualizes) the crowd is called forth – an instant Canetti dubs the 'discharge' [*Entladung*]. Such moments of collective outburst effectively enact the dissolution [*Auflösung*] of personal stings.[24] Clearly, all these images evoke a lexicon of energetic levels and energetic potentials. In this respect, it has perhaps not yet be noted sufficiently how Canetti's conceptualization of discharge and dissolution bears similarities with the early Freudian scheme elaborated in the *Project for a Psychology* [*Entwurf einer Psychologie*], the unfinished manuscript dating from 1895.[25] Well aware of the advances in neural research, Freud identified as one of the fundamental tasks of the neural system the management of the charges of excitation [*Besetzung*].[26] The quanta of excitation are managed in a consistent manner by the neurons and this in general, Freud postulates, goes in the direction of keeping excitation to the minimum. However, a major problem lies in the fact that excitation charges come from not only the external environment, but also endogenous stimuli (which later Freud would conceptualize as 'drives'). While it is, at least in principle, always possible to flee from unwanted external stimulations [*Reizflucht*], not so from the internal stimulations. Accordingly, rather than with a simple principle of 'neuronal flush' [*N-Trägheit*] – whereby neurons would 'throw away' as soon as possible all excitation [*Abfuhr*] – the neural system has to learn how to entertain its own charges, preventing them from both reaching unwanted levels as well as from relieving all their energy at once.[27]

This means that the ground state of the neural system is not its lowest energetic state, but an intermediate state, surrounded by peaks and, beyond them, a released, or depressed, state. Because, as said, the organism is regarded by Freud as not simply impressionable from the outside, but also impressionable from the inside (autosuggestible), the existence of an inner charging pathway determines the impossibility of being durably without excitations. Temporary 'satisfactions' can only be found by way of what Freud calls 'specific actions,' which cannot be produced by the organism alone, but necessitate an 'external help': for instance, hunger can be temporarily extinguished by nutrition, sexual urge by copulation etc.[28] The extinction of the charge is therefore very limited in time, as compared to the remaining temporal span, when the neural system must continue to entertain a dose of *Besetzung*, juggling between a dangerous absence of excitation and a no less dangerous excess of it. The process of *Besetzung* described by the Freud of *Entwurf* can be said to be 'pharmacological' in the sense we have discussed above in the introduction: the posology of the charges must be accurately managed, given the non-symmetrical consequences associated with the operations of 'investing' and 'divesting': in this sense, perhaps, the notion of *Besetzung* may lie at the origin of the Freudian notion of ambivalence, so crucial for his whole psychology of the unconscious.[29]

The Canettian process of 'getting rid of the stings of command' shares similarities with the process of neuronal flush [*N-Trägheit*] described by Freud, although Canetti appears here as more unilateral than Freud: indeed, in Canetti the accumulation of stings can never have positive effects. Canetti's description of the domestication of command is mostly negative, and his interest is chiefly turned towards the occurrence of discharge pathways. At the same time, if, as we are going to see, command is deeply inscribed in education and culture, then virtually no human can reclaim to be completely sting-free. So, in analogy with the Freud of *Entwurf*, the charge's 'ground state' of the system (or, the person) is always at non-zero (positive) level. At the same time, implicit in Canetti's analysis of commands lies an image of the individual psyche as deeply social: command can be thought of as a charge that constitutively comes from the outside, whereby entering a command–obedience relation, becoming part of a command machine, effectively means to associate oneself with an external source of will. On this point, Canetti is definitely more Durkheimian than Freudian, for it is Durkheim (1912) who posits that the greatest distinction is not between internal and external stimuli, but between two types of external stimuli, the non-social and the social ones.[30] At the same time, Canetti goes beyond Durkheim, by fully naturalizing the social relation, which is now revealed as not confined to the human province.[31] Even when it is accepted or welcome, a command is doomed to remain something alien inside us: this way, even exquisitely human sociation has to transit through an inhuman medium, whose nature we need to investigate deeper.

The crowd appears as a liberating figure because, in it, command is, so to speak, crushed into the possible tiniest particles, to the point of making it harmless. A pure crowd state is such that, writes Canetti, 'no-one has a right to give command to anyone else; or, one might say, everyone gives commands to everyone' (*MM* 382/*CP* 324). As the two extremes (no command on the one hand, ever-present multidirectional command on the other) coincide, we can say that the crowd is the situation where command effectively meets anarchy: at that point, stings are reduced to dust. This explains the long-lasting lure of the crowd, which people join precisely to leave their personal, 'domestic' stings behind. Even when a command falls upon a crowd from the outside, it spreads horizontally within it, so that nobody is individually affected by it in terms of stings. The crowd dynamism is quicker than sting formation, so that a new register of morality, endowed with a distinctive 'dromology,' appears here. Of course, this very fact makes the crowd also dangerously available to accept orders, given that nobody really feels utterly condemned by them. This is especially the case when a demagogue is capable of appropriating the most successful rhetorical tropes capable of mobilizing the crowd. As in the classic tradition of crowd psychology, the crowd thus appears to Canetti as a 'creature' capable of acting strongly, but incapable of feeling remorse.[32]

Humans, at any rate, do not live permanently in crowd states: the liberation made available by the intense sociality of the crowd is necessarily provisional [*vorläufig*]. Two other strategies to avoid the accumulation of stings in one's body then include *either* resisting the received commands, *or*, alternatively, passing them onto someone else. These two strategies could not be more different in terms of their overall ethical–political implications. As concerns the former, the one who does not obey is always freer than the one who obeys – but, a thick cloud of commands is launched upon him or her as an arrow-cloud meant to pierce and maim. Resistance, as we are going to see in Chapter 3, always engages one's body in the first place. The alternative, consisting of passing on commands, clearly breeds an individualist form of liberation, one that has entirely come to terms with the requirements of social hierarchy. Insofar as the latter alternative is practiced, humans but continue the game of stings: passing commands onto someone else is, indeed, what keeps them in circulation across the social body, and ultimately what makes them survive – for a command can exist only until it remains asymmetrical and in a state of 'flowing' (as also per the Freudian *Trägheit* principle).

These considerations should strike our pharmacological–cathectic sensitivity. As seen above, commands are originally hunt and war weapons, growing out of the death sentence issued during a hunting session: a command 'compels [*zwingt*] the victim to flee' (*MM* 358/*CP* 304). As a momentous occurrence of social life, command is thus contradistinguished by an immediate adherence of the commander upon the commanded: the grip of the animal predator's paw upon the prey's body, the piercing of the prey's skin by the human hunter's arrow. Here, however, a singular ambivalence must be remarked: on the one hand, the command *is* the death sentence enforcing the flight, but on the other, the command also *coincides* with the flight itself.[33] How to fully account for the uncanny relation between command and flight? Canetti is telling us that flight is command (in the sense of being its necessary consequence) but also, at the same time, the remedy against it! Digging to the bottom of the matter, we must admit that the predator does not at all aim to set the prey off to flight – it just aims to kill it. Actually, the prey's flight complicates the situation from the point of view of the predator (except of course when such strategy is itself deliberately used as a hunting technique). A crucial stage is marked by the predator's awareness – or perhaps better, the *mutual awareness* – that one's gestures can *animate* the other's motion. The veritable origin of commands lies in such a consciousness (which humans share with other animals), rather than in the sheer act of hunting – for it is such consciousness that enables the deliberate production of specific effects in the command recipient. Precisely at that point can command become prospective, future-oriented, that is, capable of orienting conduct. However, regardless of the (certainly important) prolongation of the biological expression into a logically imperative order, the cathectic–pharmacological ambivalence of the flight remains pivotal: insofar as it exists, the flight does not fully belong to either the predator or the prey. The flight is, and is always bound to remain, the contested terrain between subjection and liberation.

Variable geometries of affect

Canettian epistemology suggests that commands are not only relational undertakings but, above all, energetic ones. Accordingly, the question we have to address concerns the type of energy being expressed in a command. Earlier in this chapter, we have seen how easily command can generate tensional situations: command is, indeed, among the prime protagonists of human trauma. It entails intensity levels discharged from commander to the commanded – with the latter, as we know, the one who largely bears the brunt; but with the former, too, not immune from the force of command in terms of its powerful 'recoil.' Both the commander and the commanded, in other words, experience grave biological and emotional alterations – including higher blood pressure, muscular tension, sweating, agitation, excitement, fear, anxiety, humiliation, resentment etc. Add to this that often command does not just come in one single 'shot,' but is repeated over and over again. Such are, for instance, the activities of training, dressage, education, performance rehearsal, etc. The 'efficient' dose can sometimes only be reached by an accumulation of many repeated commands through time, just like the fatal hit of the predator inflicted upon the prey may require a previous number of tearing blows. Of course, in the case of domesticated commands, the scene appears less dramatic, but not completely unrelated to the original one: in fact, we are still dealing with an accumulation of stings, whose ultimate prolongation is the creation of situations so completely walled-in that, paradoxically, command is hailed as a blessing as a liberation. If, anyway, a command is not effective at its first shot, it means that it is met with resistance, or is otherwise somehow rejected, or at least tentatively *defused*. Resistance is likely to generate frustration in the subject issuing the command, leading to an ensuing intensification of interaction – we have amply noticed above the rapidly escalating situations that follow from the repetition of command.

The tension engendered by command thus enjoys a peculiar temporality strictly correlated to its affective nature. The affective energy typical of both short-term and long-term tensional situations (momentums and stings), highlights the role of the affective dimension at large, which is so central to Canetti's view of social life. That commands are grounded in an archaic psychosocial stratum – one which, however, remains operative in everyday interaction – is now recognized by primatologists, too. Frans De Waal asserts, for instance, the evolutionary primacy of emotions as crucial mediators of the social intercourse: 'Emotions clearly precede language in both evolution and human development' (de Waal 2019: 126). Such thesis is significantly reminiscent of Canetti's earlier idea about the original precedence of command over language. Yet, as also reconstructed above, even before affectivity, what Canetti places at the basis of command is a precise *perceptual* experience: the perception of the threatening shape of the predator by the prey. This is, wholly, a *Gestalt* issue, where the emergence of one specific form is indistinguishable from the following reconfiguration of the whole context of conduct. In turn, the visual dimension must again be appreciated as thoroughly imbued with the whole energy and the forces of social life. In this vein, Canetti can point to the direct translation into action of the *Gestalt* of the predator as perceived by the staring eye of the prey. Sheer perception, in sum, is capable of precipitating a whole new configuration – the hunt itself. With René Thom (1988), we can speak of given 'saliences' coming to be invested by 'pregnances' conferring vital significance to them. Only a pregnance can express the true meaning of a salience, and it is only when a salience becomes 'pregnant' that it becomes truly significant. A philosophy of expression – such as the one elaborated by Deleuze (1968, 1981) in his studies of Spinoza – can, in a way, be said to be entirely devoted to the examination of the outcomes of the encounters between saliences and pregnances. Within such framework, the Gestalt aspect of command can be said to correspond to the occurrence of an impregnated salience understood as an especially *expressive* event. Expression is always the expression of an affect, that is, the modification of a set of constitutive relationships that derives from singular social encounters.

Digging deeper into the fleshy embodiment of command, one special consideration must be reserved to gestures. The role of gestures is of particular importance, insofar as they stand at the polar opposite of symbols. A forceful indexical reality, the gestures of command do not symbolize power; in fact, the reverse is true: it is power itself that consists entirely of *making gestures*, like the tight finger addressed to somebody, or any other menacing gestures – 'impulsive' in the sense that they are apt to impress an impulse upon someone along a given direction or intended course of action. All the magnificent symbolic elements that garnish power can, in the Canettian epistemology, be brought back to those primal gestures of command. Rather than an encoded message, the gesture offers an opaque core of meaning related to bodies, spaces, capacities, directions. Gestures are at the same time more than eloquent, and less than univocal. Attempts at codifying gestures are certainly never-ending, most likely because they systematically fail to prove satisfactory.[34] Among the most mysterious gestures are those found in Kafka's fiction: in his essay on Kafka, Walter Benjamin (1999b[1934]) first underlined the crucial importance of such bodily expressions for the *Kafka-Gestus* itself. The reason why Kafka lingers so long in the description of peculiar, very singular, ineffable gestures lies for Benjamin in the fact that Kafka himself was personally very incapable of grasping the meaning of most everyday gestures, which looked mysterious to him.[35] Benjamin connects the odd, often awkward bodily postures depicted in Kafka's fiction to what he terms the 'optical unconscious.' The unfolding of a gesture thus amount to a particular 'test procedure' [*Versuchsanordnung*] of social interaction. The procedure is at play in each single, indescribable and yet forceful, when not *fatal*, movement: 'Each gesture is an event – one might even say a drama – in itself' (*ibid.*: 802).

The evental nature of gestures is for us here of the utmost importance. It is precisely in this direction that Canetti's search for the bodily foundations of power can be further clarified. The human body appears to Canetti as essentially fragile, permeable, 'very vulnerable in its nakedness' [*in seiner Nacktheit sehr verletzlich*] (*GW* 28/*CW* 16). Just as it can be injured by external bodies, so it can be pierced through by gestures. As seen above, commanding gestures encapsulate two elements, momentum and sting – or, if one prefers, impulse and thorn. As the command's impulse impels its execution, it also pushes the command's thorn into the victim's flesh. One single thorn is usually not deadly, but it leaves an enduring pain, a specific 'preoccupation' and the psychological torment that comes with it. This is what the sting is ultimately about: slow-motion poisoning. Its end point is the body of Gruenewald's Christ, fully pierced through: a body that cannot feel anything else, a body brought to the *extreme* of what is humanly acceptable.[36] The body saturated with stings is entirely dominated by the mnemes of all the gestures that, as a swarm of singularities, have flashed up and entered into one's existence.

For how much Canetti distrusted Nietzsche, it is undeniable that the Canettian predominance of the physiological register in the description of psychosocial phenomena resembles Nietzsche's (1994[1887]) earlier treatment of morality as grounded in corporeal matters. Indeed, Nietzsche sought to develop a whole 'physiology' of the genesis of moral sentiments, a 'somatology' conceived of as the veritable ground for human psychology.[37] In his controversial, captivating description of the utter contrast between master morality [*Herrenmoral*] and slave morality [*Sklavenmoral*], Nietzsche sees the whole apparatus of moral value as being grounded in vital expressivity. Specifically, the masters are characterized by the fact of recognizing themselves in a 'positive basic concept, saturated with life and passion, "we the noble, the good, the beautiful and the happy!"' (*ibid.*, 20: I, §10).[38] Whereas the masters are contradistinguished by their direct and unrestrained assertion of life and action, a morality of resentment – or, as Nietzsche writes, employing the French word, *ressentiment* – is typical of the slave, insofar as it derives from the condition of someone who has been previously commanded *and* has obeyed for a very long time. Resentment always harbours a dream of revenge, and for Nietzsche it remains the hallmark of an 'ill' physiology.[39]

At the same time, command for Canetti cannot be reduced to sheer physical violence. If it were so, it could not accomplish its main function, namely, initiating someone else's action [*eine Handlung auslöst*] (*MM* 358). Command implies a *threshold* that is *preliminary* to the occurrence of violence. As already considered, such threshold – which is initially very tenuous, but can be hugely expanded – is the threat, or menace. Since the momentum's immediacy is intimately linked to the directionality of the physical violence directed against a victim, the threat inherits directionality as a special capacity to impart a social tropism. In this sense, the threat stems from the very initial part of the manifestation of strength that inflicts violence, such as the predator's gesture inducing the recipient to flee: it can be compared to a medium that, so to speak, 'fills the air' between commander and commanded. A full-fledged command, however, only arises when this initial movement-space becomes autonomous and acquires its specific features. An *amplification* [*Verbreiterung*] from proximal to distal, as well as from actual to virtual, is essential to have a shift from physical force to veritable power. Amplification implies enhanced distances in space and time. Social distances are never neutral, nor merely metrical: they are *active media* that alternatively relate and sever, expose and immunize. It is from such vantage point that one can appreciate Canetti's claim about the solitude of the powerful.

'The powerful' [*Machthaber*] under consideration here is not necessarily an exotic figure of some Asian despot, but can be applied to many mundane situations: for instance, one can consider the condition of modern urbanity as one that creates 'powerful' – in the sense of separated – individuals. Students of car traffic have, in this vein, long observed that 'once tied to the car, people themselves become less sociable, cooperative, rational, considerate, and kind' (Ritter 1964: 34). Is this not another way of saying that they become more 'powerful' in Canetti's sense? It is as if the car adds a layer of distance between us and others, introducing a distance that is material, atmospheric, experiential, more than simply metrical: in cars, we certainly feel more protected, but also more remote, more estranged from the others. Cars thus produce a whole 'immunology,' a way in which people can grow more disconnected from others by retreating into 'capsules' amounting to a 'privatized, cocooned, moving environment that uses up disproportionate amounts of physical resources' (Sheller and Urry 2000: 744). Before the car, it was arguably verbal commands that defined a similar socialized 'hodology,' a knowledge of trajectories accommodating, not simply movement in space, but the affectivity that comes with it – indeed, as observed above, commands produce ways for channelling both spatial trajectories and emotions.

The relationship between command and movement can be better specified in its twofold signification. On the one hand, command is possible at all because, as already remarked, the human being is permeable: she is open to a becoming that transforms her; during her transits, thorns can sting her skin. Considered externally, then, command represent just one of the many elements of becoming, of the world's transformation – an element among many others, which humans transit across. Thus, the very possibility of the existence of commands, of their taking place at all, lies in the continuity of human transformation. Yet, on the other hand, powerful command (or, the command of the powerful) appears as an enduring attempt to *freeze* metamorphosis in order to preserve and amplify the structures of power in place. The more the command interweaves with status hierarchies, the more the powerful is him/herself constrained within the narrow limits of already-established power configurations. By compelling the others to change only in strict accordance to the asserted command, by arresting their free transformations, it is the powerful him/herself who can no longer transform, who is locked in his/her own power – hence, incidentally, his/her poor mental health.

We can trace back this image of command and its negation (metamorphosis) rather straightforwardly to our initial hypothesis. The command–machine functions as a compound entity, whose elements are at the same time ontologically diverse and tightly woven in continuity. A single flow, an ongoing ontological extravasation contradistinguishes the working of command, as is made clear in the case of the Asian tribes (section 'The Horse and the Arrow' [*Befehl–Pferd–Pfeil*]). Describing the nomad Mongol hunters from the wide Asian meads, Canetti indicates the compound of hunter, horse and weapons as a compact unit of command, a veritable command–machine. Here, command takes place through direct physical transmission, without any space of manoeuvre, without possibility of missing the mark. Just as between the horseman and the horse there is no interpretive space, but immediate transmission of command, likewise, the arrow shot by the hunter is an instance of that same infallible command, projected at distance, a 'total command' that works like a death sentence: it either grips and sinks deep into the flesh, or is lost forever. As we can see, wherever a distance, a space for manoeuvre, is created, infallibility is no longer granted, and command may fail to its target. Sometimes commands do not simply have a grip, arrows can be thrown in vain. Unlike the infallible command between horseman and horse, the single arrow is more error-prone and must be backed-up, reinforced, multiplied until the prey can no longer escape. As discussed above, something similar happened in the Milgram experiment. During the experiment, a number of subjects tried to subtract themselves from the imparted commands, while simultaneously avoiding an explicit act of defiance; specifically, they were looking for some desperate way to stop electrocuting the victim while at the same time not displeasing the authority figure of the 'experimenter' commanding them to do so. They were trying to exploit the space of fallibility of command. The special cruelty of the experimental design resided in precisely making such attempted escape moves impossible, with the consequential dramatic, anxiety-ridden outcomes we know about. In other words, Milgram's situation was designed in a way so as to make it impossible to disobey without a blatant and radical violation of the definition of the situation guaranteed by the experimenter, along with his authority as expert, and his place of command.[40]

In terms of its affections, then, command seems to be the opposite of freedom: when one is commanded, one is also thereby inherently *restricted*. Interestingly, however, command should also be recognized as what makes freedom *actual*, in the sense that only by entering a determination can one's virtuality of freedom become an actual freedom. Completely blocking an individual means blocking his/her breathing: it means killing that person, as per the infamous choking position during police arrests. But, while command is certainly a restriction to movement and action, it also provides a way of channelling them in sometimes extremely efficient ways. It is in this sense that, as noted above, command can be received as a 'liberation' by someone whose existential situation is *stuck* – such as prototypically, soldiers, prisoner, hostages ... Perhaps, new fervent admirers and adepts can be recruited this way. In other words, whenever the 'predisposed' situation is suffocating, command seems to become 'liberating.' Such a cathectic relation between command and freedom can perhaps be illuminated by comparing it with the case of certain quantum states in physics: as Feynman (1985: 55) put it, 'When you try to squeeze light too much to make sure it's going in only a straight line, it refuses to cooperate and begins to spread out.' 'Obeying in order to breath' is the paradox that ultimately brings us upon pharmacological terrain. Indeed, by designating a reality that is ambiguously both part of the illness *and* part of the cure at the same time, command leads us into the complex territory of a 'recalcitrance' that predates any 'will.'

The ideology of command

The reconstruction provided so far has laid the ground for an understanding of command that takes its social energetics seriously. The next crucial step is to consider the inscription of command within the horizon of language. Curiously, the 'second' Wittgenstein, who so insightfully declared that 'to imagine a language means to imagine a form of life' [*eine Sprache vorstellen heißt, sich eine Lebensform vorstellen*] (1953: §19), did not attach any specific importance to imperatives. So Wittgenstein, who put the *Lebenswelt* theme at the centre of his inquiries, does not have a word to say about the actual qualities of the *Lebenswelt* created by the experience of commands. It so happens that, while his *Logical Investigations* is replete with examples where people are ordered to perform certain actions or calculations, there is not a single occasion where the philosopher stops to ponder whether people are happy with following those orders or not, or even why they should be interested in obeying at all, with which consequences. Certainly, a command is a life form – but, which life form is it? The thread on 'following orders' that runs across *Logical Investigations* seems designed to suggest that, logically speaking, a command is impotent in specifying its own conditions of felicity. Wittgenstein repeatedly slows down the order sequence, installing the reader inside the logical gap between language and the world, only to rescue the same reader out of the predicament thanks to the transformation of language into its grammar-as-pragmatically-used. Canetti does not need this strange detour: for him, command is a directly meaningful anthropological reality.

As recalled above, Canetti's general idea is that, *stricto sensu*, commands do not need language to exist: 'Commands are older than speech [*älter als die Sprache*]. If this were not so, dogs could not understand them' (*MM* 357/*CP* 303). This is an important theoretical assertion, which in turn, however, requires several clarifications. On the one hand, as already discussed, the claim has the merit of widening the workings of social life beyond anthropocentric exceptionalism: social life does not belong to humans alone, nor for that matter to any single living species, but cuts across the boundaries of different species, as well as the barrier between the living and the non-living. On the other hand, the type of sophisticated orders which we see at work in modern society – for instance, in technical instructions, technological projects, legal stipulations and bureaucratic procedures – would be inconceivable without detailed linguistic articulation. In short, one needs to explain how the here-and-now of command can successfully be inserted within the larger organization of social coexistence. To do so, a more encompassing notion of command is needed, capable of embracing its prolongations, transformations, evolutions, its patterns and 'embedding' operations. Once more elaborate versions of command are taken into consideration, one can appreciate how language comes to be increasingly co-articulated with them: at some level, it may be said to turn into a constituent part of them. First, then, one wonders what transits between creatures *in the absence of speech*. Second, one must question whether one is really dealing with an actual lack of speech, rather than with some *unrecognized forms* of speech. Third, one would like to specify how different speech formations, different linguistic modulations and so on, can transform the intrinsic structure of command.

At stake here is a redefinition of what counts as speech and, more generally, as language. Canetti, writing in the 1950s, assumed a notion of *Sprache* as a distinctively human feature. Yet advances in the study of animal communication and biosemiotics have since made clear that, not simply do animals have *their* speech, but inter-specific encounters also exude phenomena of communication and semiosis. Concurrently, since the 1960s, the 'linguistic turn' in the philosophy of language associated with the second Wittgenstein has sought to overcome the flat image of language as based on the sheer logic of representation, pointing to its wide pragmatic variability. If, as concerns the latter, Canetti can be regarded as a forerunner (we return below to this point), as concerns the former his sympathy for animals would have presumably led him to be open-minded towards recognizing their cultural competences (in Chapter 2, we return on his notion of 'animal civilisation'). That said, what remains valid and distinctive in the Canettian take, is the fact of having outlined the command's capacity to flow from one body to another without codifying mediations, without necessarily being transcribed into a formalized symbolic system.

Early on in his discussion, Canetti introduces command as having to do essentially with a manifestation of the will. Precisely at this point does he attribute to speech a secondary role with respect to intention, citing the case of the animal trainer, whose will is 'notified' [*kundgegeben*] to the animal with short, concise commands. At first, the evoked imagery seems to resonate with Max Weber's 'voluntarist' theory of power. Famously, Weber (2019[1922]) based his definition of power upon the enactment of command–obedience chains. In particular, Weber distinguished the generic phenomenon of power [*Macht*], which he measured on the basis of the factual translation of certain desiderata into state of things, from a more specific type he called *Herrschaft*, which he characterized as the conscious acceptance of the transference of will from one person to another.[41] Thus, in both authors, commands appear to be placed in the 'element' of voluntariness. If flags are wind made visible, by analogy, we could say, commands are 'will made visible.' *Prima facie*, then, Canetti seems to subscribe to a psychologistic kind of theory; however, looking more carefully, one finds that the causal order is inverted: as it becomes progressively clearer throughout his discussion, there are no pre-constituted psychological entities which would subsequently enter social relations. The case of children education, which he evokes, reminds us that the individual psyche is thoroughly shaped by social interaction. Commands are, in other words, deep-seated in our elementary constitution as social animals. The 'depth' of commands is, consequently, not only psychic, but social, bodily and 'retentional.' Over time, commands have become part of our own psychic build up, they have become *us*: not that we have interiorized them, rather, they have made us what we are[42] – out of so many stings, a scaffold. That is why above we have insisted on *mutual awareness* as the veritable *element* of command. Awareness is a deeply social feeling, much more so than a 'wilful' act: awareness indicates that minimal co-presence that makes the 'testimony' of the social relation undeniable to both parties, despite all the dramatically asymmetrical consequences that follow – sting on the one side, recoil on the other.

Consent to command, we can now see better, derives in substantive proportion from the phenomenon of domestication, whereby docility and the acceptance of commands are, chiefly, products of habit rather than of conviction and explicit adherence. Here one realizes how the horizon of language ultimately equates with the horizon of domestication itself – which is true not only at the individual level, but also fundamentally at the level of the species.[43] With V. Gordon Childe (1951[1936]) and Peter J. Wilson (1988), we should speak of a long-term 'human domestication' originating in the Neolithic period since around 13,000 years BP.

Humans have domesticated themselves by settling into houses, implementing farming and agriculture, and engineering the state. Far from occurring at the same time, or along a linear sequences, domesticating processes oscillated and were for a long time piecemeal, uncertain and reversible (Scott 2017). One could perhaps even venture to say that, in fact, domestication is still somehow incomplete today, and is never just a destiny. Certainly, however, the 'adoption of the house' constituted a crucial process that spanned a period between about 18,000 and 13,000 years BP. With 'the household,' a whole domestic economy developed, which was not only an alimentary one, but also a complete aesthetic and moral one. *Food* then came to act as a crucial link between economy and morality. In parallel, in Canetti we see the flight-command prolonging into the domesticated command, once *food* is introduced as a common medium between commander and commanded. At that point, the dynamics is upturned: instead of *eating* the body of the commanded, the commander now *feeds* it. A completely new intimacy between the two can then be established: the commanded turns into an 'obeyer.' Here is precisely where the ground of all authority (Weber's *Herrschaft*) can be retrieved: domesticated command is, indeed, a kind of 'voluntary captivity' [*freiwillige Gefangenschaft*] (*MM* 363/*CP* 308).

By and large, raising children and educating them is enacted through such domesticated commands. While twentieth-century pedagogy has most insisted that children should be guided to adhere to general rules, learning to recognize and apply general rules of conduct and fairness to the specific instances of life (in a way that curiously resembles Hart's positivist theory of law), the reality of both formal and informal education remains such that most of the time children are quite directly commanded through dos and don'ts – and the meal is unsurprisingly often a crucial part of the negotiations concerning obedience.[44] That is why Canetti sides emphatically with children, whom he describes as snowed under tons of commands each day: 'it is a miracle that they ever survive the pressure and do not collapse under the burden of the commands laid on them by their parents and teachers' (*MM* 360/*CP* 306). Domestication does not change the fact that commands remain a force external to the recipient, weighting upon him or her from the outside: rather than 'interiorised' as norms of one's conduct, commands received by the youth will be spit out as soon as possible – even though, in practice, this means that they will be repeated after many years to the following generation, thereby perpetuating the game of impulses and stings. In this respect, an interesting parallel between Canetti and Hannah Arendt can be outlined: for both authors, the domestic realm is a domain of hierarchy and oppression, a realm of stings accumulation; by contrast, only the public domain – the realm of the crowd and of collective action – can provide a relieving moment, a hopeful embodiment of freedom and equality among humans. Especially in her reflection on politics inspired by the Greek polis, Arendt (1958) remarked how the public domain could invent freedom and equality only by deliberately breaking with the domain of the natural necessities encapsulated in the household.[45]

The domesticated command represents a coordinating tool in social life, enabling an efficient performance of action in synchrony with others. From the phenomenology of command and the existential situations it originates, we progressively move towards a whole ecology, whereby commands establish orderly circulations across the social body. In this respect, Tarde (1898: 116) cited commands, and more precisely the command–obedience couple, as an instance of 'elementary social harmony,' along with other couples such as teaching–learning and producing–consuming: they all constituted cases of what he called 'adaptation.' An interesting theory of commands in this vein was formulated in the first half of the twentieth century by the French psychiatrist Pierre Janet (2005 [1929]: 107 ff.), who suggested that commands embody a type of earlier division of labour. For Janet, a command can be imagined as a plan split into two subsequent segments: the first segment is linguistic, the second operational. Command precisely evolves from assigning to two different persons what is originally a single course of action. A single command looks to Janet as composed of two moments: (a) saying what I am going to do (plan) and, (b) doing it (execution). The linguistic moment belongs to the commander, who forces the second moment (operational) upon the commanded.[46] In this model, language features as preparatory of action: rather than just a description of the following action (the 'carrying out' of a plan as commonly understood), it involves a kind of *summoning* of the action to come: an order is, as Janet puts it, a 'starting cry' [*cri du commencement*] – a rallying call. The verbal aspect of command appears as a form of propitiatory preparation, whose aim is to coalesce the environmental conditions for an effective action to follow. The division of labour begins this way: one specializes in asserting, the other in implementing the assertions. While such a plan-oriented theory of command is certainly suggestive, anthropological evidence teaches us that decision-making processes can take on an aspect quite different from the one we are accustomed to in Western thinking. For instance, in a passionate monograph on the British Columbia native tribes of semi-nomad hunters, Hugh Brody (1998[1981]: 37) observes that

> The decision [to go hunting] is taken in the doing: there is no step or pause between theory and practice ... The hunter, alive to constant movements of nature, spirits, and human moods, maintains a way of doing things that repudiates a firm plan and any precise or specified understanding with others of what he is going to do. His course of action is not, must not be, a matter of predetermination.

Brody documents how the congregation of the hunting pack proceeds: once the team is reunited, various declarations about setting out to hunt are made by the members, and yet nothing happens during various subsequent days. 'Cries' (in Janet's terminology) are launched to which no clear action responds. These earlier calls to action sound, in fact, more like *boutades*, memories of the glorious hunts of the past and boasts about the super-rich hunt that lays ahead. Everybody contributes to a propitiatory imagination that has no immediate translation into practice. In other words, it seems as though we need to account for the existence of a zone of indeterminacy, or zone of indistinction, between the two parts of command outlined by Janet, whereby the element of decision or determination can virtually loom over the situation for quite a while, without ever becoming actual. Although decision and command are usually taken as the clearest manifestations of a deliberate 'will,' in fact, a much more elusive element is at play.

The elusive quid we are looking for may have something to do with *ideology*. In particular, it is Louis Althusser's notion of ideology as something that 'hails' and 'recruits' subjects that seems most resonating with the ordering pattern of command we are examining. Although commands are clearly not at the centre of Althusser's theory, his explanation of ideology offers us a glimpse into what a structural-Marxist explanation of command in modern society might look like. In the context of his analysis of the social reproduction of power relations, Althusser argued that ideology has a fully material existence, in that it is always embodied in social practices, institutions, and the series of what he called 'state apparatuses.' Looking into how ideology concretely works, Althusser's central claim is that 'all ideology addresses concrete individuals as concrete subjects, through the category of subjectivity.'[47] The peculiarity of how ideology approaches 'its' subjects is thus located in the act of 'addressing' subjects *qua* subjects: it is the occurrence of such a direct address that turns individuals into fully entitled subjects. And because the 'entitlement' of subjects proceeds from the very fact of being addressed directly, subjectivation and subjection are effectively intertwined: after Gramsci, and before Foucault, Althusser is the theorist of the production of 'autonomous' subjects under modern capitalist conditions. Resorting in particular to the term *interpellation*, Althusser implicitly evokes the French legal expressions *interpellation de police* – which equates with arrest, handcuffing and forcible transport of a person to a police station – and *interpellation de figure publique* – which corresponds to the summoning of an executive figure before a collegial body (for instance, a minister before the Parliament) for explanations (*redde rationem*). In this sense, the term 'interpellation' includes not only the act of hailing – 'Hey, you there!' – but the full force of a command that brings the subject into a specific position vis-à-vis its interlocutor – a 'position' that can be either physical or institutional, or both. Interpellation is an extremely efficient device, which 'never misses its man,' as Althusser (1995[1971]: 226) puts it (although he later sets its success rate at '90%'). Notably, for our concerns, the ideological result of interpellation is achieved without *any interpersonal relation* at play: the nature of ideology is that of a fully *impersonal* command capable of driving individuals to 'work by themselves.' That is why Althusser insists on the fact that there is never a first interpellation, given that subjects appear as 'since-always' interpellated (even before they are born) by the many ideologies through which the social groups to which they belong waive at them.

Ideology, in this sense, seems to play a significant role in the domestication of certain ways of instructing and directing humans that appear as, at the same time, personally motivating and, so to speak, impersonally grounded. Its effects are distinctive, in that they appear to involve a mode of imagination and language whose ontological qualification still baffles us. The three famous categories of firstness, secondness and thirdness outlined by Charles S. Peirce

(Peirce 1931–58[1857–66]: §1.300), designed to capture, in a 'cenopythagorean' fashion (§1.351), three distinct 'modes of being,' (§1.23) may help illuminate the peculiar status of commands as located – so to speak – *on the thresholds* of semiotics. The semiotic domain is defined, according to Peirce, by the phenomenon of 'thirdness' – or, as he also calls it, 'mediation' or 'transuation.' The sign is a medium that links three elements – sign, object and interpretant – bringing them into a single take, irreducible to any sum of actual couples (secondness). The category of mediation can thus only appear in a world that exceeds purely mechanical actions of couples of actors. Any concept of law and lawful regularity, Peirce stresses, necessitates such a triadic articulation. Peirce also explicitly mentions commands in his discussion of thirdness: specifically, he describes the command given to our dog to go and fetch a book and bring it back to us (incidentally, it also seems significant that Peirce, too, points to an interspecific instance). Every logical understanding of an action diagram requires the category of thirdness; and, insofar as the dog's action is guided by some sort of comprehension of the triadic connection dog-book-master, which cannot be broken down into smaller units without changing nature, it can be said to be a semiotic animal.

But, on the other hand, it also seems to us that command 'flows through' thirdness, lingering as a residue of the semiotic operation – an indelible residue at that. The difference between a command and a simple a script is non-negligible: to the extent that commands act immediately by 'impulsing' their subjects, they necessarily bypass the symbolic mediation of thirdness. The 'impulsive' quality of commands and their capacity to initiate action bring to the foreground elements of Peirce's secondness. Secondness – which Peirce also called 'obsistence' and 'actuality' – is the domain of forces acting upon one another, involving 'a two-sided consciousness of effort and resistance' (§1.24). All forms of 'constrain' prove the existence of secondness. If law is third, all of its actual manifestations in terms of active force must be second. As Peirce (§1.328) put it, 'pure dyadism is an act of arbitrary will or of blind force.' The forceful, impelling nature of commands clearly equates with the immediate duality of effort and resistance. Our previous discussion has indeed highlighted the tensional element at the root of command, revealing in it a *corps-à-corps* of social forces (and, accordingly, a good deal psychological strain for the parties). Furthermore, not simply does command participate of thirdness and secondness, it also possesses a strong inflection of Peirce's firstness – 'originality' or 'orience.' Firstness indicates a mode of being that is not in reference to anything else, but rather constitutes a pure quality, a pure intension – a 'priman.' The first, in Peirce, is less than an actual occurrence: it is the 'possibility' of a 'quality of feeling,' a pure '*posse*' (§1.351). The non-contractual, non-binary nature of command fits with such pure pre-relational quality, which Peirce also termed a 'new simplicity' without subject, without object and without interpretant: such is the command quality, its immediate 'impulsive' aspect, the 'virtual' aspect of command discussed above.

As we progressively venture into the overlaps between, and the co-implications of, language – or, more generally, semiosis – and command, what changes is perhaps not so much the image of command, as that of language. To understand commands, it seems, we must contemplate the image of an 'efficacious' language, a language capable of attaining an immediate grip on things, situations and persons. Once we ponder how such a language might look like, we notice, for instance, that *algorithms*, mathematical entities increasingly encoded in digital platforms and the hi-tech devices surrounding us, are of command-like nature.[48] In other words, the imperative aspect of commands places them at the root of the very notion of 'programme' so ubiquitous in contemporary informatics. Programme should be literally understood here as 'pre-gramme': first writing, then executing what is written – with no possible unriveting between the two steps. The algorithm then appears as an instantiation of a special command language: as described by Robert Rosen (2000: 45), 'an algorithm … is nothing but a strong of imperatives, ordering us to apply specific production rules to specific propositions, assuring us that if we do so, some definite end will thereby be entailed.'[49] It is possible that such a non-symbolic, efficacious root of the command language, endowed with fully 'entailing' capacity, is best expressed by a *realist* philosophy of language. But, the realism of commands stretches well beyond their pragmatics: from Wittgenstein, we have to regress to the Medieval doctrine standing opposed to nominalism. At this point, a different, more ancient realism materializes before our eyes – certainly an ancient pursuit, if magic can truly be understood as the earliest realist language. Already Frazer's (2009[1890]) definition of magic put at the core of the magical operation the assumption of accordance between nature and magical practice itself, grounded in its basic laws: the spell offers in this sense a perfect case of efficacious, command-like language. The relentless quest for the 'natural' – *sive* perfect, or universal – language is a recurrent feature of the European Middle Ages (Eco 1993).[50] In the Biblical tradition, the language spoken before the destruction of the Tower of Babel was supposed to be the primal and perfect 'realist' language: Adam's language must have been as perfect as God's own, which equated with God's own will and deeds (the latter two being, in turn, equivalent). In short, one should not overlook that God's language *is* command.[51] The Kabbalistic tradition pushed to the extreme the idea that the structure of language corresponds to the structure of the world, and Wittgenstein's *Tractatus* was but a late rediscovery of such simple and powerful idea. All versions of linguistic realism are necessarily grounded in this idea of *mathesis*, at the same time conceptual and mathematical, given the substantial unity of letter and number notation in Hebrew.

From this perspective, modernity but intensifies such a quest for a type of 'control language' capable of endowing its possessor with special powers of action. This always comes with a nemesis. Faust's *The Sorcerer's Apprentice* [*Der Zauberlehrling*] (written 1797, based on classic folktale repertoire, probably of Oriental origin) offers the most renowned illustration of a situation where forces are magically evoked that rapidly escape one's control. But one can also recall the Golem myth, originating in early-nineteenth-century Jewish folklore. The Golem creature acts as a strictly literal executor of received commands, regardless of consequences, with potentially threatening outcomes. A clay creature, Yossele the Golem was subsequently activated and deactivated on the Shabbat by its mythical creator, the Prague Hohe Rabbi Löw, who alternatively applied and removed from his forehead, or mouth, a Shem token (i.e., inscribed with one secret tetragram combination of God's name). Besides Mary Shelley's *Frankenstein* (1818), quite likely inspired by the Golem narrative were also Karel Čapek's *robots* (first staged in his 1920 play *R.U.R.*). Čapek's robots are artificial androids made of synthetic flesh, industrially produced for cheap slavish labour. Indeed, the term *robota* means, roughly, *corvée* work: as such, robots are creatures quintessentially destined to be commanded at will.[52] And perhaps unsurprisingly, Čapek's play tells the story of the first robot revolt against humans.

Always in Prague, not many years before Čapek, the power of language to have a direct grip on bodies finds its strongest literary illustration in Kafka's early short story *The sentence* [*Das Urteil*], dated 1913. As the old, apparently fraying father – but who suddenly stands up from bed claiming to be 'always the strongest' [*der viel Stärkere*] – condemns his son to death, action follows swiftly: in the next few lines we see the son – who up until that point had no apparent reason to do so – throwing himself from a bridge into the river. The 'sentence' mentioned in the story's title is thus at least three things at once: the pronouncement, the condemnation and its execution.[53] Maybe with reference to Kafka's story, *The Tongue Set Free* (volume 1 of Canetti's memoir), similarly stages the narrator's grandfather cursing the father for his decision to leave the native Danubian village Rustschuk – and by the next sentence (although it occurs in a different section), the father is actually dead. The pronounced word always carries its omen along. Taken in this sense, linguistic realism fully integrates a magical worldview, and more precisely the idea of a 'natural magic.' The same, perhaps, holds true of commands for what they have in common with *spells*.

Humanizing command

The above discussion leaves us with the impression that the dominant tone in Canetti's treatment of command in *Crowds and Power* is meant to highlight the grave ethical and political threats posed by the command–machine. Such analysis is presented by Canetti as only preliminary to an invitation to 'break its tyranny' [*seine Herrschaft zu erschüttern*] (*MM* 393/*CP* 333). Command is denounced as dangerous to freedom and, even more compellingly, to life. However, as we have also hinted at, command is not always described negatively by Canetti. Discussing in particular the 'writer's vocation' [*der Beruf des Dichters*], Canetti employs the notion of 'commandment,' or 'exigency.'[54] The term *Gebot* (*GW* 8/*CW* viii) seems quite a distinct notion from *Befehl* – and yet, some noteworthy similarities between the two exist. In particular, the author highlights how the artist cannot but find him/herself in a situation of 'lack of freedom' [*Unfreiheit*] before the task of creating (*GW* 13/*CW* 3). This inherently resembles the situation of someone who is commanded. Specifically, artistic creation cannot but bear testimony of all humans who find, or have ever found, themselves in a condition of *minority* – which means, mostly, people who are subjected to hierarchical command.[55] Far from a leisurely activity, creation is a moral imperative, a psychological necessity and even an existential compulsion. It is impossible not to be reminded of Kafka's famous phrase about writing, 'the task nobody has assigned': precisely insofar as it has not been ordered by anyone, the task becomes unavoidable – fatal, so to speak. This must be read in connection to the other Kafka's notorious claim, namely, that his own existence was entirely devoted to writing, to the point that existing and writing coincided for him – he was *made of* literature.

For Canetti, the *Dichter/Dichterin* has no choice but to assume upon her/himself an 'irrational claim to responsibility' [*irrationale Anspruch auf eine Verantwortung*] (*GW* 275/*CW* 238): as a sort of compelled activity, one which always sets for itself an impossible standard ('if I were really a writer, I would have to be able to prevent the war'[56]), poetic creation paves the way towards the possibility of a more humane command to come. Art thus appears as a constant defence of human multiplicity, recognizing the talent for transformation as a most precious asset of the humankind. Deploying such a talent to the fullest extent, the artist turns into a veritable 'keeper of metamorphoses' [*Hüter der Verwandlungen*] (*GW* 276/*CW* 240): s/he dives into numberless social manifolds, rehearsing as many metamorphoses as possible, becoming *whomever* – anyone amongst the most distant and dissimilar persons, and especially the humblest, the poorest, those who cannot read, write, nor even speak properly.[57] Melancholia and depression correspond to the incapacity to transform oneself. To guard metamorphosis thus requires special skills and special procedures. Whereas, for instance, sociological ethnography cannot be dissociated from the task of *being there*, artistic creation implies a veritable *becoming that*: the *Dichter* is 'master transformer' [*Meisterverwandler*] (*MM* 452/*CP* 381). But to do so, the artist must preliminary operate *by subtraction*. It is in this vein that we have described *flight* as the contested terrain between subjection and liberation. Subtracting her/himself from all sorts of external commands, s/he escapes from any undertaking aimed at achieving 'success' (public recognition, sells, fame etc.), as well as more generally from any goal-oriented means–end scheme: as we are going to explore more fully in Chapter 3, the *Dichter*'s vocation entails resisting the present as *the present of power*, and, with it, resisting all that exists insofar as it presents itself in the guise of external and alien commands. In their place, the new commandment of the *Dichter* comes to coincide with the unissued imperative to create. Canetti himself writes about *Crowds and Power* (nearly 40 years in the making, let us recall) that he '*had* to write it.' All genuine writers, all artists, find themselves in such condition: they have no choice *but to create*, for creation is the form the vital process itself takes in these persons. An order issued by nobody, a task that exists without any specific *will* that would have set it – a 'law' that is truly 'individual,' as Simmel (2010[1918]) framed it. A law that is verified only in just *one* case effectively means the colouration of one's existence as a special, singular 'ought.'[58]

We have here the instance of a command that does not shrink the breadth of life. On the contrary, it is writer's command that pushes her/him to stand up for life's dignity, rescuing as many persons as possible from withering away in oblivion, thus enlarging the domain of life. Not only keeping away from death, but also brushing aside the debris people are covered with, *dusting them* so as to let them shine as their unique original singularity would allow them to: this is what art is about, and it is the only way an artist can attend to her/his *century*. Of course, however, even in the sphere of poiesis, command retains its pharmacological–cathectic complexity. For instance, while defining what aphorism notebooks mean to him, Canetti admits that this sort of painstakingly slow production in the long run induces fatigue in a writer; but he also notices that it is precisely when one feels walled-in in one's work, becoming a slave of one's goal [*Sklave seiner Absicht*], that the impulse to relinquish all command [here *Regiment*] over one's production and let oneself go to ephemeral, unequipped, potentially awkward, contradictory, blundered improvisation becomes all the more valuable (*GW* 56/*CW* 42). Letting command go, temporarily relinquishing the studied organization of one's production (*discipline* as the other intrinsic component of creation), might, perhaps, resonate with the famous expression by Hannah Arendt, *denken ohne Geländer*, thinking without banister: at that point only, thinking – or creating, which is the same – turns into a risky activity, whose effect is unknown, and not assured by any system of thought, any religion, nor any ideology.

Could such artistic–poetic mode of existence help us mould a different type of command? In *Crowds and Power*, the possibility of a 'humanised command' is evoked, but – as earlier on noted by Iris Murdoch (1962) in her review of the book – not much elaborated upon. It is indeed true that the humanized command looks like a magical apparition at the end of a rather sombre discussion. It is even possible that Canetti himself wanted that apparition to look *magical*. After all, we are told about the direction where rescue might come from, but we are not told when and how it might come about. Accordingly, we are provisionally left with Canetti's own ambivalence: on the one hand, he certainly subscribes to various elements of a politically realist view of humans – an essential a-historical view where human vicissitudes endlessly revolve around the same dynamics, with butchers and victims simply swapping their positions.[59] On the other hand, such a pessimistic realism coexists in Canetti with an intense wish to find and valorize at most the transformative moments of the human experience. It is this *transformative* view of social life that animates Canetti's inquiry into the potentials of art. Some degree of magical thinking is, in any case, required by a Canettian epistemology.

Also, the transformative potential of artistic creation may be extended besides its specific domain. But, how could transformation infuse command, which looks like its very antithesis? Perhaps, we suggest, the strength of command can be *exploited* to new ends. After all, evolution cannot but tinker with the elements at hand: the means always have to be 'perverted,' so to speak, or subverted, to produce the ends. As considered above, domesticated command already defines a shared social interior, as is visible, for instance, in education and morality, but also in the collective synchronization of action. Undeniably, command appears as a wonderful social clock. Even individuality might be said to somehow emerge from it – for in fact, what are proper names if not commands? Names are created in the *vocative* form, to the extent that pronouncing a name equates with summoning a person: the named one who answers 'I'm here!' is, in this sense, already obeying.[60]

If command can be so strongly motivational, it is because, in its aspect of *cri du commencement*, it is deeply ingrained in our species. Once commands are naturalistically understood as grounded in 'social callings' of pre-individual nature, they reveal the existence of a *social life* that runs profounder than any biological process or psychological experience. Far from being paradoxical, the real question then sounds as: How can such a social life be *made human*?

It is true that command is, as we have seen throughout, contradistinguished by asymmetry; yet, its sought-for humanization does not necessarily amount to a complete demise of it. Rather, it points to the possibility of a *command without stings*. This is precisely what the last sentence of *Crowd and Power* calls for – and of course the difficulty lies in the fact that a 'command without stings' does not equate with simply an accepted command, or a 'legitimate' command – since willing submission will never spare the stings. The requirements for a liberated command lie at a much higher standard than that. The stings, we have seen, are the veritable 'burdens of distance' that set humans apart, thinning out commonality. What originates them is the feeling of resistance or, more precisely, *the long-lasting resentment of giving up one's resistance*. As remarked above, a clear resonance of the Nieztschean theme of *ressentiment* as the 'slavish feeling' can be heard. *Ressentiment* is, for Nietzsche (1994[1887]), the nihilist feeling par excellence – where slavish feeling means, above all, a feeling that enslaves the one who experiences it. The only chance for command not to become a toxic, poisonous machine is to overcome resentment. This calls for powerful inventions – both psychological and institutional – that, perhaps, have not yet seen the light of the day. Even so, new ways of flowing, along with new modes of articulating continuity and discontinuity in the social relation, can be experimented in terms of alternative 'elemental' compositions: new milieus, new media, new atmospheres rest ahead of us. If this is possible, then conceivably not even the stings should be regarded as our enemies in the absolute sense, but rather as elements of a larger cathectic problem: What to do with our stings? How to *transform them*?

As a concluding remark, it is possible now to return to the expression 'seize the century by the throat.' Applying Canetti's own theory of the organs of power, there is no doubt that the act of 'seizing by the throat' *is* one such act of power. As can be better appreciated now, however, this expression encapsulates a number of tensions and predicaments in the development of knowledge about social life – that is, in terms of episteme. Seizing the century by the throat, then, seems to hint at the huge disproportion of forces between the individual and the masses. At the beginning of the twentieth century, Georg Simmel had argued that anything like a science of society was itself a consequence of the practical power the masses had achieved over the individual during the course of the nineteenth century. Indeed, the dominant trope in the imagination of early sociologists like Simmel and Durkheim is precisely the *forcing* of the individual enacted by society (an image also quite dominant in Freud). The individual is *shocked* by social life; its personal boundaries are assaulted by the social forces. For Simmel, this sort of violence was typical of the modern urban world, whereas in his latest book, Durkheim attributed it even to primitive rituals, thus placing such a *collective command* at the root of social life at large. Canetti's image of 'seizing the century' reverses these roles, and presents us with a rather assertive individual who dares to ask tough questions. The author wants to be on the attack as he confronts collective dynamics – importantly, though, what he attacks is not other humans, but *the century* itself. In order to do so, a *radical* social critic cannot but appropriate the tool of command, and *exploit* it – once again, *force it* – to an aim quite different from its intended one.

Chapter 2

INCREASE

Figure 2 The pack wants to grow, but cannot.

Sources of increase

'The myth of increase' is an expression employed by Canetti to describe an ancestral drive towards the formation of crowds.[1] The underlying idea is that, for humans, crowds are not just a neutral occurrence, but they represent the end point of a long history that has been instrumental to evoke and prepare their actual formation. Before ever existing, crowds have been *desired*. By whom? Following an imagery also to be found in Durkheim and Freud, Canetti endorses the thesis that, before crowds ever materialized, humans existed prehistorically in small groups known as bands, camps or 'hordes' (the latter being a term widely employed by Durkheim and Radcliffe-Brown, for instance, but discarded by later anthropologists). As summarized by Peter Wilson (1988: 28), 'hunter/gatherer nomadic groups are small, face-to-face units that range over vast, relatively empty spaces.' In classic anthropology, this conception has been rendered with the notion of 'segmentary society', developed by Durkheim (1895), Evans-Pritchard (1940) and Lévi-Strauss (1949) to describe stateless, 'acephalous' societies – although there are clearly major differences between hunter/gatherers, such as the Australian aboriginals studied by Durkheim, herders, such as the Nuer studied by Evans-Pritchard, and agricultural societies, such as the ones where state formations first – although intermittently – developed (Scott 2017).

In the segmentary model, a tribe, or equivalent social whole, is presented as split into several basic, relatively independent segments. These segments are adjacent to one another – sometimes peacefully, sometimes clashing. The various 'tribal sections' consider themselves related in terms of lineage and common ancestry, and, as classically explored by Lévi-Strauss (1949), are interlocked in a more or less complex system of intermarriage relations. Local groups ('tertiary segments') are bands, each of which represents an extended family (kin group) composed by a number of about 30–50 members. Each band has a more or less stable core, but remains fluid in its overall composition: people may join or leave the kin group, essentially because the notion of kinship is not imputable to biological facts, but rather meant to assert friendship, alliance and affinity. The camp of a band is characterized by enhanced intimacy between the members, given that, as effectively put by Evans-Pritchard (1940: 142), 'the smaller the tribal segment the more compact its territory, the more contiguous its members, the more varied and more intimate their general social ties, and the stronger therefore its sentiment of unity.'

Typically, bands congregate on important ritual occasions. Rituals make the very notion of 'tribe' become tangible: such are, for instance, the famous *corrobbori* described by Spencer and Gillen (1899) and amply used by Durkheim (1912) for the elaboration of his sociological theory of religion. It has been questioned whether the Australian aboriginal model can serve as representative of hunter/gatherer societies at large – which is probably not the case. Nonetheless, the Australian aboriginals, together with the African Bushmen, feature prominently in early anthropological theory, and are amply referred to by Canetti. As a general methodological caveat, for the sake of this argument one should not place too much emphasis on the anthropological reliability of the sources: in other words, it is indeed possible that, even though the ethnographic details were revealed as faulty or misinterpreted, a number of underlying social patterns can still be successfully identified across the different settings under consideration.

It is within the bands typical of hunter-gatherer societies that Canetti places the emergence of what he calls *the pack* [*die Meute*]. Packs incept as functional subunits of the band. At the same time, speaking of human pack also clearly evokes the packs of wolves and other gregarious carnivores. While *prima facie* the choice of the term looks controversial – seemingly buying into a certain primordialist, immutable view of humanity, modelled upon animal behaviour – its aim lies, as we shall see, with stressing a naturalistic approach to the social phenomenon – specifically, one that does not assume human exceptionalism. The most important requirement for Canetti is to remain faithful to the concreteness of phenomena. A pack is a unit consisting of about ten to twenty members, specialized in a joint task, such as hunting, fighting, or weeping. We now know that many herd mammals are capable of doing this, including the lamentation for the deceased, which has been documented among elephants and apes (de Waal 2019). The pack is a unit of great importance, in that it provides the basic blueprint for teams and operational units of all sorts, from street gangs to sports teams, from religious sects to music bands. Not only do the humans who belong in this type of formation know each other personally and intimately, but they can be said to be all 'obsessed by the same goal' [*alle von selben Ziel besessen*] (*MM* 110/*CP* 93). Small and extremely cohesive units, packs always exist in a state of excitement, agitation or arousal [*Erregung*]. All packs seem to share such an overcharged state covering a rich emotional palette that includes sadness, lament, wail, buzz, frenzy, aggressiveness, ferocity, speed, and even delusion, compulsion and psychosis.

In short, we could say that the pack is an instantiation of social intensity, where the excited state both manifests and contributes to enhanced interaction and shared feelings. The pack's arousal is related to the type of immediate action that is currently uniting its members – for the pack is above all a unit of movement, a *war machine* in Deleuze and Guattari's (1980) sense: it is the shared obsession (for the prey, the enemy, the departed, etc.) that imparts to the pack its distinctive directionality. From its own direction, the pack receives its unique individuality. At the same time, Canetti stresses the metamorphic nature of packs: these formations can only be loosely codified, and easily flow and transfuse into other types. At bottom, what seems essential for their existence is, precisely, the general state of excitement-arousal. It is as if different pack formations correspond to as many ways in which arousal is concretely given shape, made sense of, and treated accordingly. Contrarily, once the excitement is extinguished, the pack naturally dissolves and withers away.

Among the pack's goals, a particularly important one is the aim to spur the augmentation of the group itself [*Vermehrung*]. Such goal is, so to speak, beyond spatial directionality. Canetti stresses that, for early human formations, increase is doomed to remain an unfulfilled dream. Indeed, a substantial increase is out of reach for the small groups of humans belonging in what have also been called homeostatic societies. Nonetheless, it was the desire to become-more animating the pack that provided the ground for the actual historical accretion of human groups. Increase is thus initially rooted in the dissatisfaction and restlessness vis-à-vis the group's current size and power of action. The outcome of such dissatisfaction is not immediate, since the pack's desire exceeds the very human reality it embodies. So, the pack dreams a larger dream than it can accomplish: that is why its dominant characteristic is that of an *intensive*, rather than *extensive*, unit. But simultaneously, even in segmentary societies, the pack acts as a sort of avant-garde for crowd formation. The pack's experience of intensity is the hotbed and the milieu where human increase is first prepared. The specific state to be highlighted here is a mix of many different feelings arising from the same early intensive state – including joy, excitation, effervescence, desire, frustration, impotence, fear and grief. Importantly, for Canetti, the 'more' of 'becoming-more' is not simply measured by the number of people in a group, but also by the maximal deployment of the physical strength of the individuals in it.[2]

Such is the case of the warrior-fighter-hero [*Held*]. In a sense, it can be suggested that such a hero is a social image that has provided the mould for the development of individuality in the modern sense: the hero stands out from the others in his/her group in that s/he experiences an increase in strength made possible by victories in fights. Warriors-heroes, reasons Canetti, have absorbed previous victories into their body, and present themselves to the next fight aggrandized by the number of survivals they have previously accumulated. The sacred energy (*mana*) deriving from past victories, together with the more or less symbolic anthropophagy of the enemy, are *incorporated* into the warrior, further increasing his/her self-reliance and ambition. We can notice, in particular, how the sacred is not produced by the individual, but is rather appropriated by him/her, precisely in the form of a psychosomatic accretion. The other members of the group confer to the individual that *mana* that becomes his or hers in the form of prestige, honour and awe.[3] So, while *mana* is usually rendered as sacred power, one could as likely speak of a very special type of embodied 'social capital,' which forms the root of the notion of 'fame.'

Each increase of energy in single individuals, though, creates tension within the pack, where equality remains a prevailing and pivotal condition. The law of distribution [*Gesetz der Verteilung*] – together with the famous primitive obligation to generosity described by Mauss and other classic anthropologists – reflects the way in which such hierarchical tension is transformed into an organizational principle of the pack and, consequently, the horde. Once again, the pack functions as a principle of incipient organizing, a blueprint to be expanded potentially to the whole group. It is the hunting pack [*Jagdmeute*] that specifically 'produces' (but perhaps better, caters) the original object to be distributed, namely the prey. While there may be different rules for sharing the prey, Canetti insists on the importance, for the group to remain peaceful, of following the established procedures scrupulously. Regardless of its substantive content, the law of distribution functions as the proto-law, the first detailed protocol of common conduct. Sharing the prey also stimulates what economists would call an 'economy of scale' type of thinking, namely, the idea that there could be an advantage in thinking large. Because human groups felt weak and vulnerable in environments that were largely beyond their control, Canetti suggests, they started mirroring themselves in animals that existed in throngs. Other swarm-like natural elements were similarly brought into such contemplation. To their eyes, swarm animals embodied the generosity and even the opulence of nature. Retrieving an expression from Walter Benjamin (1999[1933]), one could perhaps say that a strong mimetic faculty [*mimetisches Vermögen*] has been deployed in the relation between humans and animals. In its full deployment – Benjamin suggested – the mimetic faculty indicates a compulsion to 'become similar.' In other words, a zone of indistinction is established between the perception and the enactment of similarity – the point when a perception of similarity coincides with an actual performance of similarity. It is upon such ground that, in Canetti, the desire to become-more [*Wunsch nach mehr*] acquires the contours of an actual *push* [*Triebkraft*] towards increase.

Before taking place in practice, increase is evoked, visualized, played out, staged [*gespielt*]. Songs and dances, with their rhythms, melodies and refrains, are affective ways of approaching the fundamental trope of growth, fostering increase in various domains. The evoked ritual images prove capable of spurring the group towards an overarching dynamics of increase. So, even when actual human crowds are not at hand, the social group reflects itself into a number of crowd formations and crowd elements that exist in the natural world: swarms of insects, large herds, fish schools, as well as heaps of wheat and food, forests, trees, seas, clouds, stars, sands, streams, rain, fire. Such a mirroring establishes deep inter-species linkages, which Deleuze would later call 'blocs of becoming.' In this sense, a hybrid inter-species ontology is inevitably deployed by unfolding social life: each circumscribed social unit (family, ethnic group, nation, etc.) only exists through the extended associations capable of establishing a joint bloc made of heterogeneous elements engaged in a kind of ongoing conversation. Such blocs, as Deleuze also cautioned, are not based on the imitation of a static, allegedly original, model. Rather, a shared resonance is what establishes emergent zones of indistinction between the different parts of an association in the making. The bloc is not an entity but always presents itself as an association to-come [*à-venir*]. While Deleuze rejects the notion of imitation premised upon Platonicism (mimesis as the copy of an original model – see Deleuze and Guattari 1980: 17, 287 ff.; 374), for his part Canetti attributes a crucial role to the phenomenon of transformation [*Verwandlung*]: humans did not simply imitate animals – they actually *transformed themselves into* all the animals they knew. In some ways, although not in all, *Verwandlung* anticipates what Deleuze and Guattari would later conceptualize as 'becoming-animal.' For Canetti, by *passing through* animal existence, humans could better rehearse the type of *intensity* that is inherent in crowd states: this way, packs could intimate the advent of further social intensities.

Some caution is required in the interpretation of Canetti's theoretical proposal here. If one reads it as a purportedly accurate anthropological reconstruction of the beginnings of certain social institutions, then the narrative can easily be attacked as an instance of unwarranted generalization and naïve evolutionism. In his critique of Canetti, for instance, Ritchie Robertson (2000: 164) remarks that it is fallacious to suppose that 'religion (or art, or language, or any other wide-ranging institution) was separate from the rest of human development.' As Norbert Elias (2000[1968]) had previously shown, it also proves vain to look for the 'primal scene' of social life, simply because society has no beginning and no end. Sociogenesis is not the study of an idealized beginning – an alleged 'zero-degree' of civilization – but rather the identification of long-term underlying trends in social transformation. Society is better imagined, one may add in this vein, as an autopoietic system, a distinct order of life, or a plane of consistence: the approach developed by social theorists like Norbert Elias or Fernand Braudel entails an image of society that does not rule out history, but rules out the search for any primordial setting, out of which a given institution or social pattern would have emerged, just as it rules out the linear evolutionary trends of the positivist tradition.

Once these points are granted – as they certainly must be – one might still ask: does this type of criticism represent Canetti's position correctly? Perhaps, on this point, Walter Benjamin can be of help again. In his analysis of the German tragic drama, Benjamin (1974 [1928]: 226) distinguished between *Entstehung* (beginning, commencement) and *Ursprung* (origin as living source). In this respect, Canetti is probably not so much interested in reconstructing an alleged initial stage of social organization, as much as he is keen on capturing elements that are common across widely varying social contexts. These elements are primal not because they were there at the beginning, but because they underlie as active forces the ongoing proceeding of social life. Already Lévy-Bruhl (1938) and Mauss (1950[1902–1938]) suggested that, rather than reasoning in terms of successive evolutionary stages, whereby more complex and more modern stages would supplant simpler and more ancient ones, it would be better to speak of evolutionary *strata* existing within each social formation, whereby one can read the archaic as persisting inside (or below the surface of) the modern.[4] That is why it is a deep betrayal of Canetti's thought and attitude to regard him as an evolutionist: indeed, it is he who suggested that modernity's cult of itself only obscures the development of an adequate knowledge of social life. Within the framework Canetti proposes, there is no advancement nor progression, but transformation through the reassembling of a number of elements that are themselves changed by reassembly. Incidentally, such procedure is almost antithetical to the analytical sociology of Parsons, which Elias (2000[1968]: 453) famously characterized as a combinatory game of cards where the cards are limited and always the same. The forces described by Canetti are, on the contrary, not only metamorphic, but also extremely concrete, as already anticipated in the previous chapter: they are designed to be in explicit contrast to most abstract social–theoretical constructions.

The reassemblages surrounding the life of packs and their becoming are driven by a number of forces, or motifs, with increase being crucial amongst them. Propitiatory rituals have been widely described by classical ethnographers. The Intichiuma rituals of the Arunta, for instance, were characterized by Spencer and Gillen (1899: 167) as sacred ceremonies whose aim was to 'secure the increase of the animal or plant which gives its name to the totem.'[5] In general, the paramount importance of the display of food and wealth in the everyday life of non-state and non-capitalist societies has been remarked. Social status, in particular, is always written in *the element of the visible*, hence the crucial importance of display. In such social contexts, beauty seems to be more compelling than efficiency, and ornamental value prevails over the economic one. In this vein, Malinowski (1961: 58) noticed for instance that the Trobrianders systematically overproduced food in their gardens, but mostly to showcase it in a decorative manner. Later, Wilson (1988) has suggested an underlying aesthetic reason for this: displaying abundance is more important than consuming resources. Excessiveness in display is interestingly similar to what, for his part, Bataille (1967[1949]) called 'the sovereign position' (see more below). In traditional or archaic societies, feasts featuring elaborate food displays required extensive preparation – and here perhaps lies the veritable source of the 'mega-events' of today: the Olympics, the World Cup, etc. embody the continuation of such propitiatory rituals, where displayed excess gets translated into the language of 'establishing new world records.'

The priority of the aesthetic factor over the economic one does not rule out a certain 'industriousness' of the archaic group; and yet it seems as though activity is, chiefly, oriented towards impressing the guest with conspicuity. Marshall Sahlins (1972) was among the first important contemporary anthropologists to point out that archaic societies did, in fact, produce surplus resources – they embodied, in his words, the 'original affluent society' (a similar idea can also be found extensively in Ivan Illich's [1973] work on conviviality). But, if the narrative of ancient scarcity is a retrospective invention aimed at aggrandizing the achievements of the capitalist economy, the meaning of abundance must still be clarified. Ancient abundance – as perhaps, ultimately, any other social abundance – is, in the first place, offered to what the zoologist Adolf Portmann (1990) called – with reference to animal skins – a 'viewing eye.' The astonishing biodiversity of skins, scales and feathers would have never developed were it not to serve perception and perceptibility (or, conversely, imperceptibility, as in camouflage). The notion of 'ornament' as elaborated by Simmel (2009[1908]) similarly points to such wish to impress the other. Contemporary urban street cultures bear striking witness of this anthropological *tópos*: one can just recall, in hip hop, the role of showing off – the so-called 'bling.' It is also certainly not surprising that the cult of abundance – as well as overabundance – is particularly spread among the lower strata of society, i.e. among the ones most directly exposed to the threat and the reality of poverty and starvation. The myth of increase, as a cult of 'more,' finds its obvious root in the wish to survive. Turned towards impressing a viewing eye, the industriousness of the archaic group thus offers an unsolicited, and yet for some reasons 'necessary,' gift to the beholder.

Another crucial point in the institution of the increase motif is the connection to animals, and more generally to the non-human domain. In anthropology, the segmentary society model is strictly interwoven with the totemic notion. Both models have been extensively criticized since the 1950s, and mostly found wanting. Evans-Pritchard (2004[1951]) found totemism an unsatisfactory category for anthropological explanation, especially since, reduced to a set of beliefs, it can be stretched into meaning almost everything and anything. The overabundance of totemic descriptions and explanations seemed to condemn the notion to near meaninglessness. However, it is also significant that more recent anthropological scholarship in the 2000s, notably the literature on 'human-animal becomings' and 'inter-species encounters,' seems to mark a kind of return of the totem notion – and more generally, a reprise of the role of animism for the social science (Bird-David 1999; Descola 2005). Canetti uses the totem idea without much epistemological hesitations: to him, totemism is entirely made possible by the human talent for transformation. In their quest for increase, humans have been led to *transit across* the whole animal domain, in order to redouble the dynamics of accretion they observed in animals as well as other natural elements. In doing so, humans have proven to be metamorphic creatures *par excellence*, always rehearsing and further training their flair. In this context, the totem appears as but the name of an allegiance, a coalition, or a neighbouring condition ignited by a mimetic faculty that is in the process of experimenting, training and cultivating itself.

Modern increase

Canetti seems to suggest that packs as well as individual heroes-warriors have always existed to evoke some form of increase, but for a long time they could not bring it to fruition. Only the advent of the human crowd bestows substance to the old vow of increase. That is why modernity – the historical moment when the crowds have not only materialized, but have come to occupy the centre stage of social life, as well as of political history – is fundamentally interwoven with the practice of increase. The rise of mass society has indeed represented a bold, perhaps unprecedented exercise in increase. From this perspective, what has changed over the course of human history, in the passage from hunter gatherer to agricultural and historical societies, might have been, mostly, a matter of *quantities*: the pack, which longed to grow but could not grow, has given way to the crowd, a new social formation whose quintessential instantiation is infinite increase (a figure which Canetti precisely calls, the 'open crowd').

Modernity has fundamentally altered the measure of the social process. Yet while quantity matters, we have to remind ourselves of Simmel's (2009[1908]: §2) earlier insight in sociology: as far as social phenomena are concerned, quantitative changes inevitably bring about qualitative ones. Also of importance is the fact that the quantitative conditioning of the group is not linear, rather, it proceeds through specific critical thresholds of discontinuity, veritable 'phase transitions' whereby certain social formations become possible only beneath or beyond given thresholds; correspondingly, sheer quantitative change breeds the conditions for new formations to appear. Reshuffling and recombining the early pack equation, qualitatively new social formations have emerged over time. Incidentally, it is probable that there are even more formations than Canetti presents in *Crowds and Power* – to acknowledge this fact does not contradict to Canetti's spirit, which, as we have seen, was empirical, visionary and non-systematic. Combining Simmel's and Canetti's insights, one could say that, although previous formations may not be thoroughly superseded, they can mutate to the point of becoming unrecognizable: this way, for instance, the ancient cohesive pack has morphed beyond recognizability into the modern apparatus of industrial production.

Writing in the post–Second World War scenario of the *Trente Glorieuses*, in the middle of the industrial boom in the Western countries, Canetti submits that, at the root of the advanced industrial production economy lies an ancient anthropological trope. Yet, notably, the relation between these two configurations of humanity is neither linear evolution nor analytical composition. Rather, we are dealing with a more subtle process of 'prolongation' – a category to which we shall return more in-depth along this book, and which constitutes a key notion to understand Canettian transformational epistemology. For now, let us just note that, while Simmel believed that large groups are necessarily less radical than smaller groups – given the former's necessity to accommodate a larger range of individual variability and an ensuing heightened compositional heterogeneity – Canetti formulates the hypothesis that visibly large groups, such as crowds, are, in fact, always the outcome of an increase procedure that retains a deep, if non-linear, relation to the smaller and more cohesive pack who first dreamed it. The same dream is prolonged, yet by doing so also reversed, possibly betrayed – perhaps even, turned monstrous.

Some of the discontinuities in the becoming of increase are certainly momentous. The emergence of crowds, in particular, entails a different criterion of individuation. The world of the pack is one where the degree of intimacy and individuality (or perhaps better, personality) is quite high: pack members are deeply acquainted with each other, and each has a unique personal place to occupy in the small band. The dominant equality of condition does not at all rule out a strong characteriology within the pack – to the contrary, the latter is the pre-condition for their acting so single-mindedly: in modern terminology, good teamwork can only be based upon intuitive and immediate reciprocal attunement between the members. The view elaborated by Canetti contains an important idea that contradicts the modern narrative inaugurated by Adam Smith's claim that humans become more unique through the division of labour – a narrative then continued by Durkheim's dichotomy of mechanical and organic solidarity. In practice, the idea that the division of labour produces more accentuated individualities constitutes a background assumption of all classical sociology, and still undergirds many sociological approaches to morality and the economy. By contrast, in the Canettian scenario, as the population numbers increase, society becomes less personal, less 'individualist': every single one counts less – to the point that, in modernity, nobody is irreplaceable. In other words, a law of large numbers practically flanks the materialization of crowds. Modernity has perfected the notion and practice of the individual by developing a large array of technologies to individuate, such as single-user locations, ID cards, psychological profiling, personal performance metrics, legal responsibility, up to what Durkheim famously described as a 'cult of the individual.' But paradoxically, modernity is also the time that marks the demise of the heroes, of strongly characterized personalities – a loss which it compensates with the new mythology of superheroes, cinema stars, bossy politicians, and the like. Authors such as Carlyle or Nietzsche already fully belong to the field of the imaginary compensations for the weakening of personhood.

The crowd reality of modernity is, above all, the reality of a new scale of existence. In a critical study of realism in modern literature, Canetti observes that the literary realist attitude is in the twentieth century fundamentally challenged by the very nature of the new reality.[6] While nineteenth-century realism strove to get closer to the social worlds of the lower classes, twentieth-century realism finds that the reality to capture has itself become strange, creepy and unrecognizable (this way, incidentally, Canetti is probably reclaiming a realist stance for his own literary work). The twentieth century presents us, in fact, with an 'increasing reality' [*zunehmenden Wirklichkeit*], given that 'a lot more exists now ... The old, the new, and the different flow in from everywhere ... tens of thousands of new things swarm in on us like mosquitoes' (*GW* 71/*CW* 55–6). The century appears as more crowded than ever: not only, as in the past, do humans mirror themselves in animals and natural elements to propitiate their own increase; they now have organized the material world in order to plan, engineer and implement the increment: they have developed the industriousness of nature into the straightjacket of factory production. A huge mobilization of humans and things follows, where the intolerance towards imprecision becomes maximal, and utopias are turned into planning. Some of the results of this new aspirational reality are quite disturbing – one just has to think, for instance, of the debasing conditions of industrial animal farming.[7] While Canetti does not mention this example, his advocacy for animal rights is well known, and in the realism essay – dated 1965 – he mentions an even more unsettling fact, namely, the advances in scientific knowledge about 'animal civilisation', or what we today call 'animal culture'. If animals, too, are not only sentient creatures, but properly cultural creatures, then it becomes harder to rationalize the industrial farming complex (which, seen from a certain light, bears more than accidental resemblance to the Nazi extermination programme – compare in particular with Bauman's [1989] analysis) and it also becomes harder to deny – as Lévi-Strauss (2016[2013]) poignantly put it – that we have technically created a *de-facto* cannibalistic feeding system.

The increased reality of the twentieth century mirrors the fact that the modern economy is entirely premised upon a religion of growth [*Wachstum*] and a 'hybris of production' [*Hybris der Produktion*], the industrial version of which can perhaps be phrased as *more of the same*, or – as Ivan Illich (1973: 23) put it – 'the dominion of constantly expanding industrial tools'. Modernity is materially confronted with the consequences of a pursuit of quantity gone astray. Among others, Anselm Jappe (2017: 16) has recently remarked that growth is intrinsic to the capitalist system: 'Every capitalist economic transaction aims to increment a sum of money. Such a system cannot but grow: increment is not a choice, but the only real aim of the process.'[8] Jappe thus speaks of 'tautological growth', underlining the fact that the 'objective' growth of the capitalist economy is not measured as against any external reality, but only with reference to its own parameters of monetary creation. As Simmel (2004[1900]) first remarked, money is the great new crowd of modernity. The strange economic phenomena that are inherent in pure monetary games – including the uncanny world of financial transactions – seem to confirm that, in this context, the creation of value and wealth is apparently limitless, but also subject to extreme volatility. Finance is, indeed, a domain in which the slightest perturbation, the most fleeting perception of trouble or passion, an ephemeral shift of belief and desire, all get hugely amplified, both in the sense of 'euphoria' and 'spikes', as well as in the sense of 'panic' and 'depression'. Here, it becomes consequently easier to realize the extent to which social life is entirely written in the element of the visible, i.e., actualized in a sensitive, excitable, reactive medium where swarming and cascading processes are ominously likely (Borch 2019).

In the late nineteenth century, Gabriel Tarde (1890, 1902) argued that the 'natural tendency' for economic curves is the upward direction, i.e. growth and expansion. Increase, in this sense, corresponds neatly to what Tarde referred to as the fundamental 'ambition' of the social thing to expand through imitation: in his social philosophy, expansion is the natural tendency of all things social. In light of this, it does not surprise that growth has defined the economic credo of the twentieth century – whether of socialist, social–democratic, or neoliberal persuasion. The economy has, for a long time, appeared as a self-propelling force, a king Midas capable of turning into gold everything that was touched by incorporation into the economic world system, just on the condition that it kept growing, obscuring its reliance upon the energies provided to it through the suckling of earthly human, animal and material resources. While certainly the vampiristic theme was clearly present in Marx's (1976[1867]: 342) description of capitalism, a clandestine 'animistic' stance has continued to contradistinguish modern economic thinking. That is why the ancient myth of increase may help explain the constant evocative state that underpins the trend towards expansion, development, enrichment and the production of an opulence that is no less obscene just because it is a reality only for a restricted minority, and a flimsy projection for the rest.

A Canettian gaze here enables us to see that most analyses of the present have wrongly attributed to the economy and the dynamics of inequality a foundational character, while they certainly have great importance, but a *derivative* one. Digging deeper, we realize that economy is but one way to bring about the motif of increase. If we admit this, we can understand better why it is so difficult to reform the economy. While most critiques of capitalism ultimately boil down to the greedy-human-nature argument, the often overlooked anthropological foundation of capitalism in the myth of increase awaits to be fully acknowledged and unpacked. Money, it should not be forgotten, is just one crowd among others. By the end of the twentieth century, for instance, the crowd of money has come to be accompanied by the crowd of digital data, which might conceivably even supersede money in the long run. Data, indeed, provide a new instantiation of crowd formation, endowed with peculiar features. Whereas a lot of attention has been devoted to the power of data as information, an increasing recognition is also being currently given to a different aspect that comes with it – namely, data as pollution. Incidentally, the existence of the 'data detox' advice genre confirms this important facet of our relation to data: they literally intoxicate us, and not only at the psychological level. The ecological footprint of data is terrifying, as we are only too slowly realizing.[9] The huge tribute of energy that today we pay in order to store and preserve digital data, to control and excavate them, to make data *thrive*, cannot be explained by mere functionality, nor by mere economic rationale, as it certainly implies a deeper theological element – where theology stands basically for the domain of the ultimate ends. It has been suggested that neoliberalism has posited the market as a new God (Cox 2016); if so, it may also be the case that the yet-to-be-named post-neoliberal world which is taking shape before our eyes is more or less positing digital data as a newest theological entity. Indeed, the power of animation is increasingly transferred *from* the monetary dynamic *to* the algorithmic one. Even more clearly than money, that cruel ruler of so many lives, the 'deep-learning' algorithm possesses a will of its own, which is much more sophisticated than 'money will' – prefiguring the capriciousness of a god.[10] Hence, the reorientation towards a data-driven economy, a data-oriented culture and a data-infused politics has effects comparable to the deep psycho-anthropological adjustments that were first required by the rise of a pervasive monetary economy during the nineteenth century.

As we reach the third decade of the twenty-first century, we find ourselves in a time of unprecedented turmoil and structural crisis – multiple simultaneous crises, actually: economic, democratic, ecological, sanitary crises sweep through the world. As we shall examine in Chapter 4, all these crises seem to point towards an experience of 'interiority,' which is however quite unevenly felt and patchily experienced. In this context, turning back to an examination of the myth of increase may clarify some underlying threads. Is growth possible? Is it desirable, sustainable, attainable at all? And, at the other extreme of the spectrum, could humanity exist *without* growth? In Tarde's rendition of the notion, growth features as but an instantiation of imitation, that is, of repetition-made-social. Every social innovation follows a diffusion pattern, which Tarde (1890) regarded as the imitative operation subtending the multiplication of a given technique, a technology, an idea, a belief or a will spreading across a population, as well as, ultimately, across global humanity. In Tarde, as things become bigger, they also become more benign and peaceful. This is not so sure for Canetti: if growth can be distinguished from sheer repetition, it is to the extent that it becomes rougher and bouncier. The first crowd is an open crowd, whose only wish is to grow larger and stretch outward; but all institutional formations represent as many ways of encircling that open crowd, turning it into a closed form. The ritual offers an early strategy of crowd containment, which assures a centripetal closure. Spatial expansion is renounced in favour of temporal repetition. Certainly, following the Durkheimian insight, the religious ritual provides a blueprint for all forms of repeatable 'convention' – yet, it simultaneously achieves more than that. By sealing the crowd around a central totem, institutionalized religion halts unlimited growth and privileges the development of communal indoor environments. It is in this sense that the great institutionalized church-building religions have provided the primal impulse towards atmospheric construction. Cities and city life have continued the expansion of indoor life, and modern capitalism – as reconstructed in particular by Sloterdijk (2013) – is indissociable from the building of large 'hothouses' of commerce, consumption and spectacle. The closed crowd is still certainly a 'repetitive' crowd, yet one where repetition becomes selective – only certain gestures, only certain beliefs, only certain practices are accepted by the closed crowd, and this selection becomes a badge of identity; concurrently, the generic aspiration towards increase is channeled, in the closed crowd, towards more specific and quantitatively specifiable formats: the closed crowd invents 'productivity.'

This is where Canetti's invitation to overcome the avoidance of the concrete must be met rigorously. The fact that growth is a basic biological phenomenon cannot be overlooked. Digging into the fibre of the increase drive, Canetti relates it to issues of life and death. Not dissimilarly from the Maussian 'techniques of the body' (Mauss 1934), in Canetti, too, the biological can directly adjoin the social. This brings Canetti to analyse the moment of *survival* as a crucial, almost tragic dynamic inherent in social life. Survival is revealed as not a binary, but a triadic relation: not a relation between one and one's death, but between one and another, as mediated by the fact of death. Just as giving and taking are not two different acts, but the same act seen from different perspectives, so, in the survival relation, living and dying are not two different acts, but the same act seen from different perspectives. A singular facet of increase can be uncovered here: it is the power of surviving others who die. Not simply. At the cost of generating a chorus of outraged reactions, Canetti lays emphasis on an inconvenient truth: surviving can be pleasant, and from the moment one has survived once, s/he wants to survive more times. Upon these grounds, survival can turn into a dangerous addiction, even an 'insatiable passion' to some.

What is not specific to the twentieth century, but which the twentieth century put on stage in the most blatant way, is the fact that increase is related to a strange form of eating, to an 'incorporation' known, in fact, as anthropophagy. Accumulating survivals requires that one, in one way or the other, kills, and nourishes him/herself on those killings. Indeed, the first half of the twentieth century, with its two world conflicts and the scourge of totalitarianism, appears to Canetti as a vast killing factory. While only few profited from the huge concentrations of stirred increase, a large majority, as seen in the previous chapter, took part in the game of command and obedience that made that increase possible at all. In this historical context, distinct from the intimate socius of the early pack, a different type of individual and a different mode of individuation emerge in survival relations. The figure of *the survivor*, which the author considers as deriving from the fighter-warrior-hero evoked above, is a figure of *incipient individuality*. One literally becomes individual through this confrontation with other people who are first detached, then removed, then dying and finally withering away – a vision which Bauman [1989: 234] in his review of Canetti qualifies as 'spine-chilling.' Hence Canetti attaches the utmost importance to the fact that individualized life is made possible by *separation*. This individual exists only insofar as it can be separated, not only from other people (existing, that is, in a non-fusional relation to the social group) but, in the first place, from the invisible crowds of the dead.

Amongst the most tragic consequences of this dynamic, we can count the fact that an increase in the number of the dead mirrors an increase in the power of the survivor. Logically, the portrait of increase drawn by Canetti reaches an acme under the totalitarian regimes of the 1920s and 1930s, with their terrorist practices of annihilation. It becomes evident that construction and destruction, increase and war, go hand in hand. Hitler, Canetti remarks, always wanted the war, awaiting it as a blessing; and, at the same time, he engaged in fantastic construction plans. As designed by Speer, Hitler's Berlin (to be renamed Germania) should have been an apotheosis of monumentalism. All the major landmarks were set to be n times bigger than the classic references in architecture, from the Egyptian Pyramids to St Peter's cathedral in Rome (incidentally, a similar architectural gigantism can be found in Stalinism and, to a lesser extent, Italian fascism). Hitler's and Speer's urban projects were aimed at conjuring up crowds that could wait and worship the political leader: vast squares were meant to attract evergrowing, open crowds, while the mega-dome known as Kuppelberg would have hosted ritually repeated, closed crowds. A complete atmospheric management was to be deployed to keep the crowds in the desired state of excitement [*Erregung*], given that the capacity to keep those masses mobilized was essential for the realization of the political project. The arousal of the crowds could especially be assured by a false promise [*Vorspiegelung*] of increase. The relation to the dead proved essential in such delusion: the projected Arch of Triumph – the crucial landmark of the new Germania capital – would have contained the names of the almost two million German soldiers who had perished in the First World War. Because Hitler was, in the first place, a survivor of that conflict, Canetti remarks that the tribute to the fallen simultaneously constituted an assertion of survival in the sense outlined above: an act of individualization by separation and self-increase. The Arch of Triumph was therefore bound to be a reservoir for power increase. The increasing 'individuality' of the Führer, Canetti submits, required destruction – for, ultimately, destruction itself assures an increase: the increase of the dead. The terribly separated individual can feel no pity for the dying ones, as he defines himself in direct relation with the hosts of the dead (and incidentally, the word 'host' seems apposite here, given that it derives from the Latin *hostia*, namely 'victim').

Survival may look like a bare-bone reality, but is in fact a complex one. Below, we return to the cathectic–pharmacological aspect of this complexity, which makes of survival a much more ambiguous and nuanced occurrence than is usually assumed by Canetti's critics. The reconstruction of survival offered by Canetti and its entailed philosophical anthropology have been often misunderstood. Despite the startling images, it is too simplistic to censure the author as a primordialist theorist, or a cold-blooded political realist. Canetti would easily grant that most people, most of the times, are not sadistic creatures who wish the sufferings and the death of their fellows. And if we read him attentively, he is not saying that surviving always offers a perverse pleasure. Moments of survival indeed spur a wide emotional range of responses – including fear, anxiety, terror, revulsion, rage, contrition, sadness, bitterness and melancholia. If we just turn to the victims of the Nazi Final Solution plan, it is plain to see that surviving was not an experience that increased their power. Primo Levi (1986) expressed in the clearest possible way how Auschwitz survivors were marked forever by the 'shame of being human,' the shame of having been through the camps reality and having returned home, parting their ways from the many – including relatives and friends – who succumbed. The shame of having witnessed atrocity – which Levi in strong terms equates with a 'remorse of conscience' – becomes 'concrete, heavy, perennial': an indelible Angst.[11] The psychological trauma was unbearable to many survivors, including Levi himself.[12] For his part, Canetti consciously wrote as someone who could have easily ended up in the camps, and, even without being a camp survivor himself, knew very well what Zygmunt Bauman (1989: vii) has later called the 'haunted memory and never-healing scars of those whom it [the Holocaust] bereaved or wounded.'

The cathectic dimension of survival can perhaps be better articulated. Just as command generates a recoil [*Rückstoß*], inducing an anxiety in those who impart commands to others, surviving is similarly fraught with the desperation of being separated from the others – the despair, in other words, of having entertained such a deep relation with the horror of death. This is a relation that becomes unsolvable, insoluble. It is true that, by surviving, the survivor separates him/herself from the dying ones; and yet, that crucial *moment of separation* is what lasts longer than everything else. Frazer's (2009[1890]) second law of magic finds a cogent application here: in 'contagious magic,' things that were once in contact continue to be in contact, even at a distance. And it is quite significant that the archetypical illustration of this is, as Frazer put it, 'the magical sympathy which is supposed to exist between a man and any severed portion of his body, as his hair or nails.' For similarly, the individual body is always prolonged into a group body. Because of the crucial moment of separation, the survivor is *amputated*, with half of himself or herself now on the side of the dead: forever tied to the dead, s/he can never get rid of them. Since, in this configuration, nothing can disappear, survival can truly be regarded as the source of psychosis, considering that all psychotic delusions are crucially characterized by an incapacity to let things go.

And yet, the same phenomenon manifests itself in not only psychotic experiences. 'Survival,' in other words, offers Canetti's distinctive way of admitting the simultaneity of violence and fragility within and between humans. One notable epistemological advantage of the survival notion, which Canetti's critics have often overlooked, is that we can look for the experience of survival in not only extreme life-and-death circumstances, but also, and perhaps especially, in mundane everyday interaction. Survival moments, in this sense, happen whenever instances of oppression, mobbing, harassment, humiliation, vilification, smearing, etc. occur – regardless of their magnitude and apparent consequences. Similarly, as noticed above, whenever we mention the tropes of hunting, warring and lamentation, we should be able to recognize these same practices in modern everyday life – although in disguise and as they appear in peculiar 'prolongations.' Survival appears in many forms: while the experiences of totalitarianism seem remote to the 'democratic' reader, it suffices to recall how, as we listen to the daily news, we all find ourselves in the position of survivors. As the news bring us notice of another war, another attack, another destruction, another famine, another invasion, another act of oppression, we survive in the sense of relating our own life to the death, or near death, of others. All sorts of unsettling questions spark off: Is this acceptable? How could that have been avoided? Where will those dead and their surviving relatives end up? What to do next? These are the troubling questions that chase us into our only-apparently-external-to-the-facts position, as we are led – whether we like it or not – to feel ashamed of our own survival: that we are alive while so many horrible events taint this world.

At a different level, the duality of violence and fragility is reproduced in the division of labour, if one considers, for instance, workers like first-aid rescuers, nurses and doctors as professional survivors: the sense of shared humanity, which is the powerful vocational drive for all these professions, is bracketed by an acquired and trained psychological detachment between the carer and the cared-for, in an attempt to create a sort of domesticated or civilized survival. This inevitably creates a split condition. In his realism essay, Canetti evokes in particular the condition of a 'split future': no longer unified as a substantive aspiration of all, the future appears to him, in the early 1960s, as radically two-sided – catastrophe and annihilation on the one side, abundance and automatically managed utopia on the other. It is a state which, with Deleuze, we could call a *divergent synthesis*. Perhaps, a divergent synthesis is really the hallmark of every situation which, fraught with too powerful contradictions, is just about to explode. Or perhaps, instead, it is the sign that two very different conditions are for some reasons entering a superposition state. Either way, the notion of divergent synthesis may be of importance to understand the relation between increase and transformation. Just when it seems that nothing else can happen – nothing else, except *more of the same* – a sudden change, an upturning [*Umschlag*] occurs. Only at these points of reversal, under the conditions produced by such discontinuous phase transitions, can quantity revert into quality, and a different degree become a different kind. A possibility for the new springs up at this point.

Equilibrium and the politics of increase

Modernity suffers from a major problem with finding its own place in history. This may be due to the fact that, in significant proportion, modernity has itself invented the sense of historicity, and with it, the problem of 'the present.' The present appears as an always challenging time because we do not know what is its meaning, place and significance vis-à-vis other moments and periods of human existence. As we live and speak, history is in the train of happening, but has not been effectuated yet. Should we ever have the impression that history has 'already happened,' that effectively would mean that we are suppressing the very present we are trying to grasp, by prematurely 'making it history' – and, as we know all too well, early historifications are always suspicious, usually serving partisan interests. In other words, confronting the present in its full immediacy raises the crucial problem of *measure*: there is a deep interconnection between the huge, the unmeasurable, the unheard of and the monstrous, best encapsulated by the German adjective *ungeheuer*. The task of 'seizing the century' thus necessarily stretches towards capturing the monstrosity of the present. For his part, as we have seen, Canetti's view is that, in the first place, modernity but prolongs an ancient myth of increase; yet, as also said, that element of fixity in his anthropology is counterbalanced by the acknowledgement that, because of an array of technical and organizational ameliorations, in modern times the scale of the human process is transformed to the point that we cease to recognize it. As Canguilhem effectively put it in his survey of modern biology and the problem of form, 'beyond a certain degree of growth, quantity calls quality into question. Enormity stretches toward monstrosity' (2008[1951]: 135).

The problem of equilibrium can be said to emerge precisely in the context of such 'enormity.' All pivots around identifying that critical 'degree of growth' past which quantity is converted into a new, uncanny quality. Conceptually as well as ethically, the problem with measure expressed by Western modernity finds its roots in classical culture. The *hybris-némesis* complex in ancient Greek culture may be pointed out as its true harbinger. Hubris, encompassing human overconfidence and arrogance towards the gods or the natural order, represents the stance of humans who believe they can rise above their allotted measure. It is thus always met with retribution and punishment (*némesis*, the gods' revenge), which ultimately brings humans down to their knees, in a condition of defeat (*áte*) and acceptance of natural necessity (*anánke*).[13] If hubris indicates a breach of measure, the sought-after middle way is delineated by the ideal of *métriotes*, or *aurea mediocritas*, and the imperative of *méden àgan*, never too much. In short, classical culture seems to express a deep faith that any sort of excess or prevarication is going to be reverted and 'done justice with' (*dikes epíkouroi*, as Heraclitus expressed himself[14]).

A more dynamic and problematic tension between growth and equilibrium permeates the modern imagination of nature. Without attempting here a large-scale reconstruction of this imagination, it can be interesting to observe the case of the science of ecology and the analyses developed in that context about the impact of human activity upon the environment. In the early 1970s, Eugene Odum, one of the foundational figures of modern ecological systems theory (jointly with his younger brother Howard W. Odum), articulated the problem of modernity as that of the management of an excess of 'good things':

> The basic problem facing organized society boils down to determining in some objective manner when we are getting 'too much of a good thing'. This is a completely new challenge to mankind because, up to now, he [*sic*] has had to be concerned largely with too little rather than too much.
>
> (Odum 1972: 55)

The background premise of Odum's argument will sound familiar to the reader of Canetti: the ancient pack had 'too little,' and, out of its relentless desire, came the 'too much' of the crowd. For Odum, modern technical power has increased the production of things that were originally scarce and much sought-after; but, by making these things available in unbound quantities, technique has also created new problems – a typical example in this sense is food, whereby illnesses due to scarce nourishment have been replaced by illnesses caused by excessive nutrition.[15] Odum also highlighted that 'young' ecosystems have a tendency towards production and unruly growth, whereas 'mature' ecosystems – as he dubbed them – tend towards protection and stability.[16] In Tarde's (1890) innovation diffusion model, new social phenomena initially tend to spread quickly through imitation, but are subsequently slowed down because of the 'collisions' with other imitative threads, until they reach a saturation limit.[17] While not formalized, it is not difficult to recognize in Tarde's description the outline of the mathematical curve known as the *sigmoid function*, the most common example of which is the logistic curve.

The latter has been employed in ecology since at least 1838, when Pierre-François Verhulst corrected Malthus's population growth predictions. Before Odum, in the United States it was Alfred J. Lotka, who most famously reprised this model for demography. A self-regulation principle was classically formalized by the Lotka-Volterra equations, showing that predator–prey interactions follow recurrent cycles. Just as the logistic equation, the transition from 'young' to 'mature' ecosystems described by Odum presents us with a cumulative distribution, whose first stage is characterized by exponential increase, followed by a second stage, where increase slows down and becomes logarithmic (reversed exponentiation). The inflection of the curve changes according to how close it gets to its saturation values. Insofar as it tends asymptotically towards a limit, which it does not transcend, the sigmoid trajectory offers a reassuring narrative, projecting the belief that even phenomena currently looking out of control will stabilize in the long run. With its association to a bell-shaped symmetric probability density function, a general equilibrium postulate can be said to be at work in such imagery.

Not by chance does Odum's distinction between young and mature ecosystems recall Lévi-Strauss' (1962: 233-ff.) couple of 'cold' and 'hot' societies. Both were elaborated during the Western modernizing context of the 1950s, which also makes them nearly contemporary to Canetti's reflections. Lévi-Strauss proposed the cold/hot couple as a way to replace the old positivist-evolutionary distinction between primitive and civilized societies, which had been diagnosed as unsatisfactory since at least Marcel Mauss. In Lévi-Strauss's analysis, cold societies seek to annul history through an 'obstinate fidelity' to tradition that, at least ideally, tries to elide the transformative effects of temporal becoming, whereas, by contrast, hot societies fully embrace history and its effects, including path-dependence phenomena and the non-periodicity of events. Despite his best efforts, however, with the cold/hot dualism Lévi-Strauss comes close to re-propose the old binary of modern versus traditional, a trope that was foundational of the discipline of sociology at large, as well as, arguably, one of its main theoretical shortcomings. The idea that cold societies work to somehow stave off or avert history, is later reprised and transformed by Pierre Clastres (1974) in his 'societies against the state' thesis: institutions and practices in stateless societies are, either consciously or unconsciously, aimed at preventing the formation of the institutional, centralized state, in that the latter entails a concentration of power which would be neither desirable nor tolerable to them. Subsequently, Deleuze and Guattari (1980) commented extensively on Clastres's thesis and summarized his idea with the expression *société de conjuration*, or – as one might tentatively translate – 'obstructional society.' It is not – as Lévi-Strauss had hypothesized – a generic sense of historical becoming which obstruction societies reject, but a specific distribution of power which they regard as dangerous and implosive. More recently, a not-too-different idea recurs throughout James C. Scott's (1985, 1990, 2009) work on popular resistance against being governed: an array of weapons of the weak is, in his view, developed, not to counter hegemony as the ideological discourse of social domination, but to actually eschew centralized power in concrete practice. Clastres, in particular, pointed out that among the South American native tribes he observed directly, such as the famous Guayaki, the chief is deliberately kept in a weak structural position, so as to make clear that he is continuously indebted towards the group for the privileges he enjoys, but in a way that he could never arrogate for himself much substantive decisional power.

A certain paradoxical feeling, in any case, emerges once we compare more closely Lévi-Strauss's and Odum'd terminologies: for it would rather seem that, by endorsing dynamic change, modernity in fact entails a shift from mature towards young ecosystems, in a sort of rejuvenation or neoteny process, heading towards greater chaos rather than greater stability. It is in this sense that, at nearly the same time as Odum's, Jay W. Forrester (1971), the founder of system dynamics, argued that reconciling the industrial economy with a steady state, i.e. guiding 'the transition from growth to equilibrium', would be 'our greatest challenge' for the near future. From a Canettian perspective, however, no simple opposition between complete 'cold' and 'hot' systems is possible at all: in spite of their different technical setup, in fact, the moderns continue the same dream of increase that the pre-moderns first conceived. Accordingly, the intensification of the social process in modernity – first classically described by Simmel – can be understood as consisting in the singling out and the extraction of certain already-existing hot, productive trends in social life, supported by an accurate cold scaffolding (such as the one provided by institutional stability). Contrary to what Odum and Lévi-Strauss seem to have implied, there are probably not two types of ecosystems, or two types of societies, nor is there just a linear, one-way shift from one configuration to another – if ever, we should better speak of two types of forces operating within each ecosystem and each society.

It is thus necessary to interrogate more closely the lexicon of 'optimisation' and 'maximisation'. We have already been alerted by Canetti that, in modern times, the myth of increase prolongs into the myth of organization. Contrary to commonsensical ideas, it is the same basic increase motif that underpins and permeates the notion of rationality as efficiency. While Odum was elaborating his reflections on equilibrium in ecology, and while Lévi-Strauss was positing the cold/hot anthropological binary, the psychotherapist Winfried Bion, examining small groups dynamics, came up with the notion of 'the work group':

> Certain ideas play a prominent part in the work group: not only is the idea of 'development' rather than 'full equipment by instinct' an integral part of it, but so is the idea of the value of a rational or scientific approach to a problem.
>
> (Bion 1961: 99)

In Bion, the rational work group stands in opposition to instinctual deployment and the unconscious power of the 'basic assumptions' usually at play in group interaction. The true work group thus devotes itself entirely to the maximization of its own 'development.' Even a sophisticated version of psychotherapy such as Bion's, clearly replicates here an increase imperative, even if the imperative is now rendered as an increase of rational outcomes, thanks to the application of the 'scientific approach' to problems. But in the background of these considerations, one can hear the echo of Darwinianism, proclaiming that evolutionary development always works through adaptation and optimization. For his part, Canetti remarks that it is difficult for us to capture the real meaning of increase, because the notion of reproduction [*Fortpflanzung*] has in large part obscured it. This can be read as an oblique reference to Darwin and, more generally, to the Darwinian mind set in the interpretation of social life. As known, competition, selection and transmission are the cornerstones of classical Darwinian evolutionism. Reproduction offers an impoverished view of increase especially insofar as it isolates the various species as if their desire to survive through reproduction were fixed. In reality, argues Canetti, each species is inspired by the increase of the others. This way, more species are carried along together by a mutually enhanced aspiration. With Deleuze and Guattari, increase must be described as thoroughly rhizome-like – not a filiation, but an alliance.

Although Canetti does not attack Darwin frontally, his approach suggests an implicit, yet profound, displacement of perspective.[18] Reproduction and sexuality are, of course, central to human increase, and Canetti mentions them various times, while apparently never analysing them in depth. Curiously, it is probably to Bataille and fellow authors stemming from the *Collège de sociologie* one must turn to in order to gain a complementary insight into the nexus of increase and sexuality.[19] Particularly in his later work, Bataille (1957) has developed to the furthest extent an analysis of eroticism in sexual life as a form of dysfunctional, albeit fully natural, excess. His research has delved into a variegated territory stretching resolutely beyond the principle of utility across the domains of economy, religion and ethics. To the forces of production and accumulation, Bataille opposes the unproductive and the destructive, which he articulates through the categories of 'loss' [*perte*], 'wound' [*blessure*] and 'expenditure' [*dépense*]. Contrary to the Darwinian motif, we do not have a competition for survival adapting to the environment and picking scarce resources, but a competition towards always greater excess – a movement which, has we have seen, for his part Canetti would call 'outdoing.' In eroticism – which Bataille juxtaposes to the 'regular' sexuality described by biologists – a form of increase appears that has nothing to do with reproduction, but with a completely useless state of frenzy and raving: an out-of-measure of nature itself, where lust borders with other intensive states such as pain, Angst and death. By stressing these cravings that contradict demographic increase and ordered reproduction, Bataille captures, albeit in a very unilateral way, the unruly element at the core of increase. Expenditure leads to the unleashing of hardly manageable intensities: what we have is actually a generalized social intensification, a hybrid form of increase–expenditure. So, while apparently in antithesis, increase and expense find their common root in a rejection of measure, functionality and logistics – if ever, they subvert those references by forcefully asserting a new logistics, a new functionality, and a new measure. In sum, two conceptions so diverse as Canetti's increase and Bataille's expenditure find their meeting ground in the displacement of the link between evolution and the economy.

To Bataille, eros illuminates an expenditure that represents an aim in itself, impossible to subordinate to other aims or principles – hence, its 'sovereign' status.[20]

The sovereign position is not amenable to any economic balance, and rather points towards a range of 'illogical and irresistible drives towards the rejection of those material and moral goods which could have certainly been used in a rational way' (1967[1949]: 45). The problem is no longer simply – as with Odum's – to manage the 'good things' within acceptable quantities; rather, it is to explain why there is a deep, if repressed or invisible, dissatisfaction with those good things in the first place – why, in other words, it turns out that those good things are what we most viscerally hate (which was certainly Bataille's personal case, but also his theoretical take-home message for us). As with increase, what matters most with expense is not a relation to the outcome of production, but a relation to the energy invested in it. For Bataille, a similar realization comes close to what might be called (with Foucault) a *stylistics of existence* – and precisely, a style of 'luxury' [*luxe*]: 'among all living beings, humans are the most apt to consume intensively, luxuriously, that exceeding energy that the pressure of life offers to certain conflagrations that are in conformity with the solar origins of its movement' (*ibid.*: 78). The central problem of expenditure can thus be described as that of getting rid of an energy excess, a veritable 'superabundance.' One cannot miss here the importance of the fire element, which Bataille connects to the excessive cosmic energy the sun transmits to the Earth (an especially compelling idea in our overheated age), and which Canetti more ethnographically saw at work in the 1927 crowd of the Vienna civil unrest, when the Palace of Justice was set alight.

In parallel, in his work on insects, Caillois (1938, 2008[1960]) pointed out the non-economic, more-than-functional and even dysfunctional nature of phenomena like mimicry and, more generally, animal appearances.[21] Caillois evokes for instance – in a clear echo of Bataille's 'luxury' – the 'splendour' of the butterfly's wings (2008[1960]: 491), their 'sumptuous' nature (498), and suggests such a luxury is not without analogy with paintings. Although only in the latter case do we find a design [*dessein*], whereas in the former we just have a pattern [*dessin*], in both cases *who* paints is the same nature – *natura pictrix*. And since nature does so with a complete disregard for usefulness, such 'inutility' (as Caillois seeks to show through a dense literature review in entomology) is bound to remain inexplicable to Darwinian natural selection. Although nature proves to be everywhere exuberant, rich and varied, most scholars still prefer to believe in the most economic of all possible worlds.[22] In fact, Caillois suggests, one should recognize in the butterfly's wings the tendency towards the maximal deployment of an 'independent aesthetic domain.' Such a domain is guided by a peculiar type of natural force, which Caillois interestingly calls *transformation*. The complex, multifaceted notion of transformation – present as much in Darwin as in Caillois and Canetti – will be delved into more attentively in the next chapter. For now, we can content ourselves with remarking that, despite their major differences, Canetti on the one hand, and Bataille and Caillois on the other, effectively pointed out the limits of an equilibrium theory of social life.[23]

The point, therefore, is not to oppose a static versus a dynamic social pattern, but rather, to identify two different dynamic types: on the one hand, a reticular, decentred type, on the other hand, a gravitational one, endowed with a centre of reference to which all movements can be ordinated. Clastres's thesis – which unfortunately could not be developed further because of the premature death of the author – asserted that obstruction societies seek to prevent the implosive vector, which would otherwise lead to an accumulation of power in the hands of a single individual or a restricted elite. However, we can observe that if a more or less explicit orchestration of pre-emption is called forth, this probably means that the risk of a centripetal vector is non-negligible: in other words, if these societies are 'against the state,' it is because some state desire is also likely at work inside them. So, while Clastres is correct that these societies should not be characterized in privative terms ('state-less'), but rather in oppositional terms ('against the state'), in fact, the overall dynamics resembles more closely a cathectic encounter. This, in turn, enables us to regard the state, not as an outlandish, inexplicable formation appearing out of nowhere, but as an open possibility first installed by the increase motif itself.

Another point in Clastres' thesis that requires discussion is his parallelism between the political and the economic spheres, with precedence of the former over the latter: just as stateless societies obstruct the emergence of the state, so they also eschew from the enlargement of the economy: while not locked at subsistence level and chronic scarcity (contrary to the European colonialist prejudice), at the same time, they are not engaged in any growth mentality aimed to make their business prosper at all costs. This way, Clastres sought to undo several Western preconceptions, pushing for an enlargement of the political sphere beyond the command experience, and for an enlargement of the economic sphere beyond the subsistence/capitalism alternative. However, one notices here that his whole argument rests on the idea of homology between the two spheres; by contrast, what is characteristic of Canetti's notion of increase is that it does not distinguish a priori between spheres such as the political and economic. One advantage of this is that one is consequently not forced into the awkward choice of deciding which sphere is more fundamental, 'infrastructural' to which other. Epistemologically speaking, the Canettian insight thus circumvents the perilous vagueness and wide variability of such generalist categories in cross-cultural comparison. Increase corresponds to an experience of intensification of social life which may take on many different shapes. As considered above, increase is metamorphic par excellence: it is a social dream and a social urge which points to a phenomenon more basic than the economy – in fact, the economy itself is but a specification of such motif. And similarly, increase works throughout political relations, rather than being tributary to them – particularly, as noticed, in the survival motif. Regardless of the social 'sphere' or specific domain in question, we notice that both centripetal and centrifugal forces are interwoven with increase, albeit in clearly different ways.

If humans are caught in the increase dynamic in a way not dissimilar from the rest of nature, then the modern problem lies in humans' amplified technology, and the ensuing ecological footprint of their activities. In the early twenty-first century, the inescapable realization that equilibrium can never be taken for granted in ecosystems leaves us before the momentous, uncharted transformations of climate change and ecological disruption with less certainties than ever. The problem of equilibrium therefore directly impinges on how we decide to face increase – economically, politically and culturally. Indeed, this is the time when we are called to 'stare the monster in the eyes.' Here, again, it would be tempting to see a contrast between the 'pacific' increase narrative and the annihilating 'survival' motif. But, the reality of their interlocked unfolding alerts us to the complexity of social life: as considered above, even killing can be used to spur increase – which is horribly common in the practices of killing war prisoners, or in genocidal and extermination programmes, as well as in state-administered capital executions. In other words, the 'more' comes in from many different sources and directions. Of course, this 'more' is of mythical nature; for Canetti, however, far from being empty ideological talk, or a deceiving superficial narrative, myths convey deep truths about human groups.[24] Thus considering the deep narrative of modern increase leads us to admit that industrial production, liberal commerce and 'business' more generally, do not follow a principle of 'economy', in the sense of parsimony – quite to the contrary, modern economy as a whole has been increasingly moulded on a 'business' model, based on the aspiration towards unlimited increment. The point is not, as often heard, that the world has become too centred upon the economy, but rather that economy has become non-economic, pivoting around a narrowly defined, business-oriented notion of increase.

The waning of the equilibrium postulate makes it more difficult for us to decide politically what is to be admitted in terms of production and resources exploitation, and which measures of performance and growth should be deemed acceptable. A recent critique of the more-than-terrestrial measure of contemporary increase has been carried out, for instance, by Bruno Latour (2018), following ideas in part already outlined by Paul Virilio (1977, 1995) – see specifically the latter's notions of technosocial 'acceleration' and urban 'upward fall' [*chute en haut*], representing two de-territorializing vectors that amplify an unruly run towards increase. The problem outlined by the two just-mentioned French theorists can be said to concern the mismatch between the amplificatory outcomes of technology and the economy, on the one hand, and the limited availability of space, time and resources in the biosphere, on the other. A similar, previous inquiry into the aim, rhythm and limits of modern growth had been carried out during the 1980s by the social activist, early green politician and intellectual Alexander Langer (1996). Neither a nostalgic communitarian nor a sheer eco-pragmatist, Langer puzzled about how modernity has taken quite literally the motto of the Olympic games – *citius, altius, fortius* – first proposed by Pierre de Coubertin upon the creation of the International Olympic Committee in 1894 (a motto originally by the Dominican preacher and educator Henri Didon).

'Faster, higher, stronger': although, in de Coubertin's understanding, such formula was supposed to set 'a programme of moral beauty', the thrust towards achieving more – or 'outdoing', as Canetti would say – has in the meanwhile become quite practical. Langer was arguably one of the first in Western politics to address, not simply the legal framework and the policies required by an ecological politics, but the deep motivations at play: it is not enough to curb emissions by law, he suggested, until the underlying drives and desires aren't transformed. The worst ecological damages occur, for instance, when pollution is turned into a market asset to be sold and bought, albeit a negative one – not only that does not affect in the least the attitudes of voracity and predation that have created pollution in the first place, but it spurs them further. Self-restraint will emerge neither by decree nor by the laws of the market, but only in the form a new desire. A series of new desires, Langer argued, are needed to counterbalance the Olympic desires. He referred to these as being attainable through an act of 'ecological conversion': rather than a sheer technical or structural transformation, the word conversion evokes the Greek *metánoia*, a discontinuous existential moment that marks a change in one's perception of the world. Turning the Olympic motto upside down, Langer pleaded for a responsible society founded on new desires: *lentius, profundius, suavius* – slower, deeper, softer. 'With this new motto – he commented – you cannot win any face-to-face combat, but perhaps you will develop a deeper breath.'[25]

Following Canetti's and Langer's insight, a different way of inhabiting the planet may emerge from a deep questioning of the 'participationist' ideology of the modern Olympics (*l'important, c'est de participer* – another slogan De Coubertin borrowed, this time allegedly from the bishop of Pennsylvania, and made famous). Participationism pushes towards a general mobilization of resources, where not only the objective results to be attained, but the notion of limit, end up vanishing at the horizon. In a different sense, participationism is also the ideology of the new digital media. During the 1990s, the new media appeared as enabling two-way communication, in contrast with the one-way classic broadcast media. In the digital domain, however, the activity of 'sharing' has since changed its meaning: instead of indicating the gift of something precious, it increasingly means flooding the other's space with unwanted clutter, often with cognitive and emotional rubbish, if not insults and threats. Participation, which was previously regarded as the true harbinger of emancipation, has since become a much more ambiguous, even suspect notion – as most apparent in the performative turn on the workplace. The worker's participation, now defined in terms of commitment to the employer and performance maximization signify, above all, a new face of increase. The French jurist Alain Supiot (2015: 215) stresses the similarity between the new performativity of the worker and the cybernetic model of control, operated via feedback loops. To this aim, Supiot quotes Peter Drucker's 1954 management textbook, where the latter explained how to elicit the worker's 'desire do to the best, rather than just go by' (Drucker 1993[1954]: §11, 'Self-control through measurements'). Precisely, Drucker was referring there to managers, rather than workers; yet, significantly, for him the new worker had to be, more than a cog in the machine, an active and devoted participant sharing the business' mission, with the ultimate goal, made clear in Drucker's (1999) later work, of *Managing Oneself*. The 'objectives' to be simply measured and attained, in fact, increasingly recede, as the situation becomes one of maximal resource mobilization. Such outcome derives not only from the extensive calculation of performance, but crucially from a shift in emphasis toward *relative*, rather than *absolute*, performance. The imperative of ameliorating oneself – so as to become a 'star performer' (Drucker 1999: 10) – returns us to the Canettian situation outlined above, that of 'outdoing.' In other words, the self has turned into the ultimate domain of increase.

A subjective act of ecological conversion, such as the one evoked by Alex Langer, is not at all easy to attain – let alone changing a whole civilizational pattern, a task which bears so many complexities one doesn't even know where to start from. For his part, Langer pointed out that 'conversion' designates not simply a subjective attitude, but an objective process as well – in the latter sense, for instance, one speaks of 'architectural reconversion' to indicate how former industrial spaces are turned into residential spaces. Even when new desires, capable of liberating us from the participationist-performative delusion, see the light of the day, the grave problem of modern increase lies in changing the direction and speed of a whole techno-institutional cultural whole, repurposing equipment and frameworks on the go. Even slowing down such a machine that is running too fast is challenging, as braking may lead to sudden structural fractures. We enter here a kind of sorcerer's apprentice Faustian scenario, where we systematically risk failing to master our own magic.[26] Outside of the equilibrium postulate, we may still find forms of stability, some 'stubbornness' of sort – except that it is a stability, not of state, but of variation. Here is where Waddington's notions of 'chreod' (or, necessitated pathway) and 'homeorhesis' (or, flow maintenance) find their place: whereas the type of homeostasis described by Lévi-Strauss for cold societies is the preservation of constants, homeorhesis is the preservation of a given dynamic complex that does not correspond to any established quantity, but to always-changing quantities: 'Developing systems do not, of course, preserve a stationary state, but they do have a tendency to preserve a definite *pathway of change in time*' (Waddington 1972: 67). If homeorhesis is not a stability of set quantities, but a stability of overall flowing characters (valleys in a landscape rather than any single actual river), then the notion shares similarities with the 'structural stability' formalized in mathematics by René Thom (1975[1972]). The contemporary problem may, in other words, be stated as follows: because the evolution of life has certainly brought to the forefront forms endowed with structural stability, it is possible that the outcome of disturbances and stresses is not immediately noticeable. Unfortunately, that does not at all equate with saying that there will be no consequences for those disturbances. Recognizing that the process is not a linear one, amounts to admit that, when the magnitude of disturbance becomes too large, or a number of disturbances accumulate so as to reach a tipping point, the structure may collapse suddenly through discontinuous catastrophe.

In this context, two types of change can be distinguished: on the one hand, smooth diffusion (a situation in which there is near certainty of continuous but small changes in the system, contained within a 'homeorhetic' variation range) and, on the other hand, sudden catastrophe (a situation in which there is a very small possibility of a quick and radical change). And the problem is to know when and how one type of change reverses into the other.[27] At a time when the biosphere is suffering a sixth mass extinction, and the planet's climate is being irreversibly altered – all changes with a clear anthropogenic imprint on them – some have extended similar gloomy expectations to human society: 'we are the next on the list' sort of warning. So far, humans have proven to be a very resilient species; but, perhaps, we think so only because we do not see the invisible labour of catastrophe already underway. A crack is crawling in our mug, which one day, like nothing, may split it open in two. Deleuze's notion of *fêlure*, or crack-up – modelled upon F.Scott Fitzgerald's homonymous story – may have a point here: when one realizes that one's life has a crack in it, that is precisely the moment when one falls to pieces. In short, while survival and increase may have not yet revealed to us their ultimate interconnection, for both Canetti and Langer, our ignorance does not provide us with an excuse for surrendering to increase.[28]

Laws of increase, feelings of increase

We have considered above the extent to which increase remains outside of the rational means/ends scheme, and can only be understood according to the tenets of a distinct, autonomous logic. After having outlined the transformations of increase at the gates of modernity, we can now turn more attentively towards that intrinsic logic. First of all, increase is *by nature*: it represents the first and most basic way to escape death, especially because death is unavoidable at the individual level. As we explore better in Chapter 4, in the crowd, humans may experience a liberation from the burdens of interpersonal distances that confine them to individuality and block their becoming. Such experience is, however, temporally bounded: sooner or later, the crowd tends to dissolve, and only by amplifying itself into open-ended growth can it hope to protract its very existence.[29] In the year 2020, we have come to realize that it is not only the human crowd that seeks growth: *the virus, too, wants to grow*. This minimal creature at the edge of life, already knows the laws of increase. Canetti's lines about bacilli read particularly timely in this respect: 'Only a tiny minority of people have looked into a microscope and really seen them there. But everyone has heard of them and is continually aware of their presence, and makes every effort not to come into contact [*Berührung*] with them – though this, considering their invisibility [*Unsichtbarkeit*], is a somewhat vague endeavour [*etwas vages Unternehmen*]' (MM 52/CP 47). Certainly, our techno-visual set up has partly changed, in the sense that we have all become familiar with the magnified image of the virus afflicting us (although what we are provided with are very mediated and edited images, thanks to techniques of 3D rendering, artificial colouration etc.); and yet, all technological changes considered, it still sounds at the same time strange *and wholly familiar* to suggest that germs and viruses have a will of their own. Patently, Canetti even takes a certain pleasure in pointing out that such impression is due to the fact that the modern invisible crowd of bacilli is but a prolongation of the pre-modern invisible crowd of devils, which similarly used to infest humans in previous times.[30]

We live stories of animistic, intertwined increase: because of their encounter, humans and viruses now form two associated crowds, albeit within an asymmetrical relation – in fact, a parasitical relation. In other words, the parasite inside a host *merely wants to survive*; almost as assuredly, in not a few cases, its survival means the death of the host. It is in this sense that, biologically, survival can *by itself* already issue a death sentence. Humans and viruses, in other words, compose an entangled crowd endowed with a sort of grappling, cathectic dynamic: we cannot claim to understand anything that happens to one of the two crowds without understanding what simultaneously happens to the other. This is, precisely, an instantiation of Canetti's 'double crowd.' Deepening this idea, we should even say that we cannot understand what happens to *each single individual* within a double crowd without taking into account the flows, exchanges and affections – for ultimately, an infection is a type of affection – occurring within the ensemble. As momentous and tragic as it can be, the individual destiny is not all there is: due to how they interact with the host's genetic at various levels, some viruses have played a proven part in the evolution of the species they infest.[31] So, once applied to human–virus or human–bacilli interaction, the image of the double crowd gives us the image of an uneven enmity: host–guest relations cannot, properly speaking, designate a war scenario, where enemies *stand before each other*. Such a frontal stand-off is simply not given: parasitism appears as always skewed, asymmetrical, unwarlike. Indeed, what is peculiar of parasitical relations is that they are radically non-reciprocal: nested, pre-emptive, extractive, divertive, they materialize the primordial 'one-way arrow' (Serres 1980).[32] The parasite does not 'confront' its host, rather, it perverts it. Let us not forget that there is another crowd that is open and always wants to grow, another associated crowd competing for increase: the crowd of the dead. Indeed, when a crowd turns into a closed crowd, one which can no longer grow, that ultimately means the extinction of the species – or more locally, the nation, the social group, the tribe. Even in an extremely populated world, such as ours, it is estimated that currently living humans represent roughly about 7% of the total number of humans who have ever lived. It is therefore not just rhetorical to suggest that we are surrounded by 'the crowds of the dead,' since these invisible crowds surround us by a ratio of at least 10 to 1.

To understand increase, then, one needs to focus on symmetry-breaking. Once again, the scenario of the pack offers an apt starting point. Specifically, one may return briefly to Canetti's fourth-fold typology of packs, comprising hunt, war, lament and increase packs. As recalled above, it is basically through hunting that humans have come to appreciate increase: 'the large numbers of the herd which they hunted blended in their feelings with their own numbers which they wished to be large'[33] (*MM* 33/*CP* 31). Hunt and war, on the one hand, and lamentation, on the other, appear nearly symmetric. As in a full circle, the ambivalence of the human position is portrayed in these packs as swinging between hunter and hunted, killer and victim. Humans attack and kill mercilessly, but then also fear being attacked and killed: they fear being turned into victims; by feeling victims, they also begin to experience remorse for what they have once done as killers and, at this point, lamentation offers a way towards purification by allowing perpetrators to become empathic with their victims. For its part, increase breaks the symmetry of hunting-warring and lamentation, working as a kind of slant-wise vector. There is no decrease pack, no myth and no cult of decrease. This incidentally helps explain why, even as we try to curb an epidemic, we resort to war metaphors: extermination is easier to grasp than decrease – for, as considered above, extermination is *still* a form of increase.[34]

The *human energetics* – to borrow a notion from Simondon (2013[1964–89]) – that is proper to increase can perhaps be unpacked more in details. The question here is: is increase an accretion *from within* or *from without*? Canetti explicitly characterizes increase packs as an instance of 'inward pack' [*innere Meute*] (*MM* 135/*CP* 114). Outward packs have a clear external object towards which they proceed, in order to appropriate and incorporate it. This is, typically, what happens with the hunt: the hunting pack points towards the prey, and by having a prey in mind, it 'rhymes' with it. In order to 'attain' its prey, the hunt pack stretches forward towards it. In comparison, inward packs appear introverted: they are more focused on their own constituent elements than on any external reality. Such is, for instance, the case of the dying member towards which the lamenting pack turns; alternatively, the lamenting pack can focus on some asset which, while present, is at risk of being lost, and must be retained with all strengths. At first sight, then, increase is prepared by the pack by deploying its inner energies. Looking more carefully, however, one realizes that an external force is also needed.

The increase pack needs an unknown source of energy, whose force is to be attracted and exploited. In this movement, it encounters a kind of 'prey,' who however, at the same time, remains similar to a never fully overpowered 'enemy.' In other words, even when consumed, the prey remains ready to take revenge. We find here the complex phenomenon of a victim–enemy working as an ambivalent pharmakon in the energetics of the transition from pack to crowd – a transition that, as discussed above, is fundamental for the trope of increase. If the lamenting pack exhibits an agonic dynamic vis-à-vis death as its external limit, the presence of an external attractor contradistinguishes even more clearly the hunting pack (where the attractor is the prey) and the war pack (where the attractor is the enemy). From this perspective, the energetics of the pack-to-crowd transition can be said to evoke a fundamental pharmacological point: it is often the enemy the one who provides the 'combustible' necessary for increase. It does so, in the first place, by being defeated, given that the defeated enemy aliments the pack; and yet, even when defeated, the enemy's soul is never subdued: it remains with the group as a haunting, threatening presence, that works as a kind of 'trauma' throughout the pack. The power of the enemy, one may suggest, is its *memory*, as summarized by its *name*. It is in this way that, in a second and stranger step, the enemy supplies fuel for further increase attempts.

This may help explain why increase often entails the evocation of *an invisible element* – so invisible, in fact, that it is also *unnameable*. Increase packs possess a central, visible core [*Kern*], which attracts towards itself an increasing number of smaller or larger invisible additions. Not improperly then can the increase pack be characterized as a 'black hole': in energetic terms, it suckles invisible energies from the environment (yet, from an environment that is already 'individualised' to some degree), so as to turn those energies into human accretion and, more generally, into an increment in the *agendi potentia* of a social manifold. Insofar as the procedure is based on 'luring' [*heranlocken*] a number of external elements into the pack, the operation requires a strong faith [*Glaube*] that increment is possible at all, and that the incremental drive can be stimulated by resonance across different domains.[35] Therefore, a fundamental precondition is that the pack firmly believes that a number of invisible elements can successfully be enticed into joining the pack itself. Pushing this point further, it means that increase constitutes an artful activity, one almost based on a kind of artifice, or trick. Increase entertains a hidden yet fundamental liaison with deception. Looking at this fact from an epistemological perspective, the knowledge required for the luring enacted by the pack is similar to the one developed in magic. Perhaps not by chance did the Renaissance tradition of natural magic endorse precisely such a vision: the workings of magic, Marsilio Ficino and others argued, are entirely premised upon the laws of nature, even as these laws transit through an invisible element, from which thoroughly unexpected phenomena proceed. Fully naturalized in this way, magic could be conceptualized as a technology of nature capable of producing wonders through establishing alliances within the invisible.

Canetti's claim that increase and transformation 'go hand in hand' (*MM* 130/*CP* 110) can be understood in this context: for indeed, that magical technology is *totemism*. Put differently, the totem is both a function of self-increase [*Selbstvermehrung*] *and* of self-consumption [*Selbstverzehrung*]. Where does the limit between the former and the latter run? In general, we should say that the lager the circuit between one and oneself, the larger one's capacity to lure forces into one's dynamic of increase; by contrast, the smaller the circuit, the closer one gets to the precinct of self-consumption. It is consequently of vital important that the circuit is prevented from closing completely upon itself – else, one is quickly condemned. This explains why, in Canetti's interpretation, totemism necessarily entails a transformationist ontology (and, accordingly, epistemology, too): a different vision from the classic anthropological interpretations of totemism as essentially classificatory system and cognitive prop, follows. If totemism works thanks to the transformative capacity of humans, then the enactment of transformation creates zones of indistinction between human and animal, and more generally between human and non-human. The link between increase and celebration can be articulated accordingly: thanks to its excited state, at some point the pack comes to function as a 'crowd crystal,' capable of spurring the 'crowdisation' (transformation into crowd) of a currently existing social manifold – or perhaps better, a manifold that is coming-into-existence by this very same operation.

Not by chance does the increase pack often appear as a *festive* one. The evocation of a missing crowd and the propitiation of a crowd-to-come constitute the kernel of celebrations of all sorts. The atmosphere of excitement and excessiveness in the feast enables the conversion and transformation of human forces that enlarge the circuit beyond the initial domain and, thus 'luring' others into joining the circuit, support increase. However, it should not be overlooked that increase may also come from the opposite source, namely lamentation. Contrary, for instance, to the hunting pack and the war pack, which are very closed units, and similarly to the situation of the feast, the lamenting pack is open to everyone who wishes to join in.

This type of pack has the capacity to grow into a crowd of lamenters, ultimately a weeping crowd, insofar as it is not defined by any clear external boundary – except for the natural boundary of death. Ultimately, the very distinction between feast and lamentation may be not so easy to draw. This is particularly clear once we consider how many cultures of celebration and excess are deeply intertwined with contexts of crisis: consider for instance the late-1980s' UK rave party culture in the midst of the job crisis caused by Thatcherism, or, more recently, the NYC loud car culture exploded in neighbourhoods badly affected by the pandemic and an ensuing economic recession. These examples have in common the fact of producing and exploiting noise as an instance of what Canetti would call a 'crowd symbol.' In contexts where human, economic and social losses have been high, surrounding oneself with extreme noise seems to perform a compensatory increase, evoking presently missing new crowds to come.

A similar compensation, or perhaps better delegation, occurs with the acts of eating and consuming resources. On the one hand, Canetti remarks that humans have never developed a shared stomach – a fact which makes the law of distribution so essential (*MM* 115, 223/*CP* 98, 190). On the other hand, though, besides this Nietzschean-flavoured remark (morality ends where my nerves end), Canetti also advances the interesting hypothesis that chiefs' and leaders' stomachs actually function as a kind of delegated *social stomach* [*gemeinsamer Magen*]. The chief, in other words, emerges as a 'champion eater' [*Meistesser*] (*MM* 257/*CP* 219).[36] Initially, Canetti hypothesizes, the chief is the one who receives the largest share, the one who literally eats the most. His greed is welcome, with his belly as large as a barrel (*Faßbreit*) being a sign of distinction. This kind of pecking order then prolongs into the Potlatch situation: destruction of goods works as a substitution for their consummation by eating. This way, the excess of destruction lays the ground for the spectacle of power. One notices how champion-eating inevitably links increase to centralization: in order to have a more visible increase, it can be expedient to direct all resources towards one or few individuals who are then enabled to grow more than the others. This is, incidentally, the origin of social inequality.

If, as considered above, modernity associates increase with quantity, it is now possible to recognize better the place of quantity within the overall dynamic of increase. Fundamentally, increase is revealed as *tendency* or *trend*, more than any specific quantity associated with them: not the value attained, but the differential covered. Such an insight resonates with Deleuze's (1956) interpretation of Bergsonian philosophy. For Deleuze, Bergson calls for two conceptual shifts in our understanding of difference: first, we need to substitute differences of degree (quantitative differences) with differences of nature (qualitative differences): this is the most famous part of Bergson's philosophy, where he argues that duration cannot be modelled upon spatial distance, and so on. Yet, the first move does not suffice: as a second step, we need to go beyond the *difference of nature*, towards conceiving the *nature of difference* itself. The intrinsic nature of difference lies in its being more akin to action than state. Difference is *differing*, sanctioning the priority of tendency over state. In Bergson's philosophy of memory, as well as perhaps in Tarde's earlier social logic, what really matters is not the *fact* (or the extent) *of difference* but the *process of differing*. In this respect, Deleuze (1956: 47) quotes a crucial passage from *L'évolution créatrice*: '*a group will no longer be defined by possession of certain traits, but by the tendency to accentuate them.*'[37]

One may wonder how it is possible to 'differ further' without a previous degree of established difference. Ideally, one would like to know where one starts from in order to measure the delta that has been covered. This is precisely the point, though: the initial position, the zero-degree of difference, is unknown, and bound to remain so. It cannot simply be measured – even better, its measure is irrelevant to the definition of difference. In the Tarde-Bergson-Deleuze version, the trend pre-exists the states which it spans. Once we assume the hypothesis of the priority of tendency over state, the myth of increase can be looked at in a novel light, and placed in a meaningful context: such context is the vitalist tradition. Both Tarde and Simmel can be evoked as contributors. First, Tarde reprises the Leibnizian project for a monadology, seeking to explain social life as the result of the 'desired' interaction of 'open monads' (as opposed to Leibniz's closed ones). For Tarde, monads always aim at reaching out towards other monads in order to 'maximise' their interaction.[38] Social life can thus be regarded as an attempt at intensifying beliefs and desires. Second, Simmel in his late work *The View of Life* [*Lebensanschauung*] (2010[1918]: 13 ff.) observes that life always inherently tends towards *more-life* [*mehr-Leben*]; and simultaneously, because of such proper movement, life also inherently turns into *more-than-life* [*mehr-als-Leben*]. Simmel employs these two expressions to describe the vagaries associated with the becoming and the unfolding of the vital process itself: life, he points out, does not come in the positive adjectival form, but always already in the comparative form ('more-'). On top of that, more-life and more-than-life are logically contradictory, in the sense that, whereas more-life expresses the continuity of the life's flow, more-than-life corresponds to the production of discontinuous forms that are not themselves alive, and regiment the life's flow. In concrete experiences, however, more-life and more-than-life are part of the same dynamic of an 'absolute life' that includes the living as well as the non-living – forms, objects, concepts, artefacts – within its course.

The Simmelian insight may be fruitfully applied to that special type of life that is *social life*. Intrinsic to social life is, indeed, both a vector of intensification (remarked by Tarde) *and* the manifestation of thresholds of discontinuity defining veritable phase transitions (or 'reversals,' as Canetti calls them). Accordingly, rather than simply a cluster of bodies, the crowd is better appreciated as an *event*, something that unrolls – together with the peculiar state installed by such occurrence. Crowd means, in fact, always *crowding* – for crowding does not correspond neatly to any specific substance or substratum, but involves and mobilizes the *medium* of the visible. In the first place, increase is supposed to enhance the visibility of social phenomena, in the very basic sense that *more* is *more visible*. In fact, by coalescing crowds, increase transforms the visible itself: a new, swarming state of the visible is installed, where a lot of invisibility concurrently unfolds. Suffice to consider the host of invisible actors who surround the individual – which, as considered in the introduction, stirred Adorno's deep reluctance towards Canetti's work. The Canettian gaze sees the individual both coming from the crowd and returning to it (and ultimately, our rotting corpses will be devoured by hordes of critters). Even as we exist as individuals, we contain crowds within: in the literal biological sense, we entertain an ongoing relation with our microbiome, without which we could not survive. It even seems that bacteria make up about 1/40th of our body mass, so that whenever we weight ourselves on a scale, we are actually weighting not a body, but a whole society, an actual crowd.[39]

Given the non-linear laws of increase, we can hardly expect its subjective experience to be plain – indeed, here too, we are faced with points of reversal, sudden transitions and mixed feelings. Increase breeds as much pleasure as it breeds trouble; both ways, its nature appears as deeply affective. Writing from a phenomenological perspective, the psychiatrist Eugène Minkowski (1970[1993]) once pointed out that, in general, the sheer occurrence of activity is always connected to a sense of subjective 'expansion' and 'greatness.'[40] With Spinoza, one could say that activity manifests an increase in one's *agendi potentia*, engendering a feeling of joy. What is peculiar of modernity, in this respect, is the way in which the variations of *potentia* are appraised, measured and indexed, giving rise to what Canetti diagnoses in the modern human as an 'addiction to sheer numbers' [*seine Hingabe an ihre Zahl*] (*MM* 225/*CP* 193). The numbers, introduced as indices and indicators of the variations in individual and collective *agendi potentia*, take precedence over actual *potentia* – or better, they surround it and mirror it, as if capable of bringing about by themselves a real increase. This explains even more cogently the feeling of failure every time increase does not materialize. During unpredictable disruptive and catastrophic events, such as natural disasters, epidemics, recessions or wars, it becomes palpable that the veritable opposite of increase, is *fear*. Whenever increase falters, whenever an expectation of it is suddenly betrayed, anxiety and even panicking take over. Contraction, crisis, nervous breakdown, psychotic episodes and mass delusions form a vast range of psychosocial reactions to the experience of fear cause by the perceived lack of increase.

Monadology is, of course, *also* a theory of existential desperation, as it conveys the sensation that everyone is fundamentally alone and powerless. Since between one monad and the next there's an impassable abyss, the connection to the other is the greatest trouble that affects all monadological approaches. In his astute reformulation, Tarde altered the original Leibnizian layout to the point of effectively betraying it: by positing open, instead of closed, monads, Tarde opened the way to a whole host of twentieth-century sociological approaches, including cellular automata, agent-based modelling and actor-network theory. With networked reacting agents, the monadological horizon appears strangely twisted – for whereas classical monadology was concerned with the possibility of order and cooperation in a world where everyone is shut out of the others, within the Tardeian horizon, the problem is solved by removing any central harmonizing divine providence (and, by analogy, any national central governance). The pattern of order is thereby reconstructed in terms of decentralized 'emergent properties' exhibited by a swarm of unsupervised local interactions. This way, subjectively, the Angst of existential solitude is substituted with an ambivalent consolation – namely the idea that, with or without a shared plan, we are bound to always affect one another in multiple ways, remaining perpetually interlocked. 'Monadic' and yet open to all sorts of influxes: such is the new monadology of connectionism. 'We cannot but be connected' – no surprise that such idea undergirds the technological set up of the present.

As the above considerations illustrate, connectionism can therefore be regarded as a thoroughly 'increasist' ideology. The emergence of a 'performance stratum' (McKenzie 2001), or a performance-oriented society, subjectively corresponds to the feeling of being under the constant pressure to outdo, not only the performance and achievements of others, but above all *our own*. It is increasingly recognized that such a pressure to outperform ourselves often has pathological consequences. Canetti reminds us that Hitler and Speer, dreaming of unprecedented buildings to erect in an unprecedented capital city, were led by a veritable 'compulsion to outdo' [*Zwang zu übertreffen*]. And the external appearances of outdoing should not distract us from the truth that the ultimate psychological framework of increase is the psychotic state. Pushed to the extreme, we enter President Schreber's paranoid condition: the domain of a logic where even the dead ones continue to augment, where nothing can really vanish, where everything remains and accumulates in an oversaturated, wholly cluttered present. Schreber was a connectionist through and through: everything in his universe was tied together by invisible yet unbreakable 'divine rays,' the air surrounding him crowded with invisible malign agents powerfully coordinated and activated by their reciprocal ties. One of the most staggering components of his delirium was certainly what he himself called 'compulsive thinking.'[41]

The compulsion to outdo and overcome the others and oneself does not uniquely concern totalitarian states and psychotic delusions, though. On the contrary, Canetti suggests, a general compulsion of this kind has turned into a defining feature of modern society. Not by chance, an animistic world similar to Schreber's offers a realistic description of what happens in the domain of the social media, with their cascading, often malignant pseudo-news and obnoxious commentaries, along with cascading reactions to them. The addictive dimension of increase can be fully recognized here: increase breeds a kind of exhilaration – an exaltation, even: an incapacity to halt what one is doing without undergoing fearful psychic disruption. The Faustian *furor* in the final part of Goethe's poem has been finely reconstructed by Marshall Berman (2010[1982]), who suggested that, after his metaphysical and romantic stages, Faust finally reaches an *industrial* stage, turning into a veritable construction developer. Faust the developer undertakes a sort of landfilling megaproject, unscrupulously getting rid of the local residents who are in the way of his plans, and whom he deems incapable of adapting to the new conditions of existence he himself has envisaged for the world. And indeed, *Faust*'s Part Two is replete with evocations of the huge masses of workers needed for land reclamation works as well as the further masses of happy inhabitants to lodge in the new developments. Goethe himself warns that such fantasy comes at the expense of the blood of a lot of people: whoever stops to rest, or cannot cope with the rhythm, is swept away by a merciless increasist imperative. Further, as Berman remarks, Goethe's *Faust* is not a melodrama, but a real tragedy, because Faust himself is aware of the outcome of his own actions, as it becomes apparent in his final encounter with the four spectres of Need, Want, Guilt and Care.

In the light of the above discussion, addiction to increase appears as not just a triumph of repetition (a 'coaction to repeat,' in psychoanalytic language), but as the very triumph of *trend* over steady state, the pre-eminence of relative over absolute performance. Tendency takes precedence over the repeated things or acts. As 'pure tendency,' in Bergson's parlance, the force of trend becomes intrinsic to life, not as an external *télos*, but as its inner dynamic. Generalized addiction can thus be observed as a phenomenon of increase – addiction, addition. The increase compulsion preludes to a form of disposophobia, or hoarding. Psychiatry has diagnosed the painful condition of people who cannot discard anything, and are led to accumulate clutter to the extreme consequences. The unsettling question raised by the disposophobic condition can be phrased as: What is the limit between us and waste? The hoarder is a self-polluter, since the treasure/waste that grows around him or her is a major source of intoxication. Disposophobic patients themselves tell how accumulating initially seemed to offer them a kind of protection (against indigence, nudity, intrusion …) but, progressively, became a threat to their own mental sanity. Not dissimilarly, the compulsive collector often lives a life on the verge of psychic chaos: as the collection expands, one is increasingly caught in one's 'creature.' The collection is not only an object, or a series of gathered objects, but also a territory – a home territory, a mazy den, as featured in Kafka's famous story – and always, a childhood land. Typically, the hoarder dies under his or her own house crumbling down upon him or her, due to too much accumulated stuff crushing the floor. The den turns into a grave – and a grave is a home, too, or at least, what remains of a home when its inhabitants are consumed.

Now, considering the humankind as a whole, are we not in the same situation of the disposophobic with respect to planet Earth? We are now fully aware that 'throwing away' is no longer a sustainable illusion. Individually, we praise ourselves for being sane persons who can throw stuff away, instead of being condemned to hoard waste; but collectively, as a species, we have reached the limit of disposability of the planet. In this context, the ecological activist, as well as everyone conscious of the eco-climate crisis, experiences the awful sensation of being a 'disposophobic of humankind.' The myth of increase may have led humanity to a situation of global disposophobia: there is no way to make our waste magically disappear. The stocking of nuclear wastes is perhaps the most extreme example: for however we ditch them in the deepest caves, or dilute them in the oceans, they will never be far enough from us.[42] And even as we shift to consider the 'immaterial' domain of contemporary digitality, should we not admit, as hinted above, that the so-called 'big data' represent a further, enhanced form of pollution? Not only has the maintenance of data centres and the construction of ever-larger memory storage units terrible ecological consequences, but the absurd amount of private data stored by governments and private companies dwarves the dreams of any disposophobic patient. In terms of 'waste,' surveillance companies really possess a lot of 'dirt' about everybody, and are also turning into specialists in the extraction of 'value' from that dirt – but to be true, it is a purely negative value, a thoroughly perverse scheme of valorization that does not make any good to anybody.

To conclude, once all the negative and worrisome aspects of increase have been taken into account, one cannot deny that increase heralds a positive valence, too. In a perhaps more mysterious sense, increase designates the vertical tension of self-transcendence and self-amelioration, the struggle toward bettering oneself. It is this very element that, as hinted above, makes of Faust a tragic character: at bottom, his story raises the question of whether 'amelioration' should be an externally or an internally driven process.[43] Along the fine line between striving for moral amelioration and self-consciousness on the one hand, and giving way to the unrestrained hubris of increase on the other, lies the real crux of the matter. According to Simmel, even thinkers as diverse as Kant and Nietzsche – for there could hardly be more diverse thinkers – are in accord with a vision of self-improvement. Ultimately, Simmel contends (1995[1904]: 281–2), what Nietzsche accomplishes is nothing but taking the Kantian argument about self-mastery 'one step further.' If increase as self-transcendence signifies the ethical tension towards self-amelioration, such requirement mirrors the condition of a subject who cannot simply rest upon the received arrangements and the current measures in place, but wants to have a say in how these arrangements and measures are formed, as well as with the consequences of such formation – a more exposed subject, one with self-chosen greater responsibility.

Chapter 3

RESISTANCE

Figure 3 Marronnage as resistance.

Non mi passa mai, non mi passa mai.
Anonymous worker

Locating resistance

Through and through, Canetti is a writer of resistance. Now, what is resistance? One finds in Canetti a deep rethinking of the meaning and the scope of such a basic human gesture, along with the social relations it shapes. The peculiarity of his approach will become more evident once we compare it to more widespread views in the social and human sciences. By and large, resistance is understood as a practice that stands *against change*: the main characteristics ascribed to it are usually identified in refusal and rejection. For instance, famously, psychoanalysis conceived of itself as a struggle against the resistances of the patient to be analysed, along with the assumption that one prefers clinging to one's 'bad ways' rather than submitting to much-needed change. As we move from the individual psyche to large-scale historical situations, it becomes more apparent that change is, in many cases, *externally imposed*. In this sense, we may consider, for instance, the thrust towards performativity on the workplace, which has been emphatically accompanied by the neoliberal rhetoric and its companion policies. Seen in this light, resistance reveals itself as an act *against imposition* or even, as is the case with colonial contexts, *against oppression*. Yet, even once this point is granted, the implicit premise remains that resistance expresses inertia *vis-à-vis* some active force operating from the outside of the subject.[1] This way, resistance is framed as a practice essentially based on *negation*, or as the negative term in a dialectic of power. Regardless of the social status of the resistant actor, resistance is, chiefly, conceived of as a form of *reaction*: an act waged against the formal scheme of the organization or institution in question. Incidentally, the very German word for resistance, *Widerstand*, suggests precisely such an oppositional, reactive and confrontational imagery.

It will be shown here that the Canettian epistemology suggests a profoundly different conception, which reveals resistance's crucial links to transformation, creation and change. In social and political theory, the notion of resistance is certainly an uneasy one – arguably a notion which, despite the copious literature on empirical episodes, practices and histories of resistance, remains extremely contested. Ortner (1995: 175) earlier on remarked 'the ambiguity of resistance and the subjective ambivalence of the acts for those who engage in them;' this must be seen in connection to the basic sociological fact that social actors have to navigate between a number of practical contradictions in their lives. In this context, two influential traditions in the conceptualization of resistance can be identified as, respectively, the materialist and the culturalist ones. The orthodox Marxist tradition typically heralded the former conception: for pre-Gramscian Marxist authors in particular, resistance was a substantive, material action raged against, and aimed at interfering with, the functioning of the capitalist socio-economic system. By contrast, a series of authors receptive of phenomenology have privileged a culturalist explanation of resistance as primarily a matter of a stance that challenges social domination symbolically. Such a dichotomy between material and symbolic resistance has, of course, itself been challenged, at least since the revival of Antonio Gramsci's work since the 1970s.[2] Already in the 1930s, Gramsci emphasized the presence of cultural dynamics *at the very foundations* of the economy as well as at the pivot of class relations. With Gramsci and his philosophy of praxis – which he crafted as a

Marxism rescued from 'vulgar positivism' – not only is culture added to the list of social fields where domination is exercised, but it becomes *the crucial one.*

Some decades after Gramsci, Michel Foucault drew attention to the fact that a structure of power is present in not only the hegemonic sphere of cultural institutions, but also subject formation. This, to some extent, helps explain the microscopic texture of ambiguity surrounding resistance and co-optation. Particularly in his late production, and seemingly unaware of Gramsci's earlier work on modern subjectivity, Foucault described the emergence of a number of practices of self-mastery in Western culture, grounded in a twin ethical imperative towards obedience and truth-telling.[3] While the analysis of obedience as a 'practice of truth' might be easily misunderstood as shrinking the scope for resistance, Foucault is, in fact, famous for contending – on Nietzschean grounds – that 'where there is power, there is resistance, and yet, or rather consequently, this resistance is never in a position of exteriority in relation to power' (Foucault 1998[1976]: 95). In the same time span, a somewhat resonant position was developed in sociology by Pierre Bourdieu (1972, 2000) with his theory of habitus, which – as already evoked in Chapter 1 – seeks to genetically capture the emergence of specific attitudes towards authority and the societal order at large: positions in the social field, Bourdieu reasoned, generate dispositions of action that lead actors to situate themselves in specific ways vis-à-vis existent structures of power. Following the lead of Foucault and Bourdieu, and despite a measure of disagreement about the extent to which the socio-political establishment is actually capable of 'colonising' the mindset of the subaltern classes (more on this point below), subsequent authors have explored resistance as essentially located at the interplay three axes: substantive opposition, maintenance of hegemonic appearances and actual compliance.

Canetti seems to stand largely outside of these debates. As explored *passim* throughout the previous chapters, his view of power has been regarded by his critics as a crude one, while his description of totalitarian regimes – to which he devoted enduring attention – has been deemed as itself, totalitarian, i.e., lacking in socio-historical detail and organizational–institutional analysis (Arnason 1996). Furthermore, Canetti's preoccupation with myths, ancient history, biology and psychology, seems to leave him even further apart from the study of concrete manifestations of resistance in modern historical dynamics. In reality, the Canettian perspective can prove useful to detect and expose a series of inherent limitations in current theorizations of resistance, from a perspective that may resemble the one of philosophical anthropology, but that also has specific epistemological entailments for the social science. Indeed, we can use Canetti to question the two wide-ranging assumptions evoked above: first, that resistance is an act *against* something (against command, against exploitation, against imperialism, against power, against violence, etc.); second, that it is an act *from below* (resistance as bottom–up rather than top–down action).

A successful transformation of our imagination of resistance cannot proceed without also reviewing and rethinking the location of resistance in social life. The perspective from which Canettian epistemology approaches it, I suggest, enables us to enlarge the focus of enquiry, from the narrow game of cultural and political subjection towards a more encompassing social and human experience.[4] Certainly, if we adopt an Arendtian point of view on politics – whereby the latter concerns the making of a 'world in common' among humans – we are also led to reject any clear-cut separation between the social and the political domains. At this point, resistance can be better appreciated as unfolding in the totality of social space, rather than in any of its recognized institutional political arenas, forums or groups.[5] What Canetti adds to such a view of human action is, however, another essential element: the centrality of the body. Canettian epistemology stresses that resistance is neither a matter of 'sheer' existential stance, nor a skill at mobilizing political symbolism, but something one does with one's own body, something one engages one's body in. Considering the body as the veritable site of resistance does not necessarily entail the view of a combating body: from the Canettian perspective, it is absolutely clear that there is no evolution of violence. At its core, Canetti suggests, violence has always been the same, and will always remain the same – such is the realist, or static if one wants, element in his theory. But that does not mean that everything in Canetti's theory is static and primordial: what can change, what *does* change, is transformation itself, since both its origins and its becoming are grounded in heterogeneity.[6]

Admittedly, these preliminary remarks run the risk of remaining all too general. The crucial links between resistance and transformation need to be unearthed and explored more in details. Since now, however, we are already pushed towards a consideration of resistance as an instance of what might be called a 'territorial' act. What we have in mind here is that resistance can be fruitfully compared with the act of *leaving a territory*, that is, with an act of *deterritorialization*.[7] Leaving a territory means, concurrently, freeing and releasing a number of *flight lines* made virtually available by the territorial constitution itself. By doing so, resistance can be said to *probe* the very constitution of existing social territories: through its act of leaving them, it highlights *what it was truly there* in the first place. By taking into account such a peculiar 'retrodictive' operation, we begin to see better how resistance differentiates itself from stasis and refusal of change: deterritorialization here functions, in the first place, as a tool for the analysis of the present. Once we admit its capacity to diagnose what is actually 'present in the present,' what is presently before our eyes, we can also appreciate how the act of resistance is inherently interwoven with a *dialectic of visibility* in social life. Below, we return to examine the stake entailed by the movements of 'extraction' and 'subtraction' expressed by social deterritorialization.[8] What considered so far should at least suffice to provide a rationale for contending that resistance occupies a crucial epistemological location in social theory: if, as considered in Chapter 1, command always indicates a *fateful* reality, then resistance cannot but appear as the *preposterous and yet necessary* attempt to *evade the fate*.

Resistant subjectivities

As hinted above, imagining resistance as a type of transformation seems very much to run against the grain, given that everything in the word suggests stasis. The Latin word is formed by the prefix *re-*, indicating recurrence or repetition, and the verb root *sisto, -ĕre*, meaning to consolidate, to strengthen, but also to stop, to block; in turn, the verb *sisto* is itself connected to *sto, -āre*, to stay put or planted, which is a frequentative form of *sum, esse*, to be. In short, resistance is a word that speaks of endless repetition: it literally reads as 'being again and again and again …' – with strong emphasis on sameness, immobility and rigidity. If this is not stubbornness! Certainly, in the social science, intentionality is a particularly riddled term: if it means anything at all, then it must mean something different from both the cold abstractions of the philosophy of mind and the analytical classificatory clarities of psychology. In our discussion, intentionality clearly cannot be a private, inaccessible domain, imperscrutably located *in interiore homine*, but must be observable as a practice that unfolds *between actors* – a 'public' practice, to some extent. Marxian theory, and more specifically the Gramscian philosophy of praxis, first pointed out the fact that intentions and practices co-evolve. This comes in conjunction to the fact that an attribution of intentionality can be conducted via either a vertical or a horizontal strategy: whereas the vertical solution adopts a rigorously externalist, objectivist point of view, looking at actors 'from above their heads', so to speak, the horizontal solution strives to grasp the inter-subjective point of view as it unfolds practically.

These two strategies correspond, roughly, to the chasm between social physics and social phenomenology. In the case of resistance more specifically, both vertical and horizontal strategies run into the problem of the *opaque* nature of the act of resistance: only *some* actions are manifestly, consciously, outspokenly resistant, while many of them are *not* – does it mean that these other actions are simply not resistant, or should we rather infer that resistance is different from a statement of purpose? Speaking of resistance often amounts to imputing meaning that neither the actor nor, for that matter, its direct interactants, might have actually ever intended or perceived. The predicament becomes particularly visible in empirical social research: unsurprisingly, the issue is much discussed in contemporary ethnography. In an interesting contribution, for instance, Campbell and Heyman (2007) have proposed the term 'slantwise' to describe actions that fall *somewhere* along the continuum between acceptance and rejection of domination. Slant actions intersect the continuum from an unknown, oblique angle. According to Campbell and Heyman, situating actions simply along what they call the naturalization–resistance continuum, that is, simply in terms of acceptance *vs* refusal of domination, has distorted the empirically observed material in many studies, inducing ethnographers to attribute resistant intentions to actors in a way that is factually unprovable, and potentially wrong. Manifold actions have been subsumed under the heading of resistance, even when they were *not meant* to be of defiant nature. Campbell and Heyman report on their fieldwork among working-class Mexicans and Chicanos who live in the *colonias* placed in desert and remote areas along the US–Mexico border. These people adopt housing and living practices – such as irregular and informal housing patterns, ongoing moves of their mobile homes, and so on – that in many ways frustrate the attempts to control them deployed by the US Census. However, the authors claim, by and large they *do not* do so on purpose; in many cases, they appear not to be even conscious of the pattern they generate. The notion of slantwise thus promises a solution to the theoretical bias implied by the lexicon of resistance, insofar as it avoids unjustified assumptions about the aims pursued by the actors. 'Slantwise,' we may say, is not an *emic* term, but an *etic* one – not a category employed by the actors, nor even a category that we might expect them to recognize, but rather a category that admits an *opaque space of motivations* guiding observable action, without forcing the language of naturalization or resistance upon people.

The 'slantwise' notion, one could infer, invites researchers to consider resistance as if behind a 'veil of ignorance.'[9] Certainly, there are sound reasons to do so: forms of romanticization are not uncommon among self-identified critical scholars. One embarrassing aspect of contemporary critical scholarship is, in this respect, the fact that, while it specializes in criticizing power dynamics, it locates such dynamics only in the people observed, and rarely, if ever, in the scholar who observes them. An all-too-common outcome is the romanticization of the underdog, regarded as a political hero and as a morally superior, uncompromised character. The shortcoming of this way of thinking is that a number of idealized narratives of resistance are produced that conceal the ambiguity, ambivalence and contradiction present in social action. While we would like to know as soon as possible who is the oppressor and who is the victim, to tell the good from the bad guys, that is an unrealistic expectation, to which social scientists should not condescend – especially if the observed actors are made into heroes only to the extent that they mirror, or can be made to match, the researcher's own preferences. From this perspective, the concept of slantwise is helpful, in that it introduces a powerful caveat against projecting one's categories and preferences upon the actors in the field. Nonetheless, the usefulness of the notion is limited in that the power–resistance continuum is not really challenged. The main axis of reference (domination–resistance) stays the same, while a *degree of distance* from it is allowed, by removing, or temporarily bracketing, all motivational factors.

Certainly, all resistance is slantwise, insofar as it necessarily manifests itself in a way that is transversal vis-à-vis power relations, at a distance from them, rather than simply positioned at some point along the range between compliance and opposition. However, the slantwise category remains premised upon the existence of a 'bedrock' where the supposedly 'true meaning' of a practice could be ascertained: only because we contingently cannot identify its underlying meaning is an action assigned to the slantwise category. In reality, it is the bedrock that remains but a postulate. If, on the one hand, there is the risk of interpreting as 'resistant' actions which are not meant to be so, on the other hand, there is also the risk of interpreting given actions as resistant *just because* they are meant to be so! In other words, the *practice of* resistance should always be carefully kept distinct from the *discourse on* resistance, regardless of who is producing such a discourse. In this respect, the work of Albert Camus offers a powerful reminder that the very discourse of resistance can in fact *thwart* the act of resistance, transforming it into an act of power: those who set themselves the task of resisting oppression may end up being the worst oppressors, just as those who claim to be struggling against inhumanity may end up becoming themselves inhuman.[10] As, for his part, Emil

Cioran (1960) bitterly remarked, tomorrow's tyrants are recruited among today's half-beheaded martyrs. For Camus (1951), in particular, the first move of the rebel [*l'homme révolté*] is against *the discourse of resistance* and its claim to truth. Revolt consists, not in negation, but in what Camus calls a special 'consent to the earth' [*consentement à la Terre*]. Not at all quiescence towards the status quo, the rebel's consent pushes him/her beyond the ideological mists: rather than a discourse, an intention, or an ideology, resistance is an action with which one transforms oneself and the world by the same stroke.

How then to capture the specificity of the relation between resistance and power? The question must necessarily be explored within a broad anthropological frame. One of the most controversial and intriguing claims made by Lévi-Strauss, in this respect, is his hypothesis about what we might call the *inevitability of ethnocentrism*. Lévi-Strauss (1952) observed that the concept of humanity is a late creation in the history of mankind and that, even after its introduction, in most places on Earth humanity ends at the border of the tribe, or at the border of the ethnic, religious, or linguistic group. The essence of ethnocentrism should not be simply seen in the fact that one judges actions done by others according to one's code of values. More profoundly, ethnocentrism posits the group as endowed with a strong, undefeatable sense of its own intrinsic goodness. Such foundational feeling can be described as the persuasion of the goodness of being a *majority*. To craft an expression, it is the feeling of being *the majority of oneself*. There is no shortage, in groups and individuals, of such a triumphant sense of one's merits. The majoritarian attitude is precisely what Nietzsche derided in his *Genealogy of Morality*. For Nietzsche, whenever a social group asserts, 'We good people – *we are the righteous*' [*Wir Guten – wir sind die Gerechten*] (1994[1887]: XI, §14, 28), this signals, not any real assertion of life and power (Nietzsche saw power as something positive, and as essentially coinciding with life's affirmation through the capacity to feel more), but the perverse resorting to a moral justification of one's existence (where, for Nietzsche, morality is quintessentially inimical to life, and resentful). 'God is on our side' is, in other words, the basic ethnocentric claim, instituting a morality which Nietzsche considered grounded in *reaction*. Such an attitude does not only exist at the level of civilizations and nations, but also lurks in every human group in its relations to other groups as well as to its own members. Even before constituting a quantitative, numerical or percentile fact, the notion of majority thus designates a *point of view* on society and the self, as well as a specific system for evaluating the subjects. It was with this process in mind that Michel Foucault said that having defeated historical fascist regimes was a minor matter compared to the task of defeating 'the fascism we all have in our heads.' Ethnocentrism represents the operation of *impersonating-a-majority*, of breeding a majoritarian point of view on social relations and the social process as a whole. Incidentally, it should also be noted here that easy-going exoticism is itself the result of the ethnocentric operation, one where values are simply swapped ('they are more worthy than us' being symmetrical to 'we are more worthy than them').

These considerations allow us to advance in our task of locating resistance in social life. From the perspective just outlined, resistance could precisely be interpreted as the *residuum* of the ethnocentric operation: what remains outside of the constitution of a group as the *majority of itself*. Resistance is, in other words, a type of action at odds with what the ethnocentric operation accomplishes. As we are going to explore more in details below, the role Canetti attributes to crowds in their nonlinear relation vis-à-vis power approximates a situation of a commonality capable of defusing the majoritarian point of view. Resistance, in other words, emerges as the natural antibody to ethnocentrism. What is less simple to explain, though, is that at the same time resistance differentiates itself from other forms of anti-majoritarian endeavours. Mostly, contemporary social science literature regards resistance as 'rooted in an anti-capitalist, anti-imperial, anti-military and anti-colonial thinking' (Jokubaskaite 2020: 246). However, its distinctiveness within such a broad field is far from easy to determine. Resistance is sometimes likened to tactical warfare; but both tactical and strategic thinking still remain in the province of military logic, which is itself premised upon the ethnocentric operation. Warfare, in this sense, indicates a situation where more than one party contends to become a majority, and strives to trump the other party. When an organized minority fights against a majority, and eventually manages to replace it, it may succeed in tipping the power ratio (either as a coup d'état, or as a revolution), but precisely for this reason, such a reshuffle of 'heads' is something completely different from an act of resistance.

As mentioned above, in the twentieth century, leftist cultural theorists have interpreted resistance as the first step towards the revolutionary transformation of the status quo. The powerful, almost fetishized word 'revolution' shifts attention towards the level of large social aggregates and apical historical moments: as soon as one names revolution, one want to know how it ends, which new social arrangements it institutes, or why it fails to produce such arrangements, or betrays them, leaving the floor empty enough for reaction to kick back. The Canettian epistemology suggests, instead, that resistance cannot be properly understood unless we are able to articulate it at the level of its most minute psychosocial dynamics.[11] This does not at all mean that resistance must necessarily be a small-scale phenomenon – quite on the contrary, resistance can even reach the size of a mass movement, but even in that case, one should avoid measuring it against its political outcomes, or the sanctioned legal and economic gains it produces. From this vantage point, one senses again a similarity between Canetti and Camus. The latter made clear that rebellion can only be understood as a more-than-individual act – one which, in fact, is truly possible only when a crucial commons of all humans is invoked.[12] Intrinsic to resistance against totalization is the fact that commonality can never coincide with any given social group (more on this point in Chapter 4). Somewhere in-between small and large scale, an 'infinitesimal' domain emerges, irreducible to both, and yet crucial. The infinitesimal is not the small, but that which *at every scale* indicates the proximity of a critical moment. This way, the infinitesimal cannot be subsumed under the logic of the majoritarian operation. Rather than individual, the infinitesimal encompasses an undulatory domain of undifferentiated differences, where phenomena like crowds and packs – as opposed to fully institutionalized groups – occur. It is a state of thriving differences, where they are not submitted to any identification, categorization, or totalization. We can only hope to understand something about resistance once we are able to specify the peculiar relationship such infinitesimal acts entertain with the majoritarian, ethnocentric operation.

Hegemony, or else

Colonial contexts and decolonization movements have provided a most important empirical ground where practices of resistance have been developed in the course of the twentieth century. The colonial situation is prototypical, insofar as it involves two clearly differentiated parties – the settlers and the colonized – with one party *a priori* visibly stronger than the other. Such 'strength' may be due to better organization, or technological advantage, or simply a more ruthless commitment towards the exploitation of the counterpart. While colonization is a case of group domination, it clearly differs from direct confrontation: in colonial contexts, the difference in strength between the parties is ostensibly *already established* as a fact. The colonized, however, is – as Frantz Fanon famously put it – 'dominated but not domesticated.' Thus, violence appears to Fanon as the veritable *element* of the colonial relation: the settler and the colonized are inextricably connected by revenge phantasies and a physical, 'muscular' tension unfolding within the single nexus of violence.[13] Colonialism, from this perspective, is but a long apprenticeship in violence. This explains why the dialectic of domination and resistance has been observed as the hallmark of all strongly asymmetrical political relations, whereby different classes or groups are placed in positions that are simultaneously hierarchical and antagonistic. Subaltern studies have emphasized that resistance is a type of *opposition* played out in a political arena where the subaltern have very limited resources at their disposal. For instance, despite their differences, and despite the latter's critique of the former, both Antonio Gramsci and James C. Scott interpret resistance as a relation which cannot but oppose whole classes to one another. Concurrently, resistance – or lack thereof – is conceptualized as an asset in the struggle between political antagonists, favouring either one or the other party.

In social theory, such power asymmetry has been mainly theorized in terms of *hegemony*. Gramsci's (1975[1929–35]) concept of hegemony was elaborated progressively throughout his prison notebooks to explain how the bourgeois order can 'morally colonise' the rest of society.[14] Through his lens, hegemony appears as a form of power that exceeds coercion, or assertion through force. Inherently tied to prestige, hegemony is the expression of the intellectual and moral headship [*guida*] exercised by the dominant class. Class domination, Gramsci reasoned, is strongest when it appears as 'spontaneous,' i.e., as if it were 'organic' to the social body as a whole. Only in such a case can domination successfully generate a widely accepted, shared cultural framework of consent, wherein specific conflicts of interests can be accommodated without compromising the general outline. Each 'historic bloc,' in Gramscian terms, embodies a condition of hegemony that encompasses both the 'economic–corporative' and the 'ethical–political' levels: whereas the former refers to immediate economic gains the parties look for, the latter refers to the aura of legitimacy that surrounds the dominant framework and makes it hard to think otherwise. The theory of hegemony thus pictures society as a kind of slow-motion war for the conquest of the political state, a 'war of position' whose first and most important stake is the conquest of the hegemonic advantage itself. Indeed, hegemony entails the naturalization, or invisibilization, of domination: a given political project secures a crucial advantage for itself through its own inscription into 'common sense.' Gramsci contented that, in liberal-democratic parliamentary regimes, characterized by the play of political parties, hegemony is exercised in its 'normal forms' through the division of powers, the articulations of civil society and the expression of public opinion. Indeed, hegemony is mainly played out in the arena of the civil society, which Gramsci saw as the field where actual social imagination circulates. Intellectuals organic to the ruling class contribute to build and reproduce hegemony through institutions such as schooling and the mass media, in charge of co-opting, or luring, society itself into a 'will to conform.' Hegemony thus works thanks to an implicit consensus around a set of values and a whole worldview. Barrington Moore (1978) later referred to the 'conquest of inevitability' as that process through which the perspective of the dominant group is absorbed by the dominated, instilling the sense that the sufferings and pain associated with domination are unavoidable.

Accordingly, hegemony is made of unwilling, most of the time unconscious contributions to the system. In a series of political–anthropological investigations, James C. Scott (1985, 1990, 2009) has famously sought to criticize such view. For Scott, the feeling of 'inevitability' as the ultimate horizon of class colonization only portrays the official side of the relationships between dominant and dominated classes. But such official, 'public transcript' of subordinate discourse before the dominant's eye, is far from telling the whole story of their relationship. A 'hidden transcript' takes place behind the scenes, which belies and subverts hegemonic appearances. If revolts and revolutions are characterized by bursts of outright defiance, the absence of direct confrontation does not mean that hegemony truly goes unchallenged. Resistance, Scott argued, should rather be looked for in the everyday constellation of the 'weapons of the weak' – an array of unassuming practices, which include dissimulation, false compliance, lying, pilfering, feigned ignorance, foot dragging, skimming, slander, arson, sabotage, and so on. Most of these actions are motivated by utilitarian aims – in Gramscian terms, they are located at the economic–corporative level rather than at the ethical–political one. Also, they are typically unplanned and uncoordinated. This way, a proliferating range of anarchic tactical achievements is launched against the strategy of hegemony, compromising its effectiveness. Scott highlighted that even external compliance does not mean that one is effectively co-opted into cultural hegemony. By and large, resistance keeps a low profile and refrains from engaging in any symbolic confrontation with the dominant bloc. The reason is that, for subordinate people, the only effective resistance is *invisible* resistance: whenever resistance becomes visible, it attracts ferocious repression and retaliation. This idea of invisible resistance resonates across endless anarchist tracts, where invisibility is celebrated as an essential requirement in the struggle against the instituted order. According to Scott, in a kind of counter-Habermasian fashion, hidden transcripts are produced mainly in social spaces outside of the direct control of dominant discourse: traditionally, places such as the alehouse, the pub, the tavern, the inn, the cabaret, the beer cellar, the gin mill, all remain opaque to the gaze of the state, and lend themselves to host the lower classes' resistant transcripts. In sum, from Scott's perspective, hegemony only captures the public version of the dominant–dominated relationship, behind which other narratives and forms of action – such as the whole realm of folk culture, with its rumours, gossip, folktales, jokes, songs, innuendos, codes, and euphemisms – reduce hegemony to the dominants' own wishful thinking: a self-portrait of how the dominant group *would love* to be seen, but is not.

We could say Scott has sought to enlarge the field of resistance, 'flattening,' so to speak, hegemony to the paper-thin dimension of the public transcript of inter-class relations. However, the idea that hegemony is not omnipotent, and can be eroded from beneath by multifaceted forms of political resistance, does not really contradict what Gramsci maintained in the first place. In Gramsci, each social group organically expresses its own ideology, its own philosophy and rationale for existing. As a Marxist scholar, Gramsci was clearly a conflictualist, and can hardly be accused of overlooking class confrontation. At the same time, Gramsci also recognized that the struggle for hegemony is a struggle of ideologies, suggesting that the latter differ from one another not only in content but also in structure, methods and operational strategies. That different classes have different ideologies, was no surprise to Gramsci; nor can it be argued that he was unaware of the politics of visibility inherent to ideological confrontations, as his analyses of the mass media show – and in this sense, he is certainly to be credited as a pioneer in media content analysis. In other words, Gramsci never contended that hegemony functions monolithically and homogeneously: like the different 'divisions of a single army,' he held, the various social institutions and their ideological structures act on their own, in relatively independent ways. The overall mission towards which all these units converge is not mechanically transmitted, but emerges by means of resonance across a number of ideological refrains. At the micro level, people pursue individual lives in specific local contexts, which seem complete and meaningful on their own; nonetheless, the texture of each of these apparently independent local lives – even when it contains critical affirmations and points of friction – makes a contribution to the continuation of a larger hegemonic pattern. On the other hand, if hegemony were made only of sheer appearances, as Scott contends, one would still have to explain why such thin figments are so pervasive and accurately preserved most of the time. Scott believes that official transcripts are preserved only because the subaltern classes fear harsh physical repression. Certainly, violence is always present, as Fanon also recognized, and this regardless of the degree of its visibility: whether open and blatant, or nuanced and subtle, violence is intrinsic to every colonial formation. For his part, Gramsci, deploying the image of the 'war of position' for political power, admits that culture is a terrain of struggle, but also focuses on the specific *slowness* of cultural formations vis-à-vis political action. Thanks to its intrinsic slowness, which unfolds through the course of generations, cultural life penetrates deeply into the constitution of society, 'soaking,' so to speak, the social body. Of course, the lower strata of society will mistrust the higher strata and their winning discourse, but wherever we find an arena of 'popular-national' [*nazional-popolare*] culture, education, entertainment, leisure etc., we can be sure some form of hegemony is well at work.

If, on the basis of what has just been said, the theoretical difference between Gramsci and Scott must be relativized, what acquires centrality are the empirical variations across different contexts of colonization. Different social situations where colonial practices are enacted – between nations, within nations, between classes, within classes – reveal different degrees of *soaking*, whereby a given ideology becomes more or less effectively merged with the psychosocial build-up of the population.[15] Since the 1970s, the impact of Gramsci and his philosophy of praxis has been important in the articulation of the violence–resistance nexus. Several contemporary critical theorists have derived from Gramsci a commitment to the development of *counter-hegemony*, i.e. a conscious, explicit and outspoken opposition, capable of challenging domination, not only secretly, as in Scott's arts of resistance, but especially in the public realm. In the analytics proposed by Santos (1995), for instance, globalization appears as a composite plural phenomenon comprising at least four different patterns: two hegemonic forms, which he calls, respectively, 'globalised localisms' and 'localised globalisms,' and two counter-hegemonic forms, namely 'insurgent cosmopolitanism' and 'the common heritage of humankind.' Whereas the former two patterns reinforce hegemony by universalizing local patterns to be subsequently localized in colonial-imperialist ways, the latter two embody organized forms of resistance against the injustice produced and amplified by hegemony. Resistance is, for Santos, as global as is hegemony, acting on the same scale and through the same types of coalitions used by the dominators. Thus, Santos predicts that the classes and social groups who suffer the consequences of hegemonic globalization will progressively join their forces in transnational struggles against exclusion and subordination, as well as against political oppression and ecological destruction.

The life-world, as distinct from the sheer structural-economic system and its market logic, has been deemed an important site of resistance. Michael Burawoy (1991) has, in this vein, identified various possible outcomes of the tension between system and the life-world. In his model, resistance increases along a continuum that ranges from colonization (capitulation of the life-world to the system), through negotiation within institutional limits, the creation of alternatives, the carving out of spheres of self-organization, and the reshaping of the system's limits, up to collective protests mounted by social movements (reassertion of the life-world over the system). Burawoy views active protest by organized social movements as the highest degree of resistance against domination. Again, we notice that these scholars tend to conceive of resistance as an incomplete step towards the revolutionary outcome. Similarly, Hardt and Negri (2003: 115 ff.) define resistance as one of the three elements of what they call counterpower, along with insurrection and constituent power. In their conception, counterpower is ultimately indistinguishable from power, since the two are symmetrical in terms of their constitution. Implicitly – and, probably, also unwillingly – Hardt and Negri associate counterpower, rather than power, with reaction. In their conceptualization – as well as in Santos's – it is counterpower that literally merits the qualification of 'reactionary', in the sense that it represents a reaction against a previous action enacted by power. This is why, as hinted above, ultimately resistance is considered by these authors as but the negative term in a dialectic of struggle: what resistance can do, as an organic part of the power chain, is, at best, oppose the stream of global power in order to prepare the terrain for action by 'the multitude', which in Negri's Spinozist model corresponds to the political subject of emancipation. Resistance is considered important, insofar as it marks the inception of counterpower, but also denounced as *insufficient*, insofar as, allegedly, it lacks more constructive moves. In the same vein, in a discussion of environmental restoration, Light (2003) opposes to resistance an ideal of 'reengagement', suggesting that resistance by itself falls short of the positive action involved in the active engagement with environmental issues. One final influential example in this line of though is offered by Erik Olin Wright (2019: §3.5) who, in his last book before his premature death, circumscribed the province of resistance as confined to those 'struggles that oppose capitalism from outside of the state but do not themselves attempt to gain state power.' Clearly, resistance is considered by Wright as inherently unable to 'transcend the structures of capitalism', limited as it is to an attempt at *taming*, at best temporarily neutralize, the social harms produced by capitalist relations.

As seen above, Canettian epistemology places the standard of resistance higher than that of sheer opposition. On this account, in order to have an act of resistance it is not enough of stand in opposition to an enemy, regardless of whether the latter appears as stronger than us (resistance scenario) or not (war scenario). Whenever struggle is ongoing – and in spite of the fact that the forces of the contending parties may be unequal – a basic political *symmetry* between the enemies is instituted, which ipso facto prevents the occurrence of resistance. As we seek to elaborate it here, the Canettian perspective lays out a different ground for resistance, refusing to regard it as a helpful-but-insufficient step towards emancipation. Just as in colonial contexts and other situations of intergroup domination, the condition of resistance is certainly one of *lack of freedom*. As Caygill (2013: 97) has remarked, resistance emerges where one is left with little-to-no choice: 'The resistant subject does not enjoy freedom; on the contrary, the resistant subject finds itself in a predicament that does not admit the luxury of possibility.' Resistance is thus always exercised in intolerable historical contexts, to the point that *the intolerable* can be said to be the very element of resistance. However, while a certain attitude of Stoicism – albeit not necessarily a strictly philosophical one – is an intrinsic feature of resistance, such an attitude does not, by itself, suffice to make one truly resistant. The intrinsic nexus of resistance and creation is at the centre of the Canettian approach: unless one is capable of laying out a new territory, one is bound to remain existentially subaltern to the format of the existing power in place. It is precisely out of an utter lack of freedom that freedom must be invented; but a simple, unsatisfied desire for revenge remains within the premises of the Nietzschean feelings of *ressentiment* and envy, falling short of embodying an act of resistance. It is certainly not coincidental that the specific *Unfreiheit* of the resistant subject recalls the condition of the *Dichter/Dichterin* discussed above in Chapter 1. Whereas resistance is usually portrayed as a form of resignation to an unpleasant dominant reality, we can, through a Canettian lens, come to see it as the one act cast *in defiance of resignation*. Just as it does not express a direct opposition to power, resistance does not express a lack of any sort – to the contrary, it forms a meaningful, complete human act. Its completeness does not conflict with the movement of deterritorialization and subtraction outlined above: a cathectic process is at play in it, whose stake lies in finding a path for cutting *across* a domain that is uneasy and substantively inimical. More than to a revolution, resistance is akin to a *diavolution*.[16]

On patience

We may approach the notion of diavolution through a few intermediary conceptual steps. First, the temporal aspect of resistance deserves scrutiny. As remarked above, resistance initially presents itself as a sort of unmovable mountain, in its pretence to stasis quite a stubborn thing to do. However, it is possible to suggest that, far from being accidental or detrimental, stubbornness can be embraced as something that may inform the theoretical gaze seeking to apprehend these acts. In other words, in order to elaborate a suitable conception of resistance as transformation, one may need to begin by changing one's theoretical pace – one may have to become more *patient*: as Perec (1974) once recommended, *il faut y aller plus doucement, presque bêtement* … Slowing down, in this context, means not assuming that we already know enough background facts to interpret what is going on – perhaps even admitting that we know less of them than we assumed; and it might even entail that we proceed as if we actually knew little or nothing. Only once such curious methodological precautions have been taken care of, one can hope to outline the special relation resistance maintains with the human milieus where it appears. We could perhaps speak of a special type of *endurance*. Rather than either active or passive, resistance seems, in this sense, to make its way upon that peculiar terrain which is *the neuter*. Neither fully negative, nor fully affirmative, resistance evokes the power of a neuter that eludes *both* the deliberate act *and* the stimulated reaction. Resistance comes about as interruption, as suspension: an interruption of obedience, a suspension of belief. Among the few thinkers who have taken a similar reorientation seriously is Fernand Deligny, a truly unclassifiable figure and a first-class interlocutor in resistance.[17] Deligny designated as 'the arachnean' a mode of being that evades planning and organizing. He saw it at work especially in the aimless trajectories of autistic children. Between 1969 and 1986, in the Cévennes region, deep in the countryside and mountains of south-central France, Deligny was in charge, with a small group of collaborators, of taking care of a number of children with severe autism and other grave psychotic syndromes. Some of the children were given in custody to him by their families, others by various psychiatric hospitals and clinics when they could no longer be kept – for instance, Yves (diagnosed as 'deep dunce'), or Janmari ('deep-encephalopathic subject'), who would live with Deligny for almost twenty years.

It is difficult to state what the arachnean resists, although undeniably all attempts to force the pace of an autistic child clearly encounter insurmountable difficulties. Deligny set up a number of dwelling spots (*aires de séjour*) where caregivers lived with children, often outdoors, in a farm-like type of settlement. The troubled children were inserted in the flow of everyday activities carried out by the adults, living side by side with them as the latter gardened, milked goats, baked bread, and so on. They were not instructed to do anything: no educational or training programme was envisaged. While Deligny was part of a larger movement in France towards a new model of care, known as *en cure libre* – referring to situations where children could receive treatment or education outside of psychiatric wards and juvenile detention centres – in his specific case *cure libre* did certainly imply 'freedom,' but *no* therapy or educational programme whatsoever. Deligny refused to consider his children as deficient beings: he argued that they could only be considered defective if one looked at them as 'individual persons' – but precisely, he said, they were impersonal and pre-individual beings. This is a most radical teaching that even several progressive minds might regard as suspect. It is thus all the more important to elucidate his approach.

Mesmerized by spider webs, but also by those shining meshed lines that can be seen at the bottom of old used pans, Deligny opposed the arachnean mode of existence to all sorts of projects and plans. In his eyes, the arachnean net expressed a 'vital necessity,' more than any deliberate strategies. Away from functionality and efficiency, the arachnean primes acting (*agir*) over wanting (*vouloir*) or making (*faire*). 'Pure acting' is described by Deligny as a tracing activity, unled by any plan or design. Tracing, Deligny believes, is not a *secret* activity, only a *tacit* one. And the tacit proves indeed to be the most difficult dimension to understand – especially because, like drifting, it is *an objectless activity*. So Deligny was after elusive creatures, after the series of those meaningless bodily gestures which psychiatrists refer to as 'stereotypies' (tics, etc.). By his own admission, he did not know what to make of them – and truly, nobody would: for those gestures have no object, no content, no message. They are the *tacet* of communication (see, in Chapter 1, the discussion of the *tacet* of law and its relation to command). The arachnean, in other words, concerns the recognition of what Deligny called a 'commons without language.' His interest drifted towards what remains on the fringes, what reappears, or survives, in the interstices between structured discourses (expert knowledge, institutional talk, etc.). Such unknown commons, such 'commons=x' might be the veritable *locus* of resistance. An inversion of perspectives, however, does not suffice. The risk of regressing towards the myth of the good savage (that comforting imagery that recurs through Montaigne, Rousseau and beyond) is non-negligible; and Deligny was well aware of it. Therefore, he took care to disclaim a view on autistic children as models of redemption, ethical heroes, or even innocent creatures. Keeping at a distance from the moralistic language of purity and the idyllic depictions of the simpleton, Deligny's questioning ventured along a narrower, more perilous path that stretches between the ethical, the political and the ontological: what he truly laid out are the presuppositions for a new, unheard-of social theory. His project might look like a radical *utopia*; in fact, however, at the centre of his attempt in the Cevennes was a profound *topia*: the *just-thisness* of autistic children's lives. Sharing their days with the kids, Deligny and his team struggled to grasp the emergence of what, at some point, Deligny designated as 'this freedom that owes nothing to claiming.' This is a type of freedom deeply intertwined with resistance, which can only manifest itself once a passage to the impersonal and the infinitive is made – not a new point of view (*point de vue*) (still individual, still personal), but a veritable point of viewing (*point de voir*) (impersonal, infinitive). The pre-individual and impersonal layer of life seems to be entailed in a type of arachnean networking that is not specifically human; alternatively, the arachnean can be said to unsettle the limits of what we consider human (hence, again, the crucial position of autistic children).

Does it make sense to speak of freedom under such extreme conditions? In a broad and yet fundamental sense, freedom is rooted in a type of movement, namely, 'going wherever one wants' (so that all limitations to freedom ultimately turn into limitations to movement, widely understood).[18] But, the movement of autistic children is a drifting movement that stands at the polar opposite of an intended trajectory: it is an aimless roaming around, with no plans, with *no head and no tail*. The fact is that autistic children go around *without wanting*. Deligny and his collaborators started drawing maps of their movements, capturing their wandering lines (*lignes d'erre*) and curious *détours*. They so discovered that those lines of wander had a topology to them: more stable areas (*cernes* or rings) emerged, spaces of gravitation that the children never left (even in the absence of fences, or orders of any sort). And, in a similar way, a series of *keys* (*chevêtres*, literally: binding joists) were outlined, spots to which the children returned recurrently and where they indulged in their repetitive gestures. The kid's territoriology cut deep indeed: away from the grip of language, symbolism and subjectivity, Deligny's children now appeared as immediately gripped upon the land, upon the Earth. Once drawn out, their wander lines revealed the presence of a series of spatial attractors of geodesic type. To his amazement, Deligny found, for instance, that one of Janmari's key spots was where a hidden underground water fount was located (Janmari himself had always been captivated by flowing waters); another key was where in the past a now completely invisible disjunction between two trails used to be, and so on … In other words, the children's wander lines *objectively and accurately* recorded some powers of the earth unbeknownst to all the other observers. Such an unpredictable a-symbolic residuum can only emerge in the form of a *persistence*, a re-emergence – or an afterlife [*Nachleben*], as Aby Warburg called it in a different context. Deligny's attempt in the Cevennes can, in this sense, be said to coincide with the provision of a 'preliminary territory' where spontaneous arachnid networks could manifest as full, intensive, earthly and not-perfectly-human *topoi*.

This may help explain why, in the temporal register of resistance, an apparently painstakingly slow reaction coexists with very sudden manifestations. The lives of living creatures are replete with such unpredictable transformations – which we sometimes call 'miracles.' Miracles are forms of a perfectly natural magic, since they testify to a power of transformation that can be rescued from the many obfuscations in which it is usually plunged by common sense. The work of resistance is nothing but the 'clarification' of the miracles of transformation. All types of instituted and institutionalized power admit only controlled, impoverished, 'funnelled' versions of transformation. These are transformations flattened onto one single dimension. Social hierarchy works this way: within every hierarchical system, only changes in one's position through 'promotion' and 'career progression,' or contrarily, 'downgrading' and 'lowering in rank,' through hiring and firing, are allowed. This type of impoverished transformation is also present in the ascetic discourse, with its imperative *Improve yourself!* whereby one's status is measured as being lower or higher along a reference scale of moral perfection. The modern discourse has turned asceticism into the imperative of Taylorism: *Increase productivity!* And subsequently, over the last half a century, the neoliberal vulgate seems to have synthesized the former two calls into a third one: *Improve yourself so as to increase your productivity!* Since all these discourses lay emphasis on a trend to be followed, they *appear to be* dynamic: and such flimsy appearance has enabled them to disqualify those who resist as static and backward. In reality, it is the type of reduced transformation admitted and required by a similar hierarchal system that looks almost completely static when compared with the vital, magical transformations of life, their multiple, invisible temporalities and their margins of desubjectification. From this perspective, resistance exists to dismantle the many variants of the myth of increase, which all require the same thing under various disguises and pretences (see Chapter 2). One is reminded here that scepticism first appeared as stance of resistance against the too many certainties of early philosophical systems: every resistant is sceptic to a degree. Here is why the stubbornness of the resistant elicits so much uneasiness, frustration and enragement in those who wish to obtain obedience: since the resistant refuses to be channelled into increase and endless improvement, s/he is often sanctioned by hate. Yet, perhaps, hate also hides something else, namely, a secret envy. It was Cioran (1985) who suggested that, whereas we often believe that the dogmatic hates the sceptic, the one who lacks certainties may actually be more *envied* than despised: for certainties are heavy burdens to carry along, too. If the believer, dominated by a credo, seeks to 'proselitise' and 'convert' the unbeliever, it may well be – Cioran suggested – that he does so in order to *share the load* of being dominated by an idea, and its accompanying condition of servitude.[19]

It is significant that, as we progress with our inquiry into resistance, we are led to encounter a series of 'non-argumentative' beings. For his part, Canetti encounters the strange mixture of patience and protest in a donkey tied to a stick in a yard in Marrakech. The donkey is the domesticated-and-yet-resistant animal par excellence: it brays and it jibs. The humblest of all farm animals, the donkey is as much a relentless hard worker as, at the same time, a veritable champion of stubbornness. Whenever it manifests, its resistance is unparalleled: it can carry out the hardest heavyweight transport, and then, for no apparent reasons, become irreducible in refusing all orders to proceed one step farther. Due to its deeply stoical attitude, it is extremely difficult to force a donkey into something it is not convinced of. As admitted by a professional trainer, 'to be honest, in most situations it is easier to walk at the donkeys' pace rather than try and make them go at ours.'[20] Incidentally, this testimony is quite revealing about the nature of domestication: far from 'formatting' the animal, domestication entails constant negotiation with a number of untamed forces. Let us also not forget that donkeys are known to be excellent pet therapy animals, as they seem to possess an extraordinary capacity to defuse aggressiveness. For mysterious reasons, their slow and steady presence proves extremely comforting, and has been described as 'zen-like.' Donkeys are also reported to decide with whom they want to interact, and capable of developing strong personal bonds with those persons. Long before the pet therapy age, Canetti held animals such as donkeys in high esteem. He definitely also avoided all sorts of easy Disney-like moralism. In Marrakech, Canetti bore witness of one of the most striking animal transformations, namely *lust*:

> He had not budged, but it was no longer the same donkey. Because between his back legs, slanting forwards and down, there hung a prodigious member. It was stouter than the stick the man had been threatening him with the night before. In the tiny space of time in which I had had my back turned an overwhelming change had come over him. I do not know what he had seen, heard or smelled. But that pitiful, aged, feeble creature, who was on the verge of collapse and quite useless for anything except as the butt of a comic dialogue, who was treated worse than any monkey in Marrakech, that being, less than nothing, with no meat on his bones, no strength, no proper coat, still had so much lust in him that the mere sight absolved me of the impression caused by his misery. I often think of him. I remind myself how much of him was still there when I saw nothing left. I wish all the tormented his concupiscence in misery.
>
> (*Voi* 89–90)[21]

What strikes Canetti is the fact that an old, skinny, fraying, humble creature, ill-treated and flogged by its master, still contains in itself so much life, such an un-resigned preserve of desire. In one of his latest aphorisms, at 88, Canetti noted: 'The unadjusted [those who do not adapt: *Unangepaßten*] are the salt of earth, the colour of life: they make *their own* unhappiness, but make our happiness'[22] (*Aufz92–3*: 72). Those who are incapable of adjusting to the context, the unaccommodated, are the true harbingers of resistance – for resistance always means *existence without entitlement*.

Canetti knows the bitter truth about submission: it is often voluntary – or 'compliant,' as per current jargon. In Chapter 1, we have recalled that, by Weber's standards, once one adheres to an external will demanding obedience, then the ensuing power is to be regarded as legitimate. But, as we also know, a dictatorship is no less a dictatorship just because there are happy slaves. And Weber's sociological criteria ultimately make it virtually impossible to distinguish a happy slave from a free man. A sensibly different view emerges from Canettian epistemology: what truly matters, on this account, is not one's officially recorded status as a free *vs* unfree person, as citizen *vs* alien, as one-of-us *vs* one-of-them, but the occurrence of an *experience of liberation*. Only through such momentous experiences can one realize that the free person is not the person who single-mindedly adheres to a cause – no matter whether out of idealism or interested calculation (the ultimate cause being the group itself and its ethnocentric operation) – but the person who eventually breaks free of that cause, and rises to the level of destroying *one's own* false idols. Experience, in other words, only matters insofar as it is integrally *transformative*. Neither the starting point, nor the final status of an experience are determinant in themselves: the core and the crux of the matter is, effectively, *the process of liberation*. And resistance initiates this process by interrupting obedience, by inserting the most interruptive of all moves, which is doubt.[23] The experience of liberation was also at the forefront of Camus's preoccupations with the elaboration of the political stance he dubbed 'radicalism of the middle.' We notice how Canetti and Camus seem to share such a vision of a movement of resistance that is akin to a *diavolution*: the crossing of unfriendly terrains without mimetically becoming, on one's turn, an entrenched, ideologized fighter.

Similarly, becoming a *Dichter/Dichterin* must be, for Canetti, an integral experience in resistance. The specific *Unfreiheit* that characterizes the writer's position is not incompatible with the experience of liberation. What this means is that the *Dichter* can never turn into an ideologue – neither in the sense of hegemony nor in the sense of counter-hegemony. The officially sanctioned intellectual of a political regime will never be a *Dichter* in the Canettian sense. As articulated in Chapter 1, the *Dichter's* mission is to save as many human voices as possible from death, destruction and oblivion. Such a collective survival contrasts starkly with the individualizing survival that contradistinguishes power: it embodies a manifestation of *life itself* and its *vital exigency* (as Canguilhem once called it). A vitalist celebration can be seen at play in Canettian epistemology. And there is no appeasement in such a vision: the *Dichter* cannot but remain a restless creature, moving in the muddled terrain where *Unfreiheit* and resistance meet. So, the indissoluble unity of life and literature in Franz Kafka is perfectly pictured in the everyday scene of Franz unflinchingly consuming his vegetal meals at his father's table dominated by meat, before the father's disparaging gaze. The fact that resistance is always to an extent resistance to being judged, becomes clear to Canetti once he meditates on his relation to Karl Kraus, which he retrospectively depicts as his own personal 'school of resistance.' Of course, Kraus never managed any formal training, but in 1920s Vienna his cutting-edge satires and the thundering accusations he used to launch through his journal *Die Fackel* exercised an enormous influence upon the younger intellectuals. Kraus's style, Canetti recalls, was always in the mode of *sentencing*. And *sentences* are what happens when one looses patience.

We have now gained a clearer insight into some constituent aspects of the relation of resistance and its *locus* in social space; henceforth, we can focus more thoroughly on the conceptualization of power needed to account for the workings of resistance.

Non-symbolic investigations into power

Elias Canetti and Michel Foucault are two authors rarely discussed together. *Et pour cause*, some might add. Indeed, Foucault is widely regarded as the great analyst of a historically modern model of power, a type of power – soft or 'positive' – that seeks the collaboration of its subjects, shaping their intentions and placing them within a field of relations, which is also a field of intelligibility and governmentality. By contrast, Canetti has been depicted as a primordialist author who disregards historical specificities in order to point towards an ancient, obscure and violent core of power. Despite that, both authors are helpful for thinking through resistance; and sketching a comparison between their approaches may shed some light on the complex relation between power, resistance, struggle and *affirmation*.

In the famous 1982 afterword to Dreyfus and Rabinow's book, Foucault argued that power is so diffused and disseminated throughout social life that it can be considered omnipresent in it. This, however, does not pre-empt the possibility of resistance; to the contrary, power may be pervasive, but never excludes the chance of negating it. Knights and Vurdubakis (1994: 191) push Foucault's argument into the assertion that 'acts of resistance are also exercises of power.' Canettian epistemology, as we have seen, suggests, on the contrary, that resistance is *irreducible* to power: if resistance does anything at all, it is to show the *otherwise* of power, indicating a way of composing human relations that is external to the logic and the action of power. In part, I believe, Knights and Vurdubakis have forced Foucault's point: indeed, the latter placed emphasis on the reverse formulation, namely, that power is also inherently resisted. In part, however, there is a more profound misunderstanding to dispel. What Foucault really distinguished in the 1982 afterword, is not so much power from resistance, as much as power from violence and struggle. Following a trail first opened by Nietzsche, Foucault (1982) argues that power is different from both a function of consent, and a function of violence: whereas violence acts upon bodies and things by exerting a forcible action on them, power always acts upon other actions, thereby composing an active equation of forces. Thus, for power to exist, it requires an acting subject who remains identifiable and distinct. What power in the modern sense does is to structure the field where the subject will have to position himself or herself – what Foucault calls the 'field of responses.' Hence, the subject, while always existing in some relation to power, is never subsumed or determined by it to do anything in particular. Power is, most literally, a *ratio*, a proportion of forces that exists only insofar as it does not coincide with either complete victory, or ongoing struggle. Power and struggle, Foucault thus claims, constitute a 'permanent limit' to each other and, by the same token, they are also the 'point of possible reversal' of one another: 'It would not be possible for power relations to exist without points of insubordination which, by definition, are means of escape' (Foucault 1982: 225).

By contending that power relations necessarily imply means of escape, Foucault remained ambivalent – better, trivalent – about whether the means themselves belong to the field of power, to that of struggle, or to none of them. Canetti's indication, as we have seen, lies in imagining resistance as a third pole in the power–struggle complex, irreducible to both. At the same time, resistance must also be differentiated from sheer reaction: if an action, a conduct, or a stance, is either straightforwardly oppositional, or merely reactive, it becomes indistinguishable from power itself, considering the Foucaultian insight that symmetrical opposition is still a component of the power ratio. Hence, in Canettian epistemology resistance only emerges when a transformative drive asserts itself to a degree of intensity that is sufficient to breed an experience of liberation from the power relations in place. Because one cannot resist something without simultaneously resisting its opposite, resistance intrinsically exhibits a double movement – just like the Nietzschean double negation that produces an affirmation through an overall movement of *Umwertung*. Thus, the cathectic–pharmacological structure of resistance encompasses a slantwise, cut-through passage that undoes and 'resolves' the pharmacological ambivalence of the poison–medicine. Similarly, in the temporal dimension, the movement of resistance implies a liberation from the present of power, in view of opening up a now-unconceivable future in which new forms of commonality may emerge. Life always proceeds 'from the middle,' and it is in this very middle that the radicalness of action must be retrieved. Rather than from the empty extremes of yes and no, of dogmatism and nihilism – which endlessly entertain with and increment one another – the act of resistance proceeds from a middle capable of spurring a radicalism not subsumed by any already-existing categories of the social–political lexicon.

Both Foucault and Canetti locate the basic ground of power and resistance in the body. Shunning the 'avoidance of the concrete,' they both choose to point their gaze into the details of how institutions (Foucault) and ravings (Canetti) practically work upon bodies: just as Foucault was the great explorer of institutional practices and discourses (asylum, prison, police, confession …), so was Canetti a keen analyst of all sorts of delusions and eccentricities (Büchner, Schreber, Kafka, Kraus, Hitler …). Both arrive at what we may call an *anti-symbolic* conception of power, hinting at a global social–theoretical renewal. Despite the fact that they sometimes resort to the descriptive terminology of symbols, their approach is fundamentally incompatible with symbolism – i.e., with structuralism. In fact, symbolism works by establishing a parallel between some contingent material item at hand and some abstract – invisible, remote, not at hand – structure, which exists at a different order of generality. In symbolic thinking, the material is employed to recall – to make present, to 'presentify' – the immaterial, so that the contingent materiality always gets subordinated to the underlying determinant symbolic grid. Nothing could be farther from what Foucault and Canetti do: in Foucault, the symbols of sovereignty do nothing but hide the actually working diagram of government; in Canetti, postures and gestures do not symbolize power, to the contrary, power is nothing but the power to adopt postures and make gestures. It is true that Canetti has a chapter about the 'symbols of power,' yet, as soon as we examine what he means by this, we find that, for him, power is as material as the gestures that are supposed to symbolize it: there is not an abstract power that gets symbolized, but a series of 'emblematic' operations and gestures that are effective in themselves. No less than Foucaultian analysis,

Canettian epistemology offers an immanentist perspective that radically undoes the generative transcendence upon which all symbolic systems rest.[24]

In light of the attention they both pay to the body as well as the anti-symbolic view of power they hold, it may be interesting to see how Canetti and Foucault arrive at two different conceptions of resistance. Whereas Foucault advances what is an essentially *discontinuist* thesis, looking for the moments when small ruptures in the episteme of an epoch are produced (Foucault 1971), Canetti for his part elaborates a deeply *continuist* view, which considers series of prolonged formations (so that, for instance, climbing becomes commerce, the mouth becomes prison, excrements becomes morality and so on). When Foucault (1975, 1976, 2004) describes the transition from sovereign power to disciplinary power, he speaks in terms of 'replacement', 'substitution' and 'profound transformation'. Such a profound transformation consists in a shift from repressive to productive power, from a power that imposes to a power that disposes, from the power to take life or let live, to the power to foster life or disallow it to death. Since, as considered above, power needs its subjects alive, death appears as an objective limit to power; modern power, in particular, does not aim to crush its subjects but is premised upon an increase in the degree of 'docility' of bodies. The body thus appears as the place of inscription of power and its classificatory *savoirs* – such as, for instance, the *regard médicale*, the modern medical gaze based on the classification of pathologies. Whether at stake is an individual body ('anatomopolitics') or a social body, i.e. a population ('biopolitics'), the know-how of government seeks local, concrete points of application. Both disciplinary institutional enclosures and governmental dispositions are effective only if they ultimately gain a grip on bodies and the architectural and urban spaces where such bodies move about. Even in his later analysis of pastoral power, Foucault (1982) explains that, not so much are we subjects who learn to obey, but it is rather obedience that constitutes us as subjects, for it is through obedience that we come to exist in relation to a prestigious other.[25] Therefore, 'total obedience', far from crushing the subject, contributes to an increase in subjectification; yet simultaneously, since subjects are always required to position themselves in the field of responses designed by power, even when recalcitrant, they remain within such a pre-conceived field (a view that, as considered above, echoes Gramsci's notion of hegemony).

In the continuist imagination of Canettian epistemology, power represents an extension or amplification of the primal act of seizing. The same continuum ranges from the prehensile organs of the hand, to the digestive organs of the mouth, the throat and the entrails. The reason why Canetti never devotes much attention to institutional analysis probably lies in the assumption that the same apparatus for grasping and eating, for incorporating and expelling, is replicated from the most primordial forms in the exercise of power to the most institutionalized and sophisticated ones: even the most technologically advanced forms of power are but prolongations of the clutch of the hand. Yet Canetti also introduces a distinction between violence [*Gewalt*] and power [*Macht*]. Connecting the word *Macht* to the Gothic root *magan*, being able to (rather than to the more usual German verb *machen*, to do) and expanding on the paradigmatic case of the cat chasing the mouse, Canetti suggests that power is itself not an action, nor an interaction, but rather a *capacity* or possibility to act. Such a specifically extensive or projective quality of power distinguishes it from actually occurring violence. Interestingly, this idea reminds us of the conception later introduced by Deleuze (1968) whereby the domain of the real is split between *actual* and *virtual*, the latter being 'real without being actual.' For Canetti, in line with the tendency towards increase (see Chapter 2), power always wants to grow: it tends to become larger and larger, extending itself in space and time and, in doing so, it proceeds from one support to another, from the material to the psychic (not to mention, today, the digital). What does not change, is the mode of functioning of power, which remains based on clamping down on bodies. The corporeal, however, should not be considered here as a substantial reality (an assumption underlying Foucault's notion of anatomopolitics): far from being an ultimate reality, the body itself constantly stretches and prolongs into other not-simply-corporeal domains. Such are the cases, mentioned above, of the individual prolonging into a crowd, climbing prolonging into commerce, jaws into prison, excrement into morality and shelter into grave. The ultimate stage of seizing, is killing – which explains why power remains, at least in virtual terms, always bound up with death. While, strictly speaking, the dead are outside all relations of power, Canetti draws attention, not simply to the alternative between life and death, but to the precise moment of *survival*, which, as we have considered, he describes as a triadic, wholly social relation: survival confronts an individual, not with one's own death, nor with just another individual who dies, but with a whole crowd – better, with *a double crowd*: the crowds of the living and the dead.

When we compare Canetti's conception to the prima facie more sophisticated analytical framework of power elaborated by Foucault, it retains its strength. In particular, Foucault's discontinuist thesis on disciplinary power – especially insofar as phrased in terms of 'replacements'[26] – fails to explain why the nineteenth and twentieth centuries have been, in absolute terms, the bloodiest in the history of humankind. It is rather difficult, from a strict disciplinary and biopolitical perspective, to account for the persistence of the power of death – and in fact, war, totalitarianism and genocide were not Foucault's main topics.[27] They are, on the contrary, precisely the type of phenomena that drove Canetti's enquiry. Certainly, in the late 1970s, when Foucault did turn to issues concerning the biopolitical government of populations (Foucault 1991, 2004), he implicitly acknowledged that the power to seize hold on bodies has not been superseded in modernity, and is not simply a residual counterpart of disciplinary power. Even at that point, however, Canetti's analysis of the imagined relation between humans and insects can bring novel inspiration into Foucault's concept of population. Canetti suggests that mass murder is psychosocially prepared by a phenomenon of human 'inflation,' a breaking down of the bond between humans caused by the imagined transformation of scapegoated human groups into insects, with which no empathy is possible (only afterwards did biologists and anthropologists started calling this phenomenon 'pseudo-speciation'). As we have noticed, for Foucault, the modern modes of power have the peculiarity of directing bodies *at a distance*: for instance, they classify crime according to a series of 'optimal specifications,' or they design from afar the architectural spaces were bodies will be hosted and allowed, or not allowed, to move. Yet, from a Canettian perspective, we should recognize that a territorializing constraint remains a necessary requirement for the exercise of power. As examined in Chapter 1, while not all power may be of command-type, the prolongations of command are still operational inside the more distanced power diagrams. And in a similar way, the distinction between virtuality and actuality in the operations of power – which Foucault expressed through his concept of 'field of responses' – rhymes with Canetti's distinction between *Gewalt* and *Macht*. In sum, one senses that the distance between the two authors may not be as wide as it appears at first sight.

Nonetheless, differences between the two do exist. Whether one regards it as a pessimistic or an optimistic conception, for Foucault, there is no outside of power: even struggle, recalcitrance and resistance are bound to remain within its embrace. While resistance is, in principle, always possible, it is also clear that it does not produce an elsewhere, nor an otherwise. Canetti believes, instead, that an outside of power can be attained. From a Canettian perspective, resistance is precisely such a movement towards the outside. That there may exist human – or, more widely, social – relations outside of power: such is the challenge Canetti is interested in. Of course, there is no denial that humans are deeply engrained within power dynamics, that they are imbued with power just as they are with other societal requirements. Taken as individuals, humans appear to Canetti as sad creatures, patrolling their distances as if they were assets, sometimes tragically awaiting commands as if commands could deliver to them a sought-after liberation. But humanity also carries with itself a talent for transformations, revealed by its capacity to mingle with the heterogeneity of the world and its capacity to break the ethnocentric operation. These capacities point towards the outside, and initiate new becoming. Resistance, on this view, is not part of a struggle for power but part of a movement of liberation from it. As such, it implies the search for a way out: a movement of liberation from the grasp in all its different variants and sizes. The fact that such an experience can be *lived*, is the proof that power is not simply 'a name' – as per Foucault's rigorous nominalism. Not that power is a substance, but it includes a degree of intensity that cannot be explained away by the nominalistic (*sive* structuralist, discursive, genealogical, etc.) argument. Resistance takes place whenever humans seek to avoid being crushed; in this respect, Barrington Moore (1978: 125) observed that, through the centuries, the most common reaction to oppression has been *flight*. Indeed, resistance is a type of flight: a flight from command, and more importantly, the apparition of *commonality in flight*. A 'flight crowds', let us recall, is for Canetti completely different from an episode of panic: whereas in panic the crowd breaks down, with each individual looking safety *at the expense of the others*, a fleeing crowd makes it possible to *share* and jointly *dissipate* the grip of impending command. Even when worry is a dominant factor in the formation of a flight crowd, there is still some joy to it, a connection to the sense and the mood of shared movement: the flight crowd is neither helpless nor hopeless.[28]

Life: uselessness …

At the outset, we have briefly recalled how, at the basis of psychoanalytic theory, lies the idea that resistance equates with lack of courage and, specifically, the courage to change one's life: the patient 'resists' to the extent that even neurotic suffering (the 'symptom') appears more tolerable than the shocking revelations that lay ahead in the progress of a therapy. But, what if, on the contrary, resistance coincides with the very *act of life* inside a present that already denies life in the first place? We have, in this case, a resistance that is not defensive *against* life, but defensive *of* life. We know that, at the biological level, life includes resistance as one of its basic features, namely, resistance against increasing entropy.[29] On this account, resistance comes to coincide with a manifestation of the vital function itself. Within the domain of life, resistance and transformation interweave in many complex ways: a consideration of the natural sciences suggests that the function of resistance is quite distinct from that of mimesis: phenomena such as animal mimicry, for instance, do certainly imply a type of 'transformation,' yet one that ultimately results in *diminished* difference between beings; on the contrary, while resistance apparently shuts one off from external influences, in terms of outcomes it actually *increases* the diversity between beings. Resistance, in this precise and technical sense, sides with biodiversity.

Just as it represents a form of anti-mimesis, resistance also works as a form of anti-command.[30] The odd, oblique recalcitrance of Bartleby's 'I would prefer not to' comes immediately to mind: commands slip upon Bartleby, they do not have a grip on him. No doubt, Bartleby is an idiot – but, if so, one should also admit that the idiot *is* the 'conceptual character' of resistance *par excellence*.[31] Indeed, the idiot hampers the others and their work, s/he resists what everybody else accepts, what everybody else sees no reason to reject. Nobody understands what the idiot is thinking about, his/her countenance conveys a passivity that is dull and unnerving, s/he is an unpleasant, if not sinister, presence – s/he causes nothing but trouble. Simply, the idiot does not resign him/herself to what is just plainly *true*. Even unwillingly – and yet this is very hard to say: who can seriously claim to know anything about it? – the idiot eternally challenges the taken-for-granted, the consensual, hegemonic definition of the situation. One such indecipherable resistant character is 'the unseen' in *The voices of Marrakesh* [*Stim* 85; *Voi* 100], that 'small, brown bundle on the ground' in a busy square, upon which people almost stumble, who produces a single, endlessly repeated rhythmic sound: '-eh-eh-eh-eh-eh-eh-eh-eh-' – still, 'a creature.' We encounter here an important deviation from the fundamental law of imitation posited by Tarde: if social life is, by and large, imitative, there are still acts capable of undermining the imitogenic potential of action (Tarde himself called such instances, moments of 'hesitation,' which he regarded as a special type of 'opposition'). That is how, ultimately, Bartleby pushes the Wall Street lawyer to ask himself a number of unsettling questions that had never crossed his mind before. It does not matter whether, as suspected by many commentators, Bartleby turns out to be an alter ego of the lawyer himself: perhaps, after all, we all have an idiot inside, an idiot who refuses to understand, who does not accept, and does not adapt.

Every instance of resistance does signal a *failure to adapt*, a persistent lack of adjustment. In this vein, the archaeologist V. Gordon Childe (1951[1936]: 26) was among the first to stress that, overall, humans are ill-adjusted animals, 'inadequately adapted for survival in any particular environment.'[32] Of course, a completely dis-adapted animal cannot survive for long; at the same time, however, a *relative degree* of dis-adaptation may be important for the production of new adaptive measures: living, means existing on the margins of adaptation. It is a condition of restlessness and, inherently, of creation. The view of resistance as transformation elaborated here thus curiously resonates with the elemental philosophy of Gaston Bachelard: laying out a wide-ranging inquiry into the capacity of imagination, Bachelard (1942: 25) defines the latter as not simply the capacity to compose images, but, more pointedly, as the capacity to *transform* existing images so as to detect, resonate with and invent new life. After Bachelard, Deleuze (1987) suggested that what one resists is *a present* confronting one with endless hardship. To resist, a.k.a. *to exist without entitlement*: work songs and laments are the acts of a communal resistance by millions of anonymous slaves, workers and miserable humans who lay along the history of humanity – a lament enabling them to walk through Babylon. If these subjects have produced any resistance at all, it must be located in the evocation of change. To the advantage of all the creatures existing in a condition of *minority*, resistance fissures the monolith of the present, opening a crack inside it that points towards an 'untoward' becoming, an unheard-of transformation. Above, we have compared resistance to the Nietzschean double negation that produces an affirmation; we can now better specify what it negates and what it affirms: resistance is the 'no' to power, which in its turn is a 'no' to life. Through a Nietzschean *Umwertung aller Werte*, resistance, being a negation of a negative configuration of the world, enables new affirmative forces to coalesce. The present that is resisted is the present of violence, the present of subjection and power – for power always exist *in the present tense*: power is *the real*. Incidentally, that is why Canetti contends that historiography breeds an in-built cult of power: history, in a sense, records only 'the present,' i.e. the effectuated. Regardless of the subjective persuasions of the historians, who may even be quite progressive, historiography thereby inherently turns into a celebration of the present; by contrast, resistance embodies an anti-reductionist, *a-historical experience*, which looks into the ineffectuated in order to find avenues for difference outside of the repetition and the accumulation of bitter experience. Resistance is whatever distances itself from the 'seduction' and the 'false greatness' of death; and it is in this sense that, analysing the act of creation, Deleuze highlighted a fundamental similarity between *resistance* and *art*. There is not much to say about creation in itself, Deleuze noted, because it is *through creation* that one has something to say to the others: creation expresses the vital necessity to address others. As we explore more in-depth in Chapter 4, all forms of commonality originate from such assumption.

If there is an art of resistance, it must be learnt each time anew. Such learning, also, cannot but occur in critical mode, with each new generation carrying with it the inescapable awareness it could be the last one standing. Today, we know it all too well, because we have practically exhausted the ecological limits of the planet. Yet, the feeling itself is not new: in the past, people feared they had exhausted God's patience. That does not mean that history repeats itself, but that a special awareness periodically resurfaces about the intrinsic cost of 'just carrying on,' of protracting the monolithic present *as it is*. From this perspective, resistance is but a way of manifesting the awareness that the cost of 'the present' is too high, and we cannot afford it. At a time when influential social theories, such as actor-network theory, plea for the development of 'symmetric ontologies,' it is important to remind that the ethical–political pivot of resistance lies precisely in *avoiding symmetrization*: for resistance, as we have seen, cannot derive from frontal clashes – nor, however, can it be reduced to just a smooth parallel line that endorses present reality; rather, its movement is akin to a chaotic fluid flow, entailing a series of inflections, imperfect returns, swirls, diagonals, cuts through: all exercises in autonomy and escape from encaging attractors. And, to the extent that its central ethical–political concern lies in finding ways to avoid symmetrization, resistance cannot proceed through either simple denial, or simple rejection. Thus, we should take special care to distinguish resistance from disobedience, since not all disobedience is actually resistant in the sense proposed here. Resistance only occurs when one confronts a situation of power with one's own body and one's own presence in a way that differs from *both* compliance *and* struggle. In resistance, disobedience always becomes something else – one could also say: disobedience must first cease to be *nomotropic* for resistance to emerge out of it. This clarifies why resistance is such a non-effective way of conduct: on this point, Douglas Adam's Vogon guard (in *The Hitchhiker's Guide to the Galaxy*) is perfectly right: 'Resistance is useless ...' Such, indeed, is the discourse of power, and it cannot be denied that there is truth to the claim: resistance *is* useless, even futile, if we measure its utility in terms of the goals achieved, or in terms of the imperatives of production, increase and maximization. Power adheres to itself; it changes its appearances (its 'mask,' as Canetti would have it), but never allows for real transformations to occur. Not by chance does the Vogon guard go on endlessly repeating that 'resistance is useless, resistance is useless, resistance is useless ...' – there are only minor variations in this tune.

Disobedience, and even defiance, may be more profitable to power than real resistance – for ultimately opposition does not undermine power, on the contrary, it reproduces its logic, perpetuating the symmetrical struggle for power which makes possible its regular exercise. Tarde himself argued that it is impossible to order an invention (1890: 97): indeed, all veritable creation lies outside of the sphere of command; and what is needed to invent something has little to do with the sheer rejection of command – a wholly new dimension must first be introduced for invention to become possible at all. So, resistance *is* futile, but that is also why it is *of the essence*. Resistance, in this sense, is like theory-making, where a *good* theory is not one that describes or interprets a lot of things, nor one that criticizes phenomena more extensively, finding more culprits – rather, it is one that allows humans *to live more fully*, to experience more dimensions. Vital theories are neither useful nor instrumental in the strict sense, yet it is remarkable how, at bottom, they all express a need, a necessity, an exigency to flee from instituted power, from power *in the present tense*. Signifying a transformation from what is towards what could be, resistance can thus be seen a movement from being, not towards power, but towards 'potency.' On this, Bachelard (1942: 202) beautifully remarked how the 'will to power' is always a little childish, since it raves *la puissance au-delà du pouvoir effectif* [power beyond one's power], just like a child who dreams to challenge the waves of the ocean. Unsurprisingly, then, the true literature of resistance presents us with ongoing miniaturizations: Kafka dreams of becoming 'infinitely small' in order to escape from the clutch of power – for even engagement and marriage are like arrest and execution to him.[33] But there are also writers who are prosecutors, instead of runaways. Kraus 'the dictator' never actually forced his own model upon anybody, and never wished to create an orthodoxy; quite to the contrary, he progressively turned into a one-man band, editing his journal alone and remaining its only contributor; it was rather the young Canetti, along a number of young intellectual followers, who tied themselves to their demigod, and became paralysed by his intellectual model. Theirs was a servitude nobody had forced upon them: they had actually enchained themselves to their hero. Kraus was practicing his own resistance to the century, but Canetti's resistance could only come through the realization that one must break free from one's idols in the first place.[34]

Every *Dichter/Dichterin* – writer, thinker, artist, filmmaker or poet that be – must, first of all, learn to breathe independently – and indeed, nothing is more difficult. Hermann Broch's attitude is depicted by Canetti (*CW* §1) as that of a 'hound,' who restlessly sniffs the trails of the world, engaging his rhinarium in a most proximal enquiry that keeps his whole conscience engaged. The dog's nervous sniffing – which amplifies enormously his/her capacity to smell and feel – testifies simultaneously to his/her excitement *and* dissatisfaction with what s/he finds: it is, indeed, a condition of restlessness. In another famous case, Stendhal, whose most ardent wish was to 'live all lives,' illustrates a type of survival completely different from that of power, a survival which renounces killing and embraces life in its pure positivity (remembering that, as we have examined in Chapter 1, killing, surviving and 'winning' are much more diffused throughout social life and social situations than commonly recognized). Art then already indicates a mode of survival that begins when individuals somehow relinquish their position, and vanish. It is a shared form of survival, which brings into immortality, not a single human being (the famous artist), but *the largest possible number* of human beings together: all those who, with their singularity, have entered the domain of creation. No veritable work of art is a stand-alone, and that is why the cult of artworks, and the whole art market, are largely delusional enterprises. All art is a crowd formation. Because of its profound link to non-individual survival, art appeals to a whole peoplehood, and although it has no power of its own to create that people to come, it continues to address it in an act of faith that is indissociable from each effort to create. Imagining human relations – and even more widely, imagining relations *among the living* – beyond the horizon of power, may be the ultimate accomplishment of commonality (more on this in Chapter 4). Unlike the isolated genius of romanticism, the real subject of resistance is not a severed individual, even though the heralds of resistance are often strange, unadjusted, outcast characters. Unlike the officially registered ideologue or truth-advertiser, the resistant subject is neither looking for maximizing the audience, not in pursuit of social confirmation: as noticed above, the riddle of resistance lies in not becoming the copy of one's enemy.

Rather than denial and rejection, resistance calls for a stubborn acceptance-with-reworking, an intense elaboration capable of conjuring up unforeseen liberating transformations. One of the quintessential tropes of resistance is the already-evoked *marronnage*, the flee undertook by those escapee slaves upon which the Martinican poet Édouard Glissant (1997[1990]) built a theory of creolization as a unique cultural project. Born out of the brutal reality of the Plantation institution, in a world surrounded by the imperatives of silence and 'getting around,' creolization appears as wholly grounded in resistance ('within this universe of domination and oppression, of silent or professed dehumanization, forms of humanity stubbornly persisted' [*ibid.*: 65]). Through such a stubborn resistance, rather than open struggle, the oblique movement of creolization generated 'a new and original dimension,' a new language 'whose genius consists in always being open, that is, perhaps, never becoming fixed except according to a systems of variables that we have to imagine as much as define' (*ibid.*: 34). So, resistance is really the capacity to create one's own coordinates of meaning; and if we think about creole cultures, we realize that artful moments and artful acts of resistance do not necessarily define a professional domain – on the contrary, they are widely dispersed across the whole social field. The subject of resistance lies similarly scattered across a plurality of foyers, moments, compositions and openings: resistance always opens up to shared dimensions, insofar as it summons a whole palette of modes of commonality. However, an instituted social group can hardly be said to be 'resistant' in itself: a tendency towards the basic ethnocentric operation – in other words, towards implosion – is always inherent in each and every group. One cannot resist alone, but resistance cannot be exercised by a group as such, either: it is in this sense that the arachnean dimension conjures up resistance as the 'clarification' of the miracles of transformation. One can only hope to attain a degree of resistance to the extent that one gives up any attempt to *mirror* reality – either to glorify it, or to criticize it – in order to undertake new *uncharted trails* that push deeply towards the unknown and the unheard of. On this path, the ultimate risk is embodied, not by any external oppressor, but by oneself: it is the risk of ending up walled in one's own work, in one's own system of beliefs, in one's monolith (literally, one's grave stone) – a risk before which an escapist art of not being caught in one's totality is urgently called forth.[35]

What the *Dichter/Dichterin* does is not at all exceptional, nor herculean – in fact, his/hers is a situation *everybody* is normally faced with. If the thinker has to resist the completion of his or her system of thought, similarly, everybody must *resist the completion of one's individuation*. We can now see better how Simondon's (2013[1964–89]) original notion of individuation corresponds to a process that is distinct from the individuated reality that ensues from it: for

Simondon, individuation occurs *in degrees*, so that every individuated thing – be it a physical object, or a living individual – keeps within itself a reservoir of pre-individual reality, which can be used to promote *further individuations*, that is, more individuations to come. Thus, everyone is, in the literal physical sense, a *keeper of transformation*. Whence precisely the role of resistance: just as the crucial collective political question concerns how to resist the *ethnocentric* operation, in the same way, the personal ethical question concerns how to resist the *egocentric* operation – the operation, in other words, that leads to equating with *oneself's majority*, hampering the preservation of that non-individual and pre-personal source that nourishes all the further individuations that may ever see the light of the day. In a not too dissimilar way, Deleuze and Guattari (1980) evoke the possibility, for the human being, to 'flee from the face' [*échapper au visage*] as a crucial chance to achieve liberation: while the face is certainly quite important in social life, it also imposes a heavy burden, which at some points one feels the urge to discharge, even at the cost of renouncing one's name and position, of becoming *none and anyone*. That resistance has to do with a mode of transformation that relinquishes proper names was clear to Canetti, too: transformation cannot in any way be reconciled with epistemological individualism – and this despite the fact that it often takes gigantic individualistic figures to realize this: the point is precisely not to glory one's egotism, but push one's ego towards the farthest limits of social life, turning one into a *traveller of oneself* – something which may only happen when one is ready and determined to set off to unknown lands: our real home.

Resistance, we argued throughout, can only be understood thanks to transformation. We know, however, that Canetti's theory of transformation was left unfinished. Curiously – perhaps, quite appositely – the *Verwandlung* chapter in *Crowds and Power* (*MM* §IX) documents more phenomena of resistance *against* transformation than phenomena of resistance *as* transformation. And yet it is the latter that, as we have seen, represents the crucial *pars construens* in Canettian epistemology. To the extent that the transformation chapter describes mostly social regulations of transformation, as well as its functional, strategic deployment (as seen at work, for instance, in 'simulation'), but falls short of exploring the full potentials of ungoverned transformation, it will not surprise us that Canetti felt he had only dented the surface of a deeper problem, left for further explorations to come. Quite explicitly, since the outset the author proceeds in a very cautious way, suggesting to approach the phenomenon, which he qualifies as 'extremely difficult', 'from several different angles' (*CP* 337), rather than in a unitary way. By doing so, he clearly refrains from claiming to have identified the kernel, or 'true nature', of transformation – a task to which he endlessly returns in the short prose of *Aufzeichnungen*, although never in an extensive organic treatment. Accordingly, the attempt to develop a rounded conception of resistance necessarily pushes us beyond textual exegesis. In particular, I suggest it could be helpful to address more explicitly the pharmacological and cathectic nature of transformation. In the 'presentments [*Vorgefühl*] of transformation among the Bushmen,' for instance, we notice how a zone of indiscernibility is established between two bodies that remain, nonetheless, distinct: it is not the son who becomes the father, nor vice versa, according to operations that, although imperfectly, would still be subsumable under the psychoanalytical category of 'identification'; rather, it is the father's *wound* that creates a special communication between father and son. In this respect, some special 'nodal points' [*Knotenpunkte*] (*MM* 402) appear: the wound acts as a sort of very special revolving door, a veritable *point of election*, if we may say so. A point of election is not simply a recollection or remembrance; it corresponds to establishing a new level of commonality between father and son, one that is completely different from their relation of filiation, as well as all their previous knowledge of each another.

This way, a theory of transformations preludes to a theory of *events* and a theory of *moments*: the event is not an occurrence generated by a pre-existing matrix, structure, or system, but a mobile element that directly affects structure, matrix and system themselves; likewise, a moment is not a scheduled occurrence in time, nor a chosen 'location' in its flow, but the qualitative 'turn' of an atmospheric composition – a veritable *phase transition*. An elective moment, or the event of an election, is thereby not grounded in the individuals involved in it, nor in their possible 'fusion.' Rather, the election is a structuring force that reaches upon those individuals and makes it possible for them to encounter one another *anew*. This is what, ultimately, the stance of resistance makes possible: meeting one another on a new terrain. Looking at presentments from such a vintage point highlights their inherent cathectic quality: plainly, a presentment shares noteworthy similarities with a command,[36] in that it actively *pushes* the individual who feels it to act. Such a feature recalls interestingly Walter Benjamin's (1999a[1933]) earlier analysis of the 'mimetic faculty' – where, in its original configuration, the *capacity* to perceive similarities appears strictly interwoven with the *compulsion* to become-similar. In this respect, it is again essential to note how the direct contact between heterogeneous elements does not cause their fusion, assimilation, nor any ensuing uniformity: while the wound gets embodied in the son, it remains *the father's wound*, completely distinct from the son's wounds. Precisely through its not being an identification, nor a form of 'empathy,' the presentment institutes a commonality that proceeds through crowd sensations and crowd formations, inherently including a degree of resistance to individuation. Its elusive aspect, earlier on remarked by Canetti, might have to do precisely with its resistant quality: the presentment involves the transit of an impersonal pregnance across different individual bodies, whose existence manifests both a degree of resistance *and* a degree a permeability – in other words, a *coefficient of pliability*. The domain in which these bodies can be put in communication, indicates a distinct, unique mode of reality.

Canetti the *Todfeind*, the man who made denying any greatness to death and rejecting any complacency towards death his life's mission, could himself issue so trenchant judgments about people and works that they have been described as 'lethal injections.'[37] Such mini-death-sentences do not speak only of contradiction and human weakness on Canetti's own part: it cannot be by chance if – as Canetti points out elsewhere – most of the authors who have understood power, have also been *in favour* of it, as either its allies, or its eulogists. All ethical attempts call for the development of a suitable epistemology. It is not only to justify power, but to undermine it, that one needs to 'entertain' with it: it is only out of a close, almost intimate encounter with the deadly *facies* of power that the stance of resistance can be successfully crafted, finally introducing that asymmetry which alone can explain the ratio, aim and *direction* of a given pharmacological composition – where *direction* must be recognized as the ethical element of every pharmacological equation. This means that keeping alive as many people as possible (the *Dichter's* mission) also includes entertaining with the worst possible human beings, the most cruel rulers, the psychopaths. The *Machthaber*, which Canetti almost compulsively investigated, must not be denied, nor simply fought against: he must be truly *resisted*, in a way that takes the sting away from his command. By necessarily assaying and transiting through dangerous contact zones, the inherent dynamics of resistance consists of laying out new ground, new coordinates for all the transformations which have not yet been conceived.

Chapter 4

COMMONALITY

Figure 4 The enigma of commonality.

On Interiority

The renewed attention towards the commons over the past decade signals something important. Whereas nineteenth- and twentieth-century Marxist theorists *advocated* communism as a new general principle of social organization, and simultaneously *expected* it as the inevitable outcome of the crisis of capitalism, Deleuze and Guattari (1972, 1980) pointed out that, in fact, capitalism works best through crises, as a social machine that thrives on contradictions.[1] Indeed, several capitalist crises have since occurred, and predictably more we are to see, without any communist turn whatsoever in sight, in the West at least. But even the main country in the world led by a communist party is a de facto corporate–state–capitalist economy. In this context, Jean-Luc Nancy (2014: 15) remarked that, since the 1980s, it was precisely the dead end of historical communism that stimulated a round of new reflections on the promises and the limits of the notion of community. Later on, appeals to community have been interpreted by Zygmunt Bauman (2001) as compensatory vis-à-vis the lack of existential and social securities accompanied by the demise of the welfare state. Given such general historical conditions, today's renewed interest towards a plurality of *common-pool resources* (CPRs) seems to speak to the realization that they may support a number of emancipatory practices already workable under capitalist conditions – at least, to the extent that they can somehow be made consistent with private property and contract law.[2] The commons, it is believed, can be advanced 'interstitially': its supporters and sympathizers have the feeling of being at the same time, perhaps less than revolutionary, but more than just progressive. This might also mean, in other words, that one doesn't need to be a communist to take an interest in the commons. Notably, the interstitial perspective on the commons makes one of the tenets of anarchism, namely coarchic cooperation, rather cogent. Whereas in the earlier literature on natural common-pool resources – including, for instance, fish, game and forestry – emphasis had been mainly placed on questions of boundaries, access rights, exploitation rules and enforcement mechanisms, such a strictly economic–organizational perspective has since been critiqued.[3] Various invitations have been issued to attend the political practices of 'commoning,' rather than just assuming the commons as a set of pre-existing resources ready to be exploited (Linebaugh 2008; Stavrides 2016).[4] Whereas the economic perspective is premised on phenomena of scarcity and the risk of depletion, the political perspective lays emphasis on the fact that managing the commons inherently raises decisional issues that may be fraught with diverging visions as well as ensuing tensions and conflicts over the ultimate values to be pursued. Once gain, the commons looks very close to a structural condition of *anarchy*, in the etymological sense of 'lack of hierarchy': there is no way to tell in advance who has the authority to decide how to make them and what to make of them, how to create, organize and rule them. Politically speaking, then, the commons designates a situation where authority must be invented on the spot – perhaps, an instance of what Cornelius Castoriadis (1975) once called 'societal self-institution'.

Another notable thread of reflections that seems to converge around an enhanced sensitivity towards the commons, follows from an awareness of the condition of worldly 'interiority' (Sloterdijk 2013) and, accordingly, the 'terrestrial politics' (Latour 2018) needed to face the current ecological challenges at planetary scale.[5] Peter Sloterdijk in particular, in his idiosyncratic reception of the German tradition of philosophical anthropology, has retraced a whole genealogy of the process of hominization, which, he contends, proceeds through the production of 'anthropogenic islands' shaped as 'bubbles' of various sizes, each of which is always-already social, i.e. shared with significant others. So, for instance, even the smallest anthropogenic island, namely the maternal womb, is described by Sloterdijk as already entailing a shared interiority (since each of us comes to the light of day accompanied by that peculiar and unique 'twin' that is the placenta). As for Bruno Latour, whose name is most famously associated with Actor-Network Theory, he has in his more recent production turned towards a new form of rounded ecological thinking, diagnosing contemporary capitalism as being completely out-of-scale vis-à-vis available terrestrial resources. Echoing considerations already advanced by theorists such as Paul Virilio, Latour remarks that capitalism is now too large to land anywhere on Earth – which, he remarks, incidentally also explains the interest shown by large capitalist actors for space exploration. The thin layer of the biosphere represents that irreplaceable shared interior space of life that must dictate to us a fundamental and non-negotiable unit of measure; otherwise, so goes Latour, *le sol cède sous les pieds de tout le monde à la fois* [the ground crumbles below everybody's feet at once]. In this vein, Latour (2021) has proposed to interpret the lockdown experiences of the Covid-19 pandemic as an illustration of a more 'generalised lockdown' condition [*confinement généralisé*] at the planetary level that contradistinguishes our biospheric interiority: '*les terrestres se reconnaissent comme ceux qui se trouvent tous dans le même bateau* [the terrestrial recognize themselves as those who are all on the same boat]' (ibid.: §5).[6] In sum, at a historical moment when new measures of economic and ecological composition are being looked for, the commons provides a perspective from which to assess and reassess current social and technological ensembles in light of their global impact and implications.

While Canetti predates all these debates, *Crowds and Power* similarly contains a diagnosis of the twentieth century as the century that has produced an inescapable co-implication of all: indeed, it is specific of the atomic age that 'today either everyone will survive or no one will [*Alle werden überleben oder niemand*]' (*MM* 558/*CP* 469).[7] The topic of collective survival, raised in the very final page of *Crowds and Power*, signals a transformation of the meaning Canetti had previously attributed to the notion of survival, which we have reconstructed in Chapter 1. Under the new anthropological condition of the present – and with specific reference to the atomic age – survival loses its original antagonistic traits, and turns into a powerful requirement for co-implication: in other words, survival turns into a veritable commons.[8] Of course, a non-antagonistic conception of survival is still largely to be built: in this sense, Canettian epistemology contributes to the clarification of one major ethical–political requirement for 'the century.' One may find that the idea of 'shared interiority' does not immediately seem to sit well with Canetti's purported attempt to envision modernity *from the outside*. As considered throughout previous chapters, Canetti indeed sought to position himself from a perspective of *exteriority* vis-à-vis 'the century'.[9] He certainly was not alone in feeling the uneasiness tied to the modern condition: as Marshall Berman (2010[1982]: 353) acutely noticed, 'one of the weirdest facets of modernity is all the cultural energy that gets poured into a hopeless quest to get out of modernity.' Yet remarkably, for Canetti the question is neither one of becoming 'anti-modern' (a move that pushes one towards the conservative line of Heidegger, Jünger, Ortega y Gasset, etc.), nor one of moralistically judging modernity as a form of decadence (along the Nietzsche-Weininger line). On closer scrutiny, it is easy to see how all these positions still preserve modernity's exceptional place, preventing the observer from casting a truly naturalistic gaze onto its achievements. This way, Canetti's 'primordialist' sensitivity, as we have discussed it through the previous chapters, led him to consider modern social and political dynamics as *prolongations* of ancient gestures, in a way that de-exceptionalizes them *while at the same time* not denying their specificities, their peculiar *hues*.

If the commons are the harbingers of shared interiority, this is so because the condition of *commonage* can be said to revolve thoroughly around the problem of *coexistence*. The latter is, at least, a two-fold problem: on the one hand, it concerns the specification of the boundaries between interiority and exteriority; on the other, it concerns the scope and conditions of inclusion itself – the determination of the nature of its province. But, coexistence is not yet and not necessarily 'communal' by nature. That is why, in the following discussion, I suggest shifting from an analysis of the commons and the communities defined by those commons, to an analysis of *commonality* as the more general phenomenon that expresses the condition, the experience and the two-fold problem of coexistence.[10] Commonality can perhaps be described as a form of 'territorialisation' (Deleuze and Guattari 1980; Brighenti and Kärrholm 2020), since each territory corresponds to the shared issue affecting a given social manifold. At the root of all these notions (common, communal, community, commonality, as well as communication) we can clearly identify an ancient and complex notion, encapsulated by the Latin term *mūnŭs, -ĕris*. The latter is a polysemic word that covers only apparently disparate meanings: 1. Office, function, duty, obligation, product, tribute; 2. Gift, favour, offering, expenditure; 3. Public spectacle, gladiators show (Castiglioni and Mariotti 1966: 931; Benveniste 1969: 96, 187; Esposito 2010[1998]: 4). The linguist Émile Benveniste, in particular, finds a key to elucidate the notion of *mūnŭs* in the idea of 'a gift that compels an exchange': indeed, all official positions, such as typically the one of magistrate, are distinctions, honours conferred to someone, which call for particular *munificence* on the part of the one who has it bestowed upon oneself. A communitas thus literally indicates the situation of a shared (*cum* = with) *mūnŭs*, a *mūnŭs* held jointly with others.

Benveniste's linguistic analysis is imbued with the earlier sociological theory of the 'total performances' [*prestations totales*] elaborated by Marcel Mauss (1923–4), which Benveniste credits recurrently throughout his work. Events such as the public spectacles of entertainment freely offered to the population (meaning no. 3 of the word) can indeed be regarded as an instance of *counter-gift* on the part of the distinguished recipients of a honoured gift. Ancient institutions and rituals such as jubilees, liturgies, choregies, trierarchies and syssities, despite their differences, worked under a similar logic. In turn, however, Mauss's point cannot be fully appreciated without taking into account Durkheim's (1912) near-contemporary theory of societal self-institution through rituals.[11] The common is, from the Durkheimian perspective, always created ritualistically in moments of joint performance. Like the Maussian 'binding gift', *mūnŭs* indicates, at the same time, (received) favour and obligation (to give). Significantly, in this respect, the ancient meaning of *immūnis* – literally, someone who lacks or steps outside of *mūnŭs* – is not 'immune', but 'ungrateful' (and consequently, disgraced). Esposito (2010[1998]) elaborates on this trope concluding that what contradistinguishes community is neither possession nor belonging, but *lack* – or, as he also puts it, a type of *debt*: the community is regarded as the force that decentres and removes the proprietary element (the private), and creates a 'communication' based on such absence of property, in a situation therefore of debt and 'expropriation' of subjects:[12] that is why the subjects of a community are structurally *required* to relate to one another.

Now, if we take one step back, we can easily concede that all commonality contains a normative colouration, which Mauss famously expressed in terms of a three-fold set of obligations.[13] We could even more properly speak of a *tensional* element that is evinced at the core of the social relation whenever issues of *mūnŭs* are evoked. Tension is, arguably, no less important than norm – for it does not suffice that these relations create obligations, it is also necessary that they are staged and performed *as if* they were liberal and spontaneous. In the paroxysm of the potlatch, for instance, goods are destroyed, rather than given to the expected recipients, so as to make clear that one is not interested in any form of mundane 'commerce' or private gain. Public distributions of goods and exuberant expenditures [*dépenses*] are necessary to *attest* one's good fortune, one's distinction, one's honour, and ultimately one's superiority. To achieve this aim, it is necessary that they are also 'free': the deep underlying persuasion, in this case, is that all richness is *made to be given away* as a gift. In purely modern economic terms, this means a loss, waste, or (to recall Esposito's point) debt. And yet, it is still true today that all forms of richness cannot be dissociated from circulation: unless richness circulates, unless it is social, it is nothing. To return to the main point, then, one notices here that what matters most is neither the interiorization of norms, nor the indebtedness or expropriation that allegedly grounds all community, but the fact that every dynamic of commonality mobilizes sets of *open-ended expectations*. Such expectations are tensional, since nothing grants that all concerned parties will, at any point, converge or 'get even.' It was Mauss himself who, at some point, postulated the notion of expectation as a fundamental sociological category, corresponding to that time span, fraught with uncertainty, that exists *between* gift *and* counter-gift – a time locked to the uncertain calendar of a given 'term' [*terme*] allotted for reciprocation to take place. If we look at society immanently, expectations can be said to be the psychosocial device that 'recharges' societal clocks. Such in-between time can be filled with the whole emotional palette that exists between hope and despair, between fear and rage, between peace and war, between the dismissal and the renewal of a bond.

The temporal mode of the gift, understood as precisely a time bridge, is thus a chronic, rather than chronological, temporality. This in-between time corresponds to the charged, active time of *mūnŭs*. We realize this best if we just pay attention to how even the shallowest rhetorical usages of the word 'common' – of which there is no dearth in contemporary politics – clearly seek to exploit the subtended tensional–motivational force of *mūnŭs* that is coessential to its special temporality: what is common should unite all concerned parties into a joint effort, bridging a unity of vision to a unity of action. Differently from a belief – which may or may not translate into practice – *mūnŭs* already implies by nature an active engagement. Here, it may be worthy to notice how commonality always evokes 'matters of honour,' namely, the deeply affective issue of *not losing face* in the first and last resort. Hence, also, the exaggerated, pompous, theatrical staging of Maussian gift-making, which may appear quite ludicrous to an external observer. If, in matters of commonality, 'liberality is obligatory,' as Mauss put it with reference to gift-making, this means that one cannot *not* create the social relation. In *mūnŭs*, lives get mingled, and cannot subtract themselves from all the ensuing bumpiness of coexistence. In this sense, it seems fair to assume that the 'revelation of commonality' is close to the crucial mystery of social life – for whatever is 'social' cannot be severed from a dimension, or a degree, of commonality, which different historical configurations and situations enact to differing degrees, handling as they may the complexity of the intensive states that commonality itself, as a problem, evokes and spurs.

The compelling incipiency of *mūnŭs* has been addressed by Jean-Luc Nancy (1990[1983]) with his notion of 'inoperative community' [*communauté désœuvrée*] as well as by Giorgio Agamben (1990), who coined the expression 'coming community' [*comunità che viene*]: both notions probe forms of commonality that exist in becoming, and remain irreducible to any organized political society such as the State. Nancy warns us that what ensues from a situation where economy, technology and politics cooperate to produce community as a specific 'work' [*œuvre*] – which would amount to an 'operative' community – is, actually, totalitarianism.[14] Instead of either a technocratic production, or a nostalgic community of 'we' subjects, Nancy envisages a community of 'others' who are all presented with their own mortality and finitude as well as, consequently, with the necessity to step 'out-of-themselves' [*hors-de-soi*] in order to meet with others – a position which, with Bataille, Nancy calls 'ecstasy.'[15] For his part, Agamben proposes to employ the Latin designation *quodlibet* ['whatsoever case'] as a radical political subject that inherently resists statization – where the State must, on its turn, be understood as a fully accomplished community (a 'Commonwealth,' in Hobbes' phrasing). The idea that there can be a common outside of the political totality is the crucial contribution of anarchist thinking, in whose lineage Agamben's work can be read. The coming community, in this sense, can be said to constitute a communal subject that refuses to be named, and rejects any type of identity politics. Such 'whatsoever community' is explicitly set against the accomplished community. We must admit, however, that the coming community may *or may not* at all come to be: the perspective of becoming is a perspective of immanence, where nothing can be taken for granted. The coming community might as well reveal itself as but a dreamt community, a ghost community. And in this sense, commonality is inevitably *also* a commonality of delusion. Therefore, one does not even know whether any eventual coming-to-be of community should itself be regarded as a positive or as a negative thing – for ultimately, a come-to-be community is *just another* community, with all the problems inherent in the ethnocentric operation addressed above (see Chapter 3). Yet, on the other hand, what is a community that only promises to come, and always fails to materialize? Why bother to still speak of community at all?

The ambivalence of the binding gift of commonality is perhaps best conveyed by the famous expression reported by Mauss: 'one receives a gift upon one's shoulders.' That *mŭnĕra* are not always inherently pleasant to carry is proven by the fact that we can conceive of anything that affects a demos as one such *mŭnŭs*. The virus, too, is *mŭnŭs* – as incidentally the phrase 'We're all in this together' illustrates. Certainly, however, heartfelt exhortations to 'make it all together' always sound vague and a bit hypocritical – for the plain reality is that rarely, if ever, are humans all together. The British artist Banksy has played skilfully on the trope of the 'same boat,' producing two different artworks titled, respectively, 'We're not all in the same boat' (2017) and 'We're all in the same boat' (2021). The former piece is a *détournement* of Gericault's *Raft of the Medusa*, where contemporary African refugees-survivors on a raft stranded in the middle of the Mediterranean try in vain to attract the attention of a super yacht passing at the horizon. The second piece features three kids in a half-sinking rickety boat (apparently made of sheet metal, rather than paint): the first one, more elegantly dressed (commander-like), looks straight ahead, peeping into a hand telescope; the second, who wears a similar paper hat and is similarly projected forward with his body, suddenly turns his head backward, where the third one, his feet in the already-flooded part of the bilge, not wearing any fancy paper hat, face in the shadow (*is he really a child?*), is bailing water out of the boat. Even if it were true that, factually, 'we are all in this together,' problems follow from two considerations: first, we are never 'in it' in the same way; second, we may not even *feel* (although, at least in theory, we *should* know) that we are in it together.[16] The erosion of common spaces and common goods occurs, in the first place, not in terms of the enclosure and privatization of assets, but in terms of the *mentality* that subtends the very conception of inclusion, in the two facets mentioned above (*who* is to be considered included, and *how*).

The commons are the indivisible, but all sorts of difficulties spring from the articulation of such a state of indivisibility. Critically, Berlant (2016: 395) has remarked that 'the better power of the commons is to point to a way to view what's broken in sociality, the difficulty of convening a world conjointly.' Such *diagnostic* power of the commons corresponds to the enactment of its own precondition, namely the shared feeling of having a series of collective stakes that co-implicate us. As we have noticed, such a precondition is immanent and never secured once and for all. In addition, common stakes never simply amount to something that is purely and simply 'good;' on the contrary, as we have also remarked, what is collective and indivisible must be seen as something that, in many cases, *sticks to us even if we do not want it*. Whereas the literature on the commons has emphasized their aspirational side, it has become increasingly clear that the commons are just as well stuff we *can't just get rid of*.[17] As Latour (2021: §8) has effectively put it, common is but another name for *mutual encroachments*: 'If we spill over into each other, it means that we form a common [*Si nous débordons ainsi les uns sur les autres, nous formons donc un commun*].' In this sense, the commons recall the mechanism the psychoanalyst Julia Kristeva (1980) famously conceptualized in terms of 'abjection': the abject is too close to the subject to be an object and, because its proximity is perceived as troubling, polluting and threatening, it is most forcefully rejected and expelled.

Such 'abjection' of the commons may also help explain why so much 'immunity' is circulating throughout modern society: a truly 'participationist' ontology is probably not something that is behind us (as classical anthropologists believed), but something ahead of us – something that must still be envisaged. On an ethical and political level, this indicates that more effective means to rekindle participation (which perhaps, from a Durkheimian point of view, could include the creation of new rituals of commonality) are needed. It is suggested here that an alternative to the dominance of the motifs of absence, ecstasy and delusion recurring through Nancy, Blanchot, Agamben and Esposito's reflections on community, can be represented by a more 'naturalistic' approach, such as the one made possible by Canettian epistemology. Not that delusion and dislocation are absent from Canetti's work, but their role appears partial and, so to speak, functional, rather than ultimate. This is what this chapter seeks to probe.

Literature as participation

Literature, and art more generally, offer an outstanding example of *mūnŭs*:[18] art is, quite literally, *munificent*, in other words, it consists of a protracted experimentation with the problem of commonality as well as with commonality-and-its-problems. On the one hand, art – bracketing for now its incorporation into the market economy – appears as an immense gift made to humanity: in this sense, literature is a space each of us can make *one's own*, simply on condition of being able to be *moved by it*.[19] Everyone can appropriate a literary work without depriving others of it, while of course the same work of art comes to be animated and inhabited by different meanings according to the different people who come into contact with it. Art and literature join us precisely *through* – and not *despite of* – the variety of feelings, sensations and appreciations which they spur in us. One does not need permissions to generate newness with and through works of fiction and works of art, just as one does not need permissions to embody, feel and become *that uniqueness*. In light of this, Canetti's dislike for purely theoretical and academic language might be related to the limitations, inherent in specialization and professional criticism, to freely making use of the literary and artistic creation. That, however, does not mean giving in to some late-romantic myth of the artist-genius, nor to a naïf belief in art as an innocent domain of existence uncompromised with politics and the economy – for, on the contrary, art is certainly *also* an established 'art system,' it is certainly *also* big business, and of course in many places around the world it is a convenient tax-avoidance ruse, too. Still, we cannot, and perhaps must not, loose sight of Caillois's description of animal visual 'splendour' (cf. Chapter 2), of which, we could say, art and literature are an inevitable prolongation in the pursuit of an 'independent aesthetic domain.' Such a naturalizing perspective – which, for the sake of clarity, we can also interpret here as a 'microsociological' one – invites us to regard the poetic function as not confined to certain persons who, either by talent of nature or by profession, would exercise it exclusively. One could then start observing the poetic function as diffusely located throughout the whole of social life, lying scattered as it does, often unnamed, across a multiplicity of occasions, subjects and encounters.

Even when the poetic function appears condensed and crystallized in a poet's verse, or a writer's novel, or an artist's piece, its property lies in being a force that bridges, rather than separates, the personal and the impersonal domains. For instance, in *A Report from the Interior*, Paul Auster (2013) thus explains his thrust towards the biographic memoir: 'You feel compelled to give it a try. Not because you find yourself a rare or exceptional object of study, but precisely because you don't, because you think of yourself as anyone, as everyone.' Thinking of oneself as 'anyone' and 'everyone,' the writer proceeds to dig into his own self as if into a stranger. Thus considered as a condensation point of social life, the *Dichter/ Dichterin* can be anyone who, on a particular occasion and in a peculiar moment, reveals something we did not know we had in common, so that such revelation bears the mark of a *metánoia*, a 'conversion,' an apparition.

Most notably, then, every revelation of commonality is not a revelation of sameness, but of singularities, of uniqueness. Needless to say, many professional artworks fail to achieve that result, whereas a multitude of non-professional and unexpected sites and occasions may bring it about. Even when one such *Dichter* would seem to produce but 'nonsense,'[20] it is rather the inception of a sort of non-conventional *dream* – a *rêverie* in Bachelard's original sense – that is concerned. The common is, indeed, an immanent *rêve* – precisely, a *rêve général*: common dream unbound. In the poetics of the visionary German film maker Werner Herzog, this is simply and effectively articulated, when he states: 'These dreams are yours as well, and the only distinction between me and you is that I can articulate them.'[21] Articulation, however, makes a good deal of difference.

Such nexus of revelational diffuseness and munificent, immanent dream state meets the requirements for what Lévy-Bruhl (1938) once called a *participationist ontology*. As Lévy-Bruhl first conceived it, participation indicates a state of mingling of the subject with others and the world.[22] It is a mode of being that can never be confined within the rules of transparent, rational language – nor, however, should it be qualified as a simply 'pre-logical' inarticulate mindset where all entities appear conflated together. Rather than a sheer confusion of beings, participation indicates a special attitude towards perceiving a layer of existence where the principle of non-contradiction does not fully hold.[23] Such a layer is itself not *in contradiction*, but *in addition* to the layer of everyday reality, so that a shared reverie accompanies reality, and in specific moments infiltrates it from all flanks, potentially outpowering it. This line of thinking seems to naturally prolong into the Canettian perspective, whereby we could say that commonality has everything to do with a form of participation capable of revealing the power of *transformation*.[24] It is interesting to notice how the participationist-transformational perspective becomes of paramount importance whenever *deeply affective issues* are touched upon. Each time any one such issues is raised, we realize how close the 'modern mind' is to what classical anthropologists like Lévy-Bruhl still used to call 'primitive mentality.' The difference seems to be mostly perspectival in nature: what, in the case of primitive mentality, was described as 'stubborn belief' reappears in the midst of modern mentality under the guise of 'flashing awareness': participation manifests the flashing awareness that a world of invisible pregnancies accompanies the visible world of saliences as a distinct but conjoint mode of existence. On the one hand, this fact again encourages a de-exceptionalization of modernity, such as the one pursued by Canettian epistemology; on the other hand, one still must clarify which forms of experience correspond in practice to the perspective of participation. These are not necessarily pacified states only: quite to the contrary, the Martinican poet Édouard Glissant (1997: 20), searching for the deeper meaning of creolization, has evoked '*l'errance violente de la pensée qu'on partage* [the violent errantry of our shared thinking]': for the poet, commonality can never be untangled from a violent movement of sort. So, errantry has a specific topological entailment here: no artistic creation – whether it is literary, poetic, visual, musical, filmic ... – allows us to commit the mistake of conceiving of commonality under the rubric of simple reciprocity. Reciprocity tends to convey the image of balanced and harmonic relations, but in fact, commonality has little to do with such configurations: between the *Dichter/Dichterin* and his/her audience, between the storyteller and his/her listeners, there is no reciprocity. Nor is there between different members of the audience, across the many listeners, recipients, or dreamers that will spring up: a completely different geometry of relations needs to be envisaged to capture the 'violent errantry of shared thinking.'

The shortcomings of normative conceptions of community rhyme with the insufficiency of a reciprocalist view on commonality. Rather than from symmetry and harmony, commonality can be seen emerging from a condition of intrinsic exposure, a condition of loosely defined 'publicness,' whereby encounters never proceed straightforward, nor through simple binaries (such as public vs private, male vs female, etc.), but always transit through a more complex logistics. We can get a glimpse of such movements in Canetti when, in 1948, at the time of working on a lecture on Proust, he writes to his brother: 'One always prepares for great encounters in the same way: by evading, and circling around them' (Canetti and Canetti 2007: 351).[25] In a similar way, the noteworthy encounter with the Dahan patriarch in Marrakesh (*Stim* 61 ff./*Voi* 73 ff.) is wholly played out in the thin space of the introductory greetings, when the patriarch uncertainly spells his guest's name: 'In his sing-song voice my name sounded to me as if it belonged to a special language that I did not know.' Canetti is later invited by the Dahan to the *purim* celebration, but decides not to attend the family reunion so as not to disappoint the patriarch with his own ignorance of the religious ritual. Once again, we notice the fundamental difference between community and commonality: the latter never amounts to a closed or defined community. To the contrary, no commonality can emerge without transiting through a special, unknown, untranslatable language – one that never results in community language, but still mysteriously connects, relates, spurs, and above all, interrogates. Such is the uncomfortable position of 'resistance' Canetti associates with the *Dichter*.

The denial of participation produces that sort of deafness, impenetrability and incomprehension that characterizes, for instance, Karl Kraus's take on humanity: in Kraus's vision, as Canetti reconstructs it, people talking to one another are actually only *throwing words* bound to bounce back, or drop dead to the ground, in a situation where 'there is not greater illusion than thinking that language is a means of communication between people' (*GdW* 48/*CW* 34).[26] Certainly, incommunicability is a classic trope of modernist literature: on its turn, a novel like *Die Blendung* has been categorized as squarely modernist, particularly due to the satirical, tragicomic outcomes of barred communication. More precisely, Canetti has been described as the proponent of an 'analytic modernism' irreconcilable with the most influential theories of high modernism, such as those of Eliot's, Adorno's or Lukács's (Donahue 2001: 175): *Die Blendung* not so much plays with the fragmentary self typical of most modernist works, but caricatures the plot and the characters in an expressionist, dramatist way – to the point, Donahue argues, of producing a 'protest from within' aimed against high modernism. As defined by Berman (2010[1982]: 5), the larger issue of modernism relates to the attempt 'to get a grip on the modern world and make [oneself] at home in it;' in other words, the modernist question *par excellence* concerns the possibility – and above all, the impossibility – of inhabiting modernity itself. This explains why *Die Blendung* reads as an intoxicated and intoxicating novel: it is a story of impossibilities, of deception and isolation, completely imbued in violent *délire*.[27] The book seems designed to deliberately make any common sense impossible: each character looks dominated by a peculiar fixation, completely shut off from the others in psychological and emotional terms. Word-throwing is, indeed, the ubiquitous game. However, if commonality has in general the nature of a problem, rather than of a solution, it is precisely the utter lack of common sense – in the form of a stroll through the universal empire of misunderstanding, 'the *comédie humaine* of madmen,' as the author called it – that constantly re-proposes it.

The delusional, sick atmosphere of Canetti's novel and his first two plays, in other words, conjures up a sense of imprisonment and confinement that cannot but strongly suggest the trope of modernity as a form generalized internment. It is upon such background that one must also situate Canetti's later attempt to attain a regard 'from the outside' onto the century (as preliminary to 'seizing the century by the throat') – a sought-after exteriority that becomes prominent especially in

Crowds and Power and in the parallel fragmentary visions of *Aufzeichnungen*. Such a positioning is complex, yet without forcing it too much it can perhaps be restated in the following terms. On the one hand, interiority indicates participation and sharing; but, as vehemently staged in *Die Blendung*, participation often occurs at the level of the grossest and basest stereotypes, at the level of petty thinking: it is a participation in the direst traits of humanity – a *mūnŭs* not very pleasant to look at, nor to be touched by – the strength of the novel residing precisely in forcing the reader's nose into such unpleasant smell. On the other hand, exteriority is quite literally impossible to attain, unless one admits a strong theological and/ or messianic dimension, which is clearly absent from Canettian epistemology (as opposed to, notably, Walter Benjamin's); and yet, even if it were true that there is no outside, the very *gesture* of trying to get out, of cultivating a displaced, deeply naturalizing gaze onto the social process, condenses that experience of liberation which, in the previous chapter, we have found at the pivot of all acts of resistance. The *Dichter/Dichterin* figure thus cathectically embodies such an uneasy compound of interior and exterior in a gesture that does everything in its power to reject their incompatibility. Specifically, there are two sides to the *Dichter's* mission, which can prove hard to reconcile, and yet must coexist: on the one hand is the call to save everyone and everything at all costs, the artist-writer being the one who preserves the most minute singularities that ever existed, and struggles against the waning of memory. On the other hand, the artist-writer cannot but thrust to invent the new, bringing about what is yet unknown and missing from the present – a new that is so new that nobody feels its absence until it is brought into existence, and when that happens, is often received as something unwanted, outlandish, if not obnoxious. Thus, the *Dichter* structurally oscillates between a condition of unbounded participation within the world, of mixing with everyone and every story, and a condition of solitude from community, an incapacity to be absorbed by any given existent community. Resisting the community's ethnocentric operation, the poet-artist-writer can never become a mirror – least, a consolation – for any group.

The peculiar distinction between community and commonality discussed here thus speaks of the tensional encounter between art and power. In the Canettian epistemology, as we have seen, power is largely built upon survival and death – so much so that, in his relentless protestation against death, Canetti can be said to be in accord with the Camusian vision of *revolt*: 'Human revolt ... is perhaps nothing else but a long protest against death, an angry accusation of the condition defined by a generalised death sentence' (Camus 1951: 922).[28] Such a 'generalised death sentence' is also clearly Canetti's polemical target, which he substantiates in a struggle against *power* – seeing in power nothing but a deadening reality. As also considered above, *Crowds and Power* was explicitly designed as an attempt to 'find the weak spot of power': more than an analytical exercise, the book was meant to be a tool for struggle.[29] To Canetti's eyes, power stands eminently as the anti-human element present in humans: power exists to *separate* humans from one another. In the previous chapter, we have analysed how this Canettian conception shares some similarities with, but also remains remarkably different from, Foucault's. If now we turn to Hannah Arendt, who generationally was a peer of Canetti's, we can briefly recapitulate here Arendt's anti-reductionist argument directed to avoid the conflation of power and violence (as well as its confusion with strength, force and authority). Arendt (1969: 44 ff.) refers to power more positively as something that belongs to the group as a whole and reflects its capacity to 'act in concert.' In other words, rather than refraining from the risks inherent in coexistence, Arendt suggests we positively put collective power to use, in an attempt to support coexistence, and make it prosper. For instance, technological accomplishments are only made possible by extensive collaboration and co-working. If these achievements are to be regarded as common goods, then, is not the collaboration poured into them *also* a form of power? Does not the new mode of non-antagonistic survival called forth by the atomic age, discussed by both Canetti and Arendt, itself require precisely this type of power?

At this point, we must ask whether the Canettian epistemology necessarily confines itself to single-mindedly highlight only one aspect of power relations to the detriment of others. By delving into the deadly and deadening aspects of power, is not Canetti forgetting its collaborative, positive *facies*?[30] Is not his perspective, as seen through the lenses of Arendt's, too fixated on the zero-sum game model? Substantively, Canetti's challenge lies in conceiving ways of coexistence that are *not* premised on divisiveness – and in this sense, there might be an underlying convergence between Canetti and Arendt, albeit not at the level of vocabulary. Indeed, for Canetti power as such is bound to remain divisive, and can never truly lead to positively enhance commonality. With respect to Arendt's assertion of the collaborative nature of power and its collective underpinning, Canetti would point out that collaboration can also amount to collaboration in submission, and particularly collaboration in one's own submission to command. Whereas Arendt seeks to distinguish power from command–obedience relations, and courageously unveils the latter as consisting of sheer violence, Canetti, as we have seen in Chapter 1, highlights the need to think more deeply about what a command is and what it can do: considering the prolongation of the archaic command into the domesticated command, which is voluntarily complied with and may not even be perceived as such, we reach a situation where command as an interaction pattern comes to be completely infused into everyday existence, and where it becomes difficult to notice any visible traces of violence within a given social arrangement. Discerning the boundary between power and violence turns out to be more difficult than expected, and arguably Arendt herself, who set precisely that task for herself, ultimately brought home a result that is not as clear-cut as one could wish. The stark formulation provided at the outset of her essay – namely, 'The extreme form of power is All against One, the extreme form of violence is One against All' (Arendt 1969: 42) – is in practice baffled by the fact that these extreme forms tend to converge into a zone of indistinction, where it becomes ultimately impossible to fully untangle them: on the one hand, the 'all against one' scheme presupposes collaboration, but also the ethnocentric operation that totalizes the community or group, and makes it act as, indeed, *one*; on the other, the 'one against all' formation recalls the solitude of the powerful depicted by Canetti; but, in order to become effective, violence must organize itself through functioning command chains, which implies the action of small 'excited' groups, such as packs, sects, gangs, and parties, capable of articulating action and spreading mobilization. Both Schreber and Hitler conceived of themselves as 'one' in their psychotic 'onlyness,' but whereas the former remained truly alone (and thus, in Arendt's terms, truly violent) and ended up in a psychiatric ward, the latter organized a party that worked not only through repression but also through ideology, massive propaganda and consent construction (hegemony, in Gramsci's terms) so as to mobilize a whole nation (thus, undeniably, exercising power).

It is in one of Canetti's latest annotations that we find a notion interestingly resonating with Arendt's idea of collaboration as empowerment. It reads simply as follows: '*Keine Macht zu Hilfe* [No power from help; or: Assistance does not engender power]' (*Aufz* 92–3: 91). Here, help seems to correspond rather closely to what Arendt calls power – yet for Canetti it must not be considered as a form of power. Help is certainly a way of envisaging social coexistence, but what matters in the mode of Canettian epistemology is its link to transformation: true assistance unsettles, rather than reinforces, the power relations in place. In particular, the type of help evoked by Canetti does not follow from either calculation or arrogance – rather, it is, like art, a gift that uncloaks and supersedes power realities. It is no less important to remark that the nature of help, just like that of the gift, *is* asymmetrical, and does not presuppose the concerted reciprocity that contradistinguishes planned collaboration. In this sense help is, and cannot but be, unexpected, unheard of (even, to a degree, *monstrous*). The different, and to be true starkly contrasting significations Arendt and Canetti attribute to the term 'power' can be made a little more understandable through an 'elemental' perspective: power is the 'air,' the atmosphere in which violence can, each time anew, occur. Such an atmospheric quality of power is one core preoccupation of Canettian epistemology. In Chapter 1, we have already described 'threat' (a coessential component of command) as a type of ambience or 'feeling': notably, as already considered, in *Crowds and Power* what really matters for the constitution of *Macht* is not only the diagram of action it entails, but the whole 'colouration,' the special hue social situations are being imbued with. For Canetti, let us recall, power works not in actuality, but in virtuality: well before any action is undertaken, power designates a state of amplification and resonance, in other words, a virtual action. And it is exactly such amplification that blocks free-flowing transformations: forbidding metamorphosis, power is, ultimately, but 'alienation' – as seen, for instance, in Brecht's theatre (*NaH* y.1960). Conversely, imagining coexistence outside of power must always proceed through thinking – and rethinking – the transformational possibilities of life. In the previous chapter, we have considered how these possibilities are related to the movement of resistance: neither properly individual, nor fully collective, the act of resistance is the name of a relationship, the imagination of a world in common that is never to be made fully actual. Precisely through its unaccomplished status can the 'help of resistance' offer us the terms for casting a new outlook onto the present (or 'actual reality').

How can these considerations about power and help/assistance relate to the *Dichter/Dichterin*'s condition? We have noticed how the *Dichter*'s stance appears to be forged simultaneously by resistance *and* participation. By resisting power through creation, the writer-artist participates in all lives and deaths, to the point that no single existence, in its uniqueness, may leave him or her untouched. Flaubert's thrust to 'live all lives' [*vivre toutes les vies*] translates into an enhanced, extensive *as well as* intensive participation in the world. From Flaubert's perspective, this means accepting all life in a non-judgmental way.[31] In attending all life, the writer cannot refrain from also attending the enormous sufferings of humanity: this means that the *Dichter/Dichterin* cannot but be him/herself a scarred person. Flaubert, for one, grew up in a hospital, which his father, who was a doctor, directed; he himself recalls that sometimes the kids stopped their plays to peep into the anatomical theatre, where his father was performing dissections; the flies that buzzed on the corpses were later seen on the kids' toys. Such a familiarity with illness and death delineates a permanent situation of survival, where seeing others die, or dead, was an everyday encounter. Canetti inherits a similar focus, along with another trait of Flaubert's: the latter's great interest in stupidity, in the *idées reçues*, hearsay, conventional trivialities.[32] Just as they embrace all lives, writers also ingest all the *bêtises* that are the most widespread and circulating linguistic commonality – the faecal matter of thought, so to speak. It is of such humble materials, after all, that all modern art is made. Accordingly, a deep ambiguity follows: certainly, the writer wants to rescue everybody from death and oblivion, but simultaneously, his/her interest for fellow humans may turn into a strange form of opportunism, into actual greed. In this vein, for instance, Ruth von Mayenburg, who knew Canetti in 1930s' Vienna, could describe him as no less than a *Menschfresser*, a man-eater, who stalked his 'victims' for the stories he could extort from them.[33] Mayenburg's satirical portrait of Canetti's as a stalker for human stories raises a substantive problem, which brings us back, once again, to the cathectic as a crucial dimension of commonality. Indeed, we can now better see that every cathectic experience is constitutively exposed to a phenomenon which, in a very neutral sense of the word, we must designate as 'perversion.' Perversion indicates situations where means and ends, good and bad, safe and dangerous, systematically swap their places, so that no secure moral haven can be achieved. It is a condition which, in more hopeful terms, we may also call 'experimental.' Once symmetrical and reciprocalist conceptions of community are superseded, one may begin to make some room space, in the manifestations of commonality, for a disreputable figure, namely, the parasite. Perhaps, the artist and the parasite share more than a superficial similarity. The parasite is, indeed, the hijacker of flows (Serres 1980), the one who aptly redirects them into different, unexpected directions, opening up, in this way, new avenues, new combinations. In parallel, rather than cultivating the romantic image of the artist as the original and unconditional source of *mūnŭs*, it could be more helpful to regard him/her as a parasite – that is essentially a switcher of narrative energies. The *Dichter/in* does not so much mimic others' lives, nor does s/he seek to masquerade, pose or 'pass' as someone else; rather, acting as a parasite who switches energetic flows, s/he protects the path of transformation itself, allowing others to undertake it at any time.

If literature can 'reveal' anything at all, one among its first revelations may be precisely this: how deceptive is to believe that death is outside power. In the Canettian formulation, as seen throughout previous chapters, power is actually grounded in death, specifically its *facies* of survival – but, survival is also the moment when the mystery of commonality becomes most compelling. A striking illustration to this effect is offered by George Orwell's short story, *A Hanging*, set in the 1920s in a Myanmar then under the British colonial rule. The story minutely and matter-of-factly describes the carrying out of a capital execution. Absolute banality, awkwardness and clumsiness, rather than horror and despair, surround the execution. Here, the 'survivors' do not appear at all to be made more powerful by the fact that the prisoner has been executed, nor do they derive any specific satisfaction from the sight of the corpse – in fact, they strive to ignore it. Certainly, the superintendent and the jailer cannot stop congratulating themselves that the execution has proceeded smoothly: the prisoner did not oppose any resistance, and has died on the spot ('Well, sir, all hass passed off with the utmost satisfactoriness. It wass all finished – flick! like that'). But these very nonsensical congratulations, followed by a joint drink of whisky, suggest that they were quite nervous about the situation in the first place. By focusing on the procedural details, these officials were clearly trying at all cost to evacuate the meaning of what they were actually doing, namely killing a fellow human being, destroying a living creature. They did everything in their power to avoid the realization, finally spelt out by the narrator, of 'the unspeakable wrongness of cutting a life short when it is in full tide.' Such a denial of reality cannot bring any clear sense of empowerment to them; rather, they appear to remain stuck within a larger situation of power nobody seems to realize to be debatable at all: they live in inevitability.

Survival is thus far from simple, linear and clear-cut. If, in the essay 'Power and Survival,' the act of surviving others features as the foundational scene of power, one must go further and excavate its additional, invisible geometries. Some acute insights into this problem come from Georges Bataille. One of Bataille's central concerns is his – almost obsessive, to be true – idea that humans can only communicate through their wounds [*blessures*] and lacerations [*déchirures*] (Bataille 1939). A different, yet interestingly connected, conception of survival follows: 'S'il voit son semblable mourir, un vivant ne peut plus subsister que *hors de soi* [If one sees a fellow human being die, one, as a living being, can no longer continue to exist but *outside of oneself*]' (Bataille 1976: 245). Pursuing the Durkheimian approach, which he prolongs in exquisitely heterodox fashion, Bataille identifies such 'out-of-oneself-ness' with the dimension of *the sacred*. Quoting precisely the passage above, Blanchot (1983: 21) for his part glosses that what pushes one out-of-oneself is the fact of 'taking upon myself the death of the other as the only death that concerns me.'[34] In this vision, the one who survives does so in a new structural condition, contradistinguished by a denial of normality – a new spatially 'eccentric' position, namely, *out-of-oneself-ness*. Such positionality does not equate with Oriental selflessness, i.e. the dissolution of the self, but indicates a complex form of the relation to oneself – one where 'oneself' is, so to speak, never brought home. With respect to Bataille's idea of humans communicating only in extreme, lacerating situations, what needs to be ascertained is whether, in the first place, one has ever been *inside oneself*. In fact, it is possible to argue that one occupies that position only in limited portions of one's life. With Canetti, we could say that one is inside oneself ultimately only in situations of power; at all other times, when we relate and are affected, we already naturally exist out-of-ourselves. This allows us to define the space for a commonality of the affected. In survival, ways are parted between those who die and those who survive – but at the same time, those who survive come to be bound by a renewed condition of commonality: their *mūnŭs* can be better specified as an exceptional mix of imperative to remember, to bear testimony, to prolong the gesture that was shaped by the very experience of survival.

It is the same *mūnŭs* which we have discussed so far in terms of literature and art: the *mūnŭs* of creation. Survival now appears as the place where, and the moment when, *being* – suddenly, violently even – presents itself as *ought*: not an ought that is imposed on life from some transcendent position, but an ought that is coessential with it.[35] Only in this way can commonality be resurrected from its ashes. It is not necessarily an arcane situation: commonality happens recurrently, it disappears from sight only to return to the daylight after prolonged droughts and much underground flowing; and it can only be back *as and through* creation. Regarded as an act of visibilization, commonality does not confine itself to the living, but necessarily bridges the living and the dead: certainly, the living and the dead do not sit on equal ground, there is a basic asymmetry between them – and yet, they can never be ultimately and fully disentangled. Canetti praises what in the dead still refuses to die – but that is only possible to the extent that the living do not cease listening to their muttering protestation. The partition between the living and the dead is similar to, and perhaps to a degree coincides with, the partition between the individual and the crowd. The dead exist in crowd formations – the hosts of the dead. Because of their basic asymmetry, and because of their singular yet non-individual existence as 'the dead', every possible meeting ground – both between them and the living, but also amongst the living themselves – is bound to entail what, with Bataille, can be designated as out-of-oneself-ness. Commonality happens whenever we are brought in relation to crowds, and – which is the same – the dead. Literature and art then provide us with a counter-intuitive indication here: commonality must be found, not in the most familiar, but in the most alien, in the unintelligible, in the hardly-recognizable. Not that the naked voice simply 'stands for' what cannot be said; rather, the naked voice *is* that which cannot be said, and still matters the most: for it embodies that refusal, that resistance, and potentially, that assistance, too. Canetti's exploration of voices [*Stimmen*] engages the deep sensorium of existence as a way of evoking the 'destiny' of all social life. Such an ultimate, extreme point of commonality is embodied by 'the unseen' creature [*der Unsichtbar*] squatted in a square corner in Marrakesh – perhaps a beggar, invisible, since completely bundled up in rags. That unnamed something at the edge of the human frightens and revolts many. Instead, Canetti experiences a sense of great calmness [*Ruhe*] spreading through his own body: beyond all the misery and the dirt, a creature lives; there is *a life* there that will not be extinguished easily. This is what really can resonate in each one: 'I was proud [*stolz*] of the bundle because it was alive.' Some may find this a strange, even spooky type of commonality, given that there is almost no communication in the conventional sense between the narrator and the unseen – and yet, in its astounding singularity a similar encounter may tell us something of the mystery of commonality. Canetti systematically rejects any cheap sense of commiseration. It is not a question for him to look down at the 'poor creature;' his seems to be, rather, a Spinozist indication: commonality will never be achieved through sad feelings. So he concludes his note – as well as his whole travelogue – remarking that the sound of 'the unseen' 'outlived [*überlebt*] all the other' tones [*Laute*] in the square.

Here again, a conception of survival returns that is irreducible to the one formalized in *Crowds and Power* and in 'Power and Survival': for 'the unseen,' just like Deligny's kids for that matter, can hardly be reduced to an individual person. Least, can it be conceived of as simply being 'inside him/herself.' *Who* survives, then? There is certainly a source to this life, a distinctive continuation of existence; but such phenomenon can neither be located nor confined within any clearly designated biological or psychological individual. Not incidentally is the dominant register in the Marrakesh travelogue the aural one. Merging and overlapping, voices do not amount to a language, nor can they ever be cut down into coded language. Although it is never univocally clear what they mean to say, there cannot be any doubt that they *are* expressing something. The blending of anonymous voices in the African marketplace defies Blanchot's conception of community as ultimately based on the bond developed in the small group and the couple. Let us just recall that Blanchot's reference models for community are found in interpersonal friendship and the erotic couple. From a Canettian perspective, these models are insufficient. Certainly, Blanchot is perfectly aware that no community can be 'authentic' or complete, yet his very choice of the couple of friends or sexual partners proves that he cannot stop longing for complete authenticity: the result, to which Nancy (2014: 138) attracts attention, is an eternally ephemeral, elusive community. In turn, Nancy's own take on this issue counters to Blanchot's what might be called an 'iconoclastic' conception of community, based, as said above, on the rejection of every form of accomplished 'work' (the 'inoperative'). Here, contrary to Nancy's austere workless community, Canettian epistemology admits that commonality may have something to do with 'the work.'[36] For his part, Blanchot had pointed to literature as precisely constituting the essentials of such a 'work,' upon which community could be built. While Canetti would concur with Blanchot that literature can be functional to commonality, he would almost as certainly reject Blanchot's mystical attitude towards the literary work, which implies a ritualized tone of sacredness and transcendence. Canettian epistemology is clearly non-religious in the way it approaches both literature/art and myth. From this perspective, the sacredness of myth is a given that must itself be interpreted naturalistically. Rather than grounding community in the sacred, Canettian epistemology gives us the opportunity to unpack the myth as repeated narration, storytelling, travelling stories in space and time.

With Durkheim, the foundations of the sacred are to be found in the reunited collective. If so, narrated stories cannot be fully allocated to the sacred, given that they never cease to circulate in multiple modes, reaching dispersed audiences: their aptitude is to travel across, rather than mirror, a condensed assembly. Contrary to the central, static position of the sacred, which pivots around the autogenic and autotelic group, the novelty brought about by stories can never be completely communitarian; rather, it designates travelling commonalities never to be completely appropriated, each time making communities look unrecognizable to their own eyes. The kernel of myth is the telling of transformation – better, of a whole series or sequels of transformations. On many occasions, Canetti expressed his belief that the stories told by myths convey something essential about the human condition, forming one of humankind's most precious gifts.[37] Of course, myth can also be captured by communitarianism: as known, mythopoiesis easily turns into a functional component in the construction of nationalist narratives – suffice to mention, among the many examples, Leni Riefenstahl's powerful propaganda movie *Triumph des Willens/Triumph of the Will*: there is no doubt that mythopoiesis has, in the context of modernity, often strengthened irrational and regressive ideologies.

However, a different view appears once we approach myths through their *trajectology*: not the study of how myths are constituted, nor of what content they promote, but the study of how they travel and how they reach us in their specific mode of experience [*mythische Erfahrung*].[38] Once we approach commonality through trajectology, the myth gets 'de-sacralised' – or even 'desecrated': removed from the transcendence where 'the group' projects it, and brought back to the circulatory immanence of social life. What is specific of myth is not its abstraction from social vicissitudes, but rather a peculiar temporal dimension – which, above, we have sought to characterize as 'chronic.' The chronic temporality of commonality defines the experience of myths as 'contemporaneity.' The contemporary, thus, is never a given, or a starting point, but always a production and an achievement: to 'hold' something in common with others means to *become* contemporary with them. An audience can be scattered across spaces and times, yet *in stories* it finds a way to become contemporary in the fraught temporality of *mūnŭs*. Commonality unfolds in a condition of structural lack of knowledge and mastery as well as of openness towards new affects (even when these are negative affections), a condition which can only lead – and, correspondingly, push – along new avenues of creation.

The Crowd's Common

In a world that is increasingly mediated and remote-operated such as ours, in a world of global frictions and offshore capitalism, of artificial intelligence and biotechnologies, of enhanced surveillance, spectacle and propaganda, of health passports and checkpoints, and lastly of new conflicts for global hegemony, which are the new ways of experiencing commonality? In the previous sections, the ambivalence and the predicaments of community have been explored by acknowledging how the condition of atmospheric interiority of the century creates the basis for an experience of social and ecological co-implication which, in turn, acts of artistic creation encapsulate into an attitude of worldly participation. We now have to add a further dimension to our reflections, which we have only overshadowed above: Canettian epistemology also crucially suggests that commonality can never be disentangled from a politics of crowds.

In the nineteenth century, observers of crowds were struck by the latter's power to 'absorb' and 'dissolve' the individuals who joined them. The melting of individuality has ever since anxiously preoccupied crowd theorists, regardless of whether they have asserted or denied such phenomenon of effacement – whether, in a sense, they have been methodologically individualists, or holists.[39] In this respect, twentieth-century sociology can be said to have largely been a sociology of social groups and their organization, while it has been psychology's (specifically, social psychology's) task to document the suffering and/or euphoria individuals experience while living in organized groups – ranging from pressure to conform, to influence, to collaboration, and 'performance'. It is precisely such exclusive focus on the tension between the group and the individual – each of which alternatively conceived of as the building block of the social – that has made other fundamental experiences of social life appear strange and exceptional. Amongst the latter are, as we have already diffusely considered throughout Chapter 2, crowds and packs. It proves difficult to handle such formations in a theoretically satisfactory manner: a crowd is not a society, nor a community, just as a pack is not a family, nor a firm. Crowds and packs are 'unfamiliar' social manifolds whose status remains structurally ambiguous, given the difficulty of squaring them within the modern social scientific epistemological framework (Borch 2012; Brighenti 2014) – an ambiguity at the level of episteme that inevitably reverberates into an ambivalence in terms of moral assessment.

Typically, crowding states, besides being difficult to pin down theoretically, appear as 'dangerous' and 'threatening' in moral and political terms – so much so that both crowd control and crowd mobilization can be said to have been absolutely central to modern politics. And it is also not a coincidence that the perceived danger inherent in crowds recalls the question of commonality: as considered throughout, the latter does carry with it unsettling consequences for already-established social formations. In the same way as commonality resists being mapped onto a simple topographical space, so crowds and packs resist simple treatment in terms of spatial extent. Whereas social groups and individual subjects are often defined by their numerical 'extension' and their boundaries – as if, so to speak, they were sets, to be added, subtracted, or merged – one could not hope to understand crowds and packs without taking into consideration the phenomenon of *intensity* and the manifestation of a series of intensive states that accompany them. To the extent that the set-theoretical mode of thinking leads us to an imagination that emphasizes 'cohesion within' and 'separation between' units, it fails to account for the circulation of intensive states across a manifold. Once the issue of intensity is examined, crowds and packs cease to appear as either individuated 'facts' or 'containers' of individuals, and reveal themselves as more akin to unfolding processes and events. A processual philosophy like Whitehead's (1978[1929]), and an evental philosophy like Deleuze's (1969), are more suited to the task, and clearly these philosophies are more complex than intuitive set theory – in fact, they can be tantalizingly difficult. In any case, through the lenses of process and event, the epistemological unruliness of crowds and packs may be better appreciated as the transformative unfolding of intensity and of intensive states transecting a manifold; and crucially, because intensity is always manifested in and through 'critical distances,' social compositions must be assayed in terms of the distances characterizing and governing them: it is distances that make intensity visible and, so to speak, 'tangible.'

Not only is distance squarely placed as an eminent field for investigation at the very beginning of *Crowds and Power* (*MM* 13/*CP* 15), but the sense of touch [*Berührung*] is also later on examined as that which provides the bodily foundation of social life. Specifically, touch gives rise to a range of phenomena qualified as 'tension' [*Spannung*] (*MM* 237/*CP* 203). Here, for us, tension can be meaningfully linked to intensity, as one of its most visible manifestations. *Crowds and Power* does not initially give the reader the full scope of the sense of touch in terms of its variety and diversity, zooming in onto the prototypical hunting scene, where touch is clearly associated with an exercise of power that leads to seizing, crushing and eating the prey. The wrong impression has consequently sometimes been derived that Canetti viewed touch and contact in negative terms only (Honneth 1996); in fact, he acknowledged that there are multiple ways in which the socii – whether animal or human – come into each other's proximity, so that the tension generated by their intensive co-presence can take on widely differing significations. Far from being necessarily correlated with deadly outcomes, closeness may also be imbued with positive liveliness, as, for instance, in Georg Simmel's earlier analysis of interaction space: as soon as two people start interacting, Simmel (2009[1908]: 545) remarked, 'the space between them appears filled and enlivened [*erscheint der Raum zwischen ihnen erfüllt und belebt*]'.

Tenderness and intimacy are also enacted through contact, and elicited by contact, as is the case for all mammals, very much a touch-based animal class, where absence of touch from the mother is likely to create serious lifelong troubles in the newborn. In primates, notably, the whole life of the social group is sustained and strengthened thanks to social grooming; similarly, canids have evolved especially elaborate and affectionate bodily ways of taking care of the others in their pack, and the same predisposition towards touch is documented across several mammal genera (horse, mouse …). The hygienic aspects of grooming are known to be of lesser importance than its social meaning in terms of wellbeing, relaxation and emotional synchronization with others. The naturalistic analysis of distance management and touch behaviour has been extensively conducted in ethology, anthropology, psychology and animal cognition studies, with the peculiar interdisciplinary field of proxemics emerging as one of the most peculiar outcome (Hall 1966). While Canetti wrote before most of that research was conducted, he was nonetheless able to identify the primates' hands as the organs that have concentrated the most crucial gestures to sustain the social bond: it is in the contact with the fur and the skin that the hands become sensitive, and the fingertips derive a special pleasure and well-being from such contacts.[40] This way, a special 'patience of the hands [*Geduld der Hände*]' (*MM* 249/*CP* 213) has been learnt, along with a special temporality for rhythmical tasks. The latter has enabled the synchronization of joint activity, in turn conducive to a sense of togetherness and solidarity. Also, for Canetti, the patience of the hand naturally prolongs – through the development of crafts – into the construction and (literally) manufacturing of objects.[41]

Observed in terms of distancing, the problem of commonality can be said to reside in the articulation of a social space that lies *between* complete isolation *and* empathic fusion, where both extremes are excluded – although they clearly persist as 'attractors' throughout. Excessive distance turns into individual isolation, a situation where each single individual gets paralysed by the whole burden of social hierarchy, whereas on the contrary excessive closeness fatally leads to the ethnocentric operation that makes the group implode and turn into a totalitarian and fascistic endeavour. Canetti, on this point an Arendtian, clearly holds a non-fusional view on commonality. For instance, he describes the storytellers in the square of Marrakech as apparently so close to their audience, and yet so completely alien, as if their utter separation were an essential quality that made their narration possible at all. Similarly, we know that, in his personal life, Canetti lived through long periods of anticipation towards meeting his brother Georg, with whom he felt an elective relation, and yet curiously he also wrote to him that the notion of family was only bearable to him when its members were '*separated by great distances and never all together*' (*Lett.* 352, emphasis in the original).[42] This, notably, he put in practice in his London life with Veza, whom he often visited while, however, living elsewhere. In the introductory lecture on Proust, Kafka and Joyce, he remarks that 'the first thing to understand about a great writer's life is the kind and degree of loneliness he has managed to establish for himself' (*Auf.* 14). And, as already amply discussed, the commonality with native peoples such as the Australian Aboriginals was similarly exercised remotely, and never translated into any ethnographic endeavour.[43] In Marrakesh, let us finally recall, Canetti renounces to pursue his conversation with the Dahan patriarch and prefers to cultivate his admiration for him only on the basis of a single, fleeting encounter.

Rather than of mimetic nature (i.e., generating a spiral mirroring of sameness), commonality entails, in this vein, the creation of a zone of indistinction between *realizing* that we have a shared *mūnŭs* with people who are the most remote and dissimilar from us, and *pursuing* that *mūnŭs* from a distance that neither looks for further 'interested' intimacy, nor simply remains cold and disconnected – a distance, in other words, where a space of respect can be opened up. The problem here is precisely how to imagine a form of distance that does not turn into another type of avoidance of the concrete – and the only possible answer to the question is that one will only be able to assess the value of a given distance on the basis of the further commonalities it has made visible, and the further transformations it has consequently enabled. A crucial insight of Canettian epistemology is that metamorphosis walls are also empathy walls: what we cannot or just don't transform into remains affectively alien to us – this way, our attitude towards insects, and the way we crush them, is linked to the fact that rarely if ever do we transform into them.[44] Historically, the Nazi extermination of the European Jews and all social undesirables was made possible by the imaginational transformation of the hated ones into insects, with which empathy was impossible, from whose fate one could remain emotionally shut off (*MM* 214–22/*CP* 183–8). Whilst insects mostly do not matter as individuals, however, they *do* matter as crowds – for, again, crowds are not merely numerical issues, not simply matters of extensive magnitude, but always conjure up intensive states.

In crowds, distances are enacted as very specific forces that immediately evince commonality. At first sight, the crowd appears as an episode of complete abolition of interpersonal distances: 'Only together can [humans] free themselves from their burdens of distance'[45]. In fact, acceptance of being touched is itself better regarded as a *special way* of managing distances, rather than simply throwing them away. By keeping distances into the picture, we have a chance to explore the living geometries of social manifolds. Specifically, the crowd presents us with an evolving environment of bodies, movements, gestures, reactions. The crowd is, we may say, the limit-case where society becomes its own environment: from the local perspective of the participants, the surrounding is wholly made of other socii. Such a situation, where everything is in smooth flux, generates its own inner logic of movement: Milgram, for instance, took notice of the 'separation of intention and consequence' that characterises crowd environments.[46] In a crowd, even staying the same requires change: even at a basic physical level, one's movement can never be fully disentangled from the others' – such is, precisely, the meaning of the 'environmental' or 'atmospheric' quality of the crowd. And one can appreciate here all the difference between 'being in a crowded space' and *becoming a crowd*.

Although the crowd prototypically appears as 'open,' i.e. as a purely growing and expanding entity (see Chapter 2), at some point it will close on itself, or will be forcibly closed by authority: as already considered, it is the closure of the crowd that sets the beginning of the group, along with its ethnocentric operation. Many such manifestations are evoked, not only in *Crowds and Power*, but in Canetti's autobiography, too: his apprehension of crowds is, in the first place, not theoretical, but experiential. Crowd episodes are, indeed, a *fil rouge* running through the autobiography. Besides 'that brightly illuminated day' of July 1927 in Vienna, when, at 22, Canetti joined a worker demonstration that was harshly repressed by the police and degenerated into chaos and mayhem (*Mem* 484–90), even earlier crowds remerge in his remembrances: in August 1914, as a 9-year-old, he found himself along with his two younger brothers in a throng when the breaking out of the War was announced: as everybody patriotically started singing an anthem in German, he (soon imitated by his two younger brothers) sang loudly the same melody in English – 'I don't know whether it was out of old habit, perhaps it was also defiance' – causing an angry, threatening reaction – 'faces warped with rage all about me and arms and hands hitting at me' (*Mem* 96–8). This way a tough lesson is soon learnt about the fateful consequences of breaking the unanimity of the crowd, once the ethnocentric operation (instanced, in this case, by the nationalist raving) has been set in motion. In the long run, the experience of the crowd thus appears to Canetti as, at the same time, liberating and constraining – 'half delirium, half paralysis' (*Mem* 364).

The peculiar role played by memories from one's youth and childhood in recalling crowd events is not coincidental: the individual, Canetti seems to suggest, cannot but remember crowd experiences as dream states; *a fortiori*, this may also partly explain why *Crowds and Power* is so unreservedly animistic with respects to crowd descriptions. If the spatiality of a social manifold is crucial to understand its commonality, it is to the extent that a wholly atmospheric spatiality is concerned. Animism is, in a sense, the epistemological counterpart of thinking through atmospheres, whereby the threshold between object and environment happens to be often crossed in multiple clandestine ways. As already mentioned, an atmospheric conception of social life has been specifically developed by Peter Sloterdijk (2016[2004]) with his notion of 'anthropogenic island.' Sloterdijk has argued that natural islands have provided the blueprint for a type of space where humans could come to be – where, literally, they could be 'made.' From sea ships to spaceships, a number of such 'absolute islands' has been designed over the course of history (Foucault would have dubbed them 'heterotopias'). Inside similar spaces, it has become increasingly clear that the atmosphere, in its immediate materiality of air, pressure, temperature, quality etc., must necessarily be taken care of for the island to be able to sustain biosocial life. Sloterdijk seems to be inspired by Canettian epistemology on this point, especially as he stresses the crucial importance of respiration inside anthropogenic islands. The pack and the crowd, in the Canettian epistemology, seem to count as some of the earliest instances of such islands; and the intimate nexus of respiration, freedom and social rhythm is a core refrain running throughout Canetti's work. In his already-considered essay on Broch (see Chapter 3), Canetti suggests that all forms of freedom can be seen as prolongations of the original act of breathing, insofar as the latter embodies our deepest relationship to the atmosphere – and incidentally, this explains why all deaths by asphyxiation are so unbearable to imagine.[47] The rhythmic element of respiration is itself prolonged into social manifolds. Crowd-formations, for one, are each endowed with a special rhythmic temporality: an assembly is a breath-in, always followed by a breath-out. Humans, remarks Canetti specifically, cannot live in crowd-state forever: at some point, the crowd dissolves and everybody goes back home (*MM* 382/*CP* 324). Then, people return to be individuals – yet, as we know, infused with a longing for the crowd that they have been.[48]

The continuist perspective of Canettian epistemology invites us to consider how sheer physical tropism prolongs into social–moral–political constitution. So herd animals are capable of establishing a *solidarity in flight*; this means that the flight of a herd – just like that of a human crowd – along a common direction [*Richtung*] spontaneously turns into a shared attitude [*Gesinnung*] (*MM* 365/*CP* 310). In that distinctive event of social life which is the flight, the manifold appears as seized by an 'exaltation of common movement,' capable of endowing it with 'the greatest tenacity': to the extent that fleeing together thus improves the flight performance itself, it turns into an important social asset (*MM* 59/*CP* 53). But the formation where the *esprit de corps* is first moulded and best expressed is not so much the crowd as it is the pack. Because of its reduced dimensions, the pack that cannot grow to crowd size (cf. Chapter 2); therefore, in order to build its own team spirit, it needs to rely to a larger extent on the individuality of its members. It is insufficient to oppose an absolute deindividuation of the crowd to a relative deindividuation of the pack, though, given that the intensive states at play in social manifolds are simultaneously both fully sensorial (i.e., encompassing the visual, aural, olfactory and tactile sensory registers and effects) and psychological – better, with Simondon, *psycho-social*.

This explains why social manifolds must be attended also in terms of the peculiar mental states they express. The inquiry into delusion and psychosis as mass manifestations is, of course, not specific to Canetti – indeed, it is a refrain that runs across early-twentieth-century authors as diverse as Sigmund Freud, Wilhelm Reich, George Bataille, up to Hermann Broch.[49] Yet we have also underlined above that Canettian epistemology does not seek to found commonality merely on delusion. It is in the context of a continuist psycho-social theory (similar, for instance, to Pierre Janet's psychiatry) that psychotic conditions can be said to effectively *visibilize* at best the forces being played out in the social field. To begin with, the fact that the pack looks obsessed by a single thought or image (archetypically, the image of the hunted prey) suggests some similarities to paranoid psychosis, where the patient becomes fixated with a narrowed-down – or even shrinking – repertoire of motifs; conversely, the fact that the crowd is so varied and thriving with differences evokes the schizophrenic disorder, where fragments of experience fail to be put into any meaningful order. Such an idea is considered by Deleuze and Guattari (1980: 46), who however evoke the hypothesis only to discard it: for the French philosophers, what is at stake is not so much two different types of social manifold (the pack vs the crowd, each endowed with its own specific 'unconscious') as two poles, the schizophrenic and the paranoid, that compound an operational mode of being inherent in each manifold.[50]

Put differently, each manifold must be appraised in terms of opposing vectors that jointly operate across its full span: two vectors Deleuze and Guattari call, respectively, 'deterritorialisation' and 'reterritorialisation.' It is a dynamics that does not necessarily point to psychosis or delusion. Canettian epistemology, as we know, insists on the excited [*erregter*] state that contradistinguishes packs, and which can affect crowds as well. Such excited states correspond to a situation in which different manifolds are put into a state of resonance. This means that a manifold is always in contact with other manifolds, and is in fact defined by its interaction with them. That is why Deleuze and Guattari lay emphasis – quoting precisely a passage from Canetti – on the importance of the *inner movement* of the manifold as it manifests itself through the movement of its members approaching a limit.[51] The most important consequence of this fact is that the so-called 'boundaries' of a manifold are not lines that would in some sort contain the manifold, rather, they are thresholds of intensity that articulate the transition from one manifold to another. For instance, as Canetti also makes clear, the pack results from an intensification of the social group, from which it emerges for various purposes, such as hunting (see Chapter 2).

The shift from one manifold to another can be said to occur through veritable *phase transitions* that take place even without necessarily changing the manifold's members or composition, yet subjecting them to a reorganization, a re-functionalization of sort: a flight crowd can turn into a reversal crowd, a hunting pack into an increase pack – but also, an increase pack can turn into a crowd crystal that precipitates an open crowd, or a crowd may emit its war packs, etc. One should not underestimate what this entails in terms of the commonality problem – for indeed, on this account, commonality cannot be ultimately said to reside really 'inside' a manifold; rather, it is *at the edge* between one manifold and another one that it exists. This corresponds to the location where one manifold can be 'converted' – reformulated, expanded, upturned, revolutionized ... – into another. Each and all of these movements strengthen the hypothesis submitted above that the social manifold is not a thing or a set, but an *event*. The event has 'thresholds' that designate, not the border between one group and another, but the limit running across all members of the manifold who are in a critical state – between the manifold as it currently is and as it is becoming. There is no alternative for the manifold but to transform itself. It is on this point, interestingly, that Canettian epistemology can perhaps be compared to Victor Turner's work. Although Turner, who wrote in the mid 1960s, seems to have ignored Canetti's work (a stance almost *de rigueur* amongst British anthropologists: see Introduction), he similarly develops a view of the social field as highly dynamic: society is always cut through by structural as well as anti-structural forces (Turner 1977[1969]). The former, Turner famously called the forces of *societas* (which include roles, statuses, rules, institutions, rituals ...), the latter, the forces of *communitas*, which materialise the 'generalised social bond' (*ibid.*: 96), or the 'essential and generic human bond' (*ibid.*: 97).

In this vein, it may well be that the problem of commonality lies, not so much in the *creation*, as much as in the *visibilization* of commonality itself. The solitary individual, severed from the others and kept apart by too great distances, seems to stand at the polar opposite of social manifolds. Canetti, as we know, advances an extensive elaboration on the solitude of the individual, and how the latter is tied to power: insofar as power eliminates the other *qua* other, the powerful is doomed to remain *alone*. Someone who can no longer connect to others is essentially cut off from human empathy – hence, the powerful appears as an ill individual, secluded in a condition of 'onliness [*Einzigkeit*]' (*GdW* 37/*CW* 24). Such onliness seems, *prima facie*, to designate a situation thoroughly deprived of *mūnŭs*; in fact, however, this may prove an illusion – that is, illusion *and* delusion at the same time. To the extent that onliness increases the 'dangerous passion' of survival, it inevitably breeds psychotic states; but these states systematically overcome the condition of onliness: they forcefully bring the individual into contact with several manifolds: crowds, populations, race, tribes – often also animals, extraterrestrial aliens, data crowds ... The manifold, in other words, reappears *within* the individual: as in Schreber's case, the paranoid is wholly surrounded and permeated by invisible crowds impossible to get rid of. The unseizable crowds of the psychotic are unmistakably hostile, they never cease to haunt and torment him.

While commonality seems to be utterly denied by the powerful-paranoid subject, it in fact manifests itself in him in the strongest terms: at the limit, we should say that the individual is itself a creative, metamorphic manifold, and psychosis does nothing but make the compositional organization of such manifold *visible*. At the very least, the manifold is always *passing by* the individual, at a distance that is critical, and may at each moment generate outstanding events (flows, transformations …). We have already evoked Gilbert Simondon's (2013[1964–89]) theory of the individual as an ontological reality that ensues from the operation whereby an individuated entity gets progressively defined inside its milieu. In addition to physical and biological individuation, Simondon argues, psychological individuation enables an additional operation of *individualization*, that is, the furthering of individuation being carried out *by the individual itself*. Accordingly, psychic functions emerge as relatively separated from somatic functions. Individualization, in other words, recapitulates the operation of individuation, with thinking now taking the body as its own milieu of individuation: thinking becomes 'the individual of the individual'.[52]

A psychological individual is the unique outcome of its own story, thanks to the ongoing endeavour of individualization; however, Simondon also recognizes that individualization remains necessarily a partial undertaking, at least in normal cases, given that a complete individualization would destroy the very possibility of social relations, which occur precisely thanks to, and through, the non-individualized part of the individual. What Canettian epistemology adds here is the insight that the individualizing operation itself includes narration: the 'story' of individualization provides a perspective, a point of view upon the individual reality *as-it-becomes-individualized*. In other words, individualization is a narrative task: there is no individualization, and *a fortiori* no individuality, without narration. But this also means that the social relation is inscribed even deeper into the psychological individual than Simondon admits. Every individualization includes *becoming the beholder of one's individuation*, which corresponds to the emergence of what, in zoology, Adolf Portmann (1990) called a 'seeing eye', understood as a supplementary organ of the social animal that is simultaneously internal and external to it. Neither a biological organ, nor a psychological subject, the 'seeing eye' is the external point of view upon oneself, whereby the individual associates or completes itself with a regard that becomes an extra-organic social organ 'tying' the social animal to relations. Far from being on a solipsistic track, then, individualization is itself fully and integrally psychosocial, and cannot be reduced to an individual's consciousness – nor even a conscience. One could suggest that, in fact, it is psycho-social individualization itself that always accompanies the rise of *mūnŭs*.

We can now see better the reasons for one of the core claims made above: commonality is not that which is equal, but that, which is *different for each* and yet for some reasons *implicates one* in an undeniable way. Although sharing is certainly one mode of such co-implication, the motif of sharing has sometimes led observers to overlook that commonality is not and cannot be premised on symmetry.[53] In this precise sense, commonality effectively recalls the functioning of command: as considered in Chapter 1, the source of command always resides in *an alien source*, and the *proprium* of its manifestation lies in its non-negotiable, intractable character: just as command does not make issuer and receiver more alike, so the communal does not make those who are implicated by it more similar to one another. Command and the common both concern coexistence (*cum-*); and commonality addresses, as explored above, *the condition* defined by the existence of *mūnŭs*: neither a resource, nor an organization, commonality is the situation, the experience, the *problématique* of the common. Simultaneously, one cannot miss the differences between command and commonality: instead of the hermetic, metronomic, almost 'wordless' nature of command (more ancient than language …), what is the proper of commonality is its calling for stories. How much do these communal stories differ from community mythologies, though! As considered above, the lack of univocality calls for a whole trajectology, whereby the requirements of *mūnŭs* appear in a light that is no longer that of the collective sacred mythology of the group, but a much more perilous navigation into the unhomely.

Parcels and particles of sacredness certainly linger in the air, and the whole point is to understand the different shapes that atmospheric co-implication takes in the different cases. Since, as seen above, packs and crowds are formations of radical equality,[54] every hunt and every increase necessarily result in an act or a rite of sharing and distributing the obtained shares. In Chapter 2, we have noted that, according to Canetti, the *law of distribution* [*das Gesetz der Verteilung*] functions as the proto-law, the first detailed protocol of common conduct (*MM* 115/*CP* 98). However, what matters most is not the arithmetic of shares itself, but those more subtle feelings associated with fairness, unfairness, envy, and related dissatisfactions. That the frustration of fairness provokes awful resentment and rage is something that has been amply documented in primates, too.[55] The special sensitivity of human nomadic populations towards securing fair shares from the hunt is well documented as being intimately tied with their distinctive sense of honour (see, e.g., Chatwin 1989). This means that another, more subtle arithmetic, accompanies the first one: it is an *affective* and *narrative* arithmetic. The laws of the gift, as laid out by Marcel Mauss, offer an earlier anthropological attempt to consider these two arithmetics jointly: every gift necessitates a counter-gift, or return gift, which must be *both* reasonably increased *and* occur within a suitable timeframe. If the return gift is either too small, or too large, it will create a rebound effect and a series of counterproductive consequences. That is why a special *sensitivity* is required in gift-making: no simple arithmetic will ever guarantee a peaceful outcome. At the limit, we could perhaps say that commonality is mathematically impossible – *and therefore*, socially, all the more necessary.

Pharmacological and cathectic

The superposition and conjunction of the two irreconcilable arithmetics of *mūnŭs* points to a more general problem of measure-setting.[56] Here we find ourselves on a terrain we can recognize as properly *pharmacological*: it is a space where questions of 'how much' and 'when' become inextricable from questions of 'what' and 'with which effects.' One could perhaps more simply say that pharmacology is the condition of being bedeviled by measures. The ancient Greek word *pharmakon* covers an array of meanings including recipe, medicine, drug, philter, dye, charm, talisman, and tool; what they all seem to have in common is the constitutive ambivalence of their effects: a *pharmakon* is at the same time always remedy *and* poison. Famously, Jacques Derrida's 1968 essay 'Plato's Pharmacy' (Derrida 1972) scrutinized the nature Plato assigned to writing as a new technology of knowledge. In a classic passage of *Phaedrus*, writing is given as a gift by its mythical inventor, the god Theuth, to the Egyptian king Thamus. Theuth flaunts his new technology as one capable of making the Egyptians wiser and endowed with stronger memory – to which Thamus retorts that, in fact, writing only increases forgetfulness and creates but a delusion of knowledge. In doing so, Theuth and Thamus trade the word *pharmakon*, emphasizing alternatively its positive and negative entailments.

As with every other tool, one could gloss, writing operates by delegation, with each delegation entailing enhanced reliance and dependence upon the enabling support, or medium. Derrida writes that the problem of *pharmakon* evokes all 'the magic virtues of a force whose effects are hard to master, a dynamics that constantly surprises the one who tries to manipulate it as master and as subject' (*ibid.*: 97). In sum, if indeed writing is a remedy for memory, then we should be fully aware that 'there is no such thing as a harmless remedy' (*ibid.*: 99). Notably, by stressing the 'double participation' of *pharmakon* in both good and bad, Derrida develops an argument against substantialism: rather than a fixed substance, the *pharmakon* must be understood as a 'dangerous supplement' (*ibid.*: 110). The supplement is an external addition, an *Ersatz*, yet its danger lies in the fact that it comes quite close to replacing the alleged internal essence of the matter.[57] Thus, theoretically and morally, Plato rejects the *pharmakon* insofar as it fatally interferes with 'natural motion.' Typically, in Plato's Hippocratic medical model, a disease is imagined as itself a living being who has to complete its life cycle following a natural, unhampered course; and, from such a vantage point, every *pharmakon* represents an undue interference into natural processes (although Derrida is keen on revealing that, precisely, Plato is in many ways more complicit in pharmacology than he likes to admit).

The pharmakon is certainly *artificial*; however, as soon as one steps outside of Platonism, one finds that pharmacological formations abound in nature. All phenomena of parasitism are, for instance, pharmacological, just as are phenomena of animal camouflage, and so on. Therefore, in all its artificiality, the pharmakon must be recognized as also a *fully natural production*. Its status is, precisely, that of a natural artifice. Whereas Platonism sees nature as basically unhampered and free from interferences – and accordingly, something to be preserved from interferences at all cost – the naturalist perspective regards it as made of *nothing else but interferences*. That of course does not mean that all interferences are equivalent, or that one can never cause damages by intervening recklessly into complex ecosystems;[58] on the contrary, what is meant is that an analysis of 'interferences' – or more simply, of relations – must be assayed in the context of a connective medium that forms the non-neutral background hosting and rooting them. In short, pharmacology coincides with a theory of mediated interaction. This also suggests that, just as we need to overcome substantialism, we also need to overcome a purely abstract relationalism – for relations are never pure, but always affected and inflexed by the medium in which they take place and unfold. The pharmacological nature of commonality is perfectly illustrated by the ambivalence of the gift as discussed above: the gift (*gift/Gift*) is a prize *and* a duty at the same time, it is as much of a praise as it is no less than a poison.

An inquiry into the pharmacological structure of commonality can be complemented by attention towards cathectic dynamics. As hinted at in the introduction, in cathectic formations we encounter seeming opposites strangely, yet profitably, entertaining with each other. We are now better placed to see that the pharmacological situation of a medium that swerves into polar alternatives is necessarily complementary to the cathectic situation, where two polar opposites become complicit as they meet on an uncertain middle ground. On this terrain, logical short-circuits can be expected to occur in panoply.[59] Developing new ways of thinking through the riddle of commonality might proceed from attending the peculiar, idiosyncratic trajectories that are being established through the tensions of 'the middle.' In this sense, one could perhaps retrieve the most immediate antecedent to Canettian epistemology in Walter Benjamin's unrivalled work on the uncanny intersection between messianism and the cultural world of capitalism. In two distinct and yet importantly related moments (respectively, the *Artwork* essay and the autobiographic *Berlin Childhood around 1900*), Benjamin resorts to two crucial biological-evolutionary notions: such are, respectively, the notions of adaptation [*Anpassung*], and vaccination [*Impfung*]. Clearly, both also bear a pharmacological-cathectic valence. First, film appears to Benjamin as a technology capable of training the human perceptual apparatus to the novel urban conditions of existence; importantly, though, it does so by precisely shocking the senses, submitting perception to a forceful, imperative transformation [*Veränderung*].[60] Second, deciding to write about childhood recollections through the emotional prism of a double exile – from his city and from his past – Benjamin exposes himself to the risk of a most painful homesickness. Nonetheless, this very same exposure turns out to provide him with an effective psychological vaccination against the sort of melancholic-depressive nostalgia that had plagued him for years.[61] The art of *deliberately entertaining with dangers that are there in any case*, is the element of all adaptation, as well as the driving logic of inoculation.

Should we try to formalize the adaptive-immunitarian situation, we could say that a set of critical points determines the edges of regions where a seemingly 'coherent' experience is given – past which, however, sudden global transformations occur. Cathectic-pharmacological events, in other words, place us face to face with 'incoherent' transitions. Such are indeed, in Canetti, the qualitative transformations of packs. In a striking passage, Canetti, for instance, describes the Australian aboriginal Warramunga weeping pack [*Klagemeute*]: the pack congregates around the sickbed of a gravely ill person and begins its lamentation; progressively, the latter turns into clamour, manifesting itself as aggressive howling and crying. A series of expressive, extreme gestures stun the man which they purportedly seek to console. The climax is reached in a type of forcible action: since the pack above all does not want to let the sick man go away from it, in order to preserve him from being carried away by death it resorts to actually *jump on him*. So the members of the pack throw themselves upon the body of the dying man, in a desperate attempt to block him from parting ways. In so doing, they form with him a single human heap, as if such a united heap could challenge, or even revert, the fate. As the pack gets possessed by its own weeping, its gestures of desperation become frantic – in fact, remarks Canetti, more likely to harm and finish off the already agonizing man, than save him.[62] Up until a certain point, the agony of the dying man seems to be mimetically mirrored by the pack; but, as lament turns into raging clamour, sorrow borders thinly with war. It is a strange region of intensity where desperation and aggression overlap. Against whom, however, would the pack be raging war? There's no way to hunt death, and the poor dying man is still one of *theirs*. On the verge of the lament, the pack is confronted with its own actual powerlessness to overcome death – unless the dying actually *dies*: at that point, the dead man unequivocally becomes an enemy of the pack. Since, as said, those very frenzied actions with which the pack tries until the very end to rescue its member, in fact accelerates his death, the pack can ultimately be said to be complicit with death. Its strongest assertion therefore is: what really *continues*, what must go on to live, is 'the heap,' of which the living and the dying are part. Canetti deliberately calls the member that is being so forcefully 'rescued,' the pack's victim [*Opfer*], suggesting that the gestures of the well-meaning weeping pack may also be an execution in disguise. Agony certainly works both ways, against and towards death. Given the degree of individuation that is present within the pack, one cannot doubt that the pack must be in despair about the prospect of losing one of its precious members; but at some point during the progression of the lament, the death of a member must appear as a special type of 'negotiation' with death, so as to ensure the most important survival, the survival of the collective. Perhaps paradoxically, after the death of the sick man, the pack's remaining members all find themselves in the position of 'survivors' – i.e., in a position of 'empowerment.'

If we dig to the bottom of survival, then, we realize that, in humans as well as other animals, the survival of the individual can never be *fully real*, such a reality of survival being rather an attribute of the species. The latter, however, must be understood here *not* as phylogeny, but in its reality of manifold – not as a phenomenon of reproduction and descent but as a phenomenon of living populations currently distributed in given environments and given 'zones' or 'niches'. Put differently, according to a perspective laid out by the late Simmel (2010[1918]), survival is only the survival of *life itself* through the varied forms it, at each instant, takes. Such 'forms' correspond to what we have been calling here 'social manifolds.' Notably, then, the cathectic-pharmacological reality of commonality cannot be successfully reduced to the drama of community and its self-preservation strategies, regardless of how momentous the latter can be. What contradistinguishes pharmacological and cathectic dynamics is, rather, the unfolding of an uncertain terrain, a middle ground or medium, where qualitative points of reversal swiftly occur. These are critical moments, or tipping points that fundamentally alter the course and the meaning of the actions undertaken: they re-associate, reshuffle, and reshape meaning. Such points are not located within one manifold, as they would be within a set, but always on edging lines running across different manifolds. Such is, for instance, the moment when a successful capture suddenly silences the hunting pack; or, to return to the example evoked above, the moment when, once the member has died, the weeping pack sequesters everything that had belonged to him and makes it disappear. More mundanely, cathectic considerations can also explain the seeming paradox whereby the very fact of naming one's enemy actually *strengthens* the enemy – a lesson many autocratic leaders have learnt by heart, or even feel instinctively, and which, on the contrary, the various 'cancel' campaigns have fundamentally misunderstood (spending as they do most of their energies making up lists of who should be 'deleted').

All situations of commonality, considered in light of pharmacological–cathectic dynamics, raise a Camusian sort of problem: In the struggle against inhumanity, is not one becoming-inhuman oneself? In other words, *What is the limit?* The question, in its radicalness, alerts us to the fact that what really matters is not so much the limit between oneself and 'the enemy', as much as the limit between oneself and one's own potential enmity-qua-inhumanity. The quantity and rhythm of the pharmakon's intake progressively unravels a dangerous edging line. Camus in this sense gave us one of the best examples of cathectic politics with his formula, 'radicalism of the middle.' Whereas radicalism is usually associated with extremist politics, Camus put forward a radical politics that called for the utmost attentiveness to the lines of reversal running through the medium of politics. Real reversal does not occur 'at the extremes,' but right in the middle. For his part, Canetti seems to suggest that, in confronting power, two different types of courage are needed: a first type is theoretical, and consists of looking at power in the eyes, apprehending its fundamental nature, not embellishing or mystifying it in any way ('seizing the century'). Such is the courage of the political realists in the tradition of Machiavelli and Hobbes. Canetti's sustained engagement and almost – at times – indisputably fascinated attraction towards such a stance does not prevent him from recognizing that the theoretical courage pales in comparison to a second courage, which we may call a 'poetic' one: such is the courage of *not resigning* to the reality of power. Not resigning, resisting, transforming: in the previous chapter, we have already considered at length how these three moves are effectively intertwined in depth in the Canettian epistemology. If commonality is not something that needs to be created at all, that is because it predates our attempts to do so, and founds them. One can, however, change *the visibility of commonality* – and, at this point, we realize that commonality can only be made visible precisely by acts that create the new: in all its unfamiliarity, the new is, perhaps strangely, what makes *mūnŭs* truly recognizable, undeniable, and therefore all the more precious – precisely, precious in proportion to the difficulty with which it can be recognized, and the ease with which it can be spoiled.

Commonality is not something that unites individuals as a community bond would do. In this sense, again, commonality runs contrary to the constitution of community. That is why we have to return to Deligny's point about his autistic children, when he remarked that, to him, what mattered with them was their *pre-individual* and *im-personal* existence. Commonality does not concern the individuation of a person or a community, nor the personalization of a community or an individual, but rather, the visibilization of *further individuations* to come, whose trajectories and co-implications are currently unintelligible. From this perspective, individuations do not sum up one onto the other: the same person passes *through* different degrees of individuation, not as an addition, nor as a set-theoretical inclusion, but as an exercise in changing intensities in relation to a manifold, which itself is made of those transformations. That is why commonality comes in the impersonal and the infinitive – as captured by Deligny's expression *point de voir*, instead of *point de vue*. This means that commonality is not something we could expect to be personally *comforted* by. Commonality connects us through difference and faces us with the unhomely; in a way, it is *communication*, but not communication as described by twentieth-century political and media theory, which largely overlooked the cathectic–pharmacological constitution of *mūnŭs*. Deligny, let us recall, writes of a 'common without language.' If we take language away, politics as traditionally conceived seems destined to crumble, and the media would appear pointless. But, it is also under such unfamiliar conditions that the communal, the political, and the personal are connected in a way that prevents their conflation. Curiously, given such emphasis on the impersonal and the pre-individual, the discussion on commonality conducted so far in this chapter is also the one most nourished by details about Canetti's personal life – yet it is precisely by exploring the most minute life details that one can gauge the actual import of the political. There is, in other words, a trans-scalar aspect to commonality: not that the personal is un-political, but to some extent we should rather admit that the personal is also 'impersonal,' since our personal lives are constantly crossed by singularities that, while making us what we are, simultaneously keep us out-of-ourselves. The singularity of a gesture makes of a life what it is, and yet, that gesture is understandable only because it does not end within the confines of the person making it.

The 'common' addressed by commonality is, in the end, something that can never be firmly located. Its 'co-implicating' aspect delineates a peculiar spatial condition, which speaks both of 'factual' interiority and, simultaneously, of an absolute, forceful outside functioning as a strange attractor. In other words, it is not only the limitation from the inside, but also the requirement from the outside that jointly constitute the puzzle of commonality. So, commonality ultimately coincides with social life itself, insofar as the latter travels through the socii and can never be completely 'dammed up' inside them. The more general point about life here, is that it travels: where it is going to spring up next, remains unknown, and can only be assayed by attending to all those special moments of 'animation' that unmistakably signal the flashing up of commonality. That is why commonality cannot be illuminated by purely rational-cognitive-deductive means: it presupposes imageal notions that are more similar to the way of thinking of the Bororo than they are to Kant's critical philosophy (cf. Lévy-Bruhl 1938: 8 March 1938). Inherently evoking the priority of capacity over being, of multiplicity over determination, of transformation over forms, commonality only appears in the revelation of something so new that no community can successfully appropriate it, a 'new' that, each time *anew*, appears as *untimely* and *out of place*.

CONCLUSIONS

This book was conceived of as an attempt to reconstruct Canetti's *Gestus*, with the aim of figuring out its possible social–theoretical continuations – or, its *prolongations* – into the global present and the upcoming future. The highly idiosyncratic position taken by Canetti, along with his overall anti-systematic and even 'anti-theoretical' stance, has made our exploration more tentative, but also, hopefully, more surprising. Canetti, we have seen, has been accused of clinging to a primordialist, Hobbesian view of humanity, as when serving us a theory of totalitarianism itself deemed totalitarian.[1] In fact, in the course of our research, it has become visible, I believe, that what Canetti's approach resists is, chiefly, the empty rhetoric of newness that surrounds modernity talk. Modernity – here understood in the first place not as a specific historical period or geographic expanse, but as a style of thinking and communicating – has a rhetorical preference for the 'innovative' over the 'traditional,' for the 'original' over the 'derivative,' and for the 'personal' over the 'anonymous.' In this respect, Canettian epistemology, with its deeply naturalizing gaze onto social life, largely razes down modernity's own claim to an exceptional status, and reveals that the sources of everything we regard as unique to it are, in fact, quite ancient – as, for instance, is the case with the myth of increase rebranded in terms of economic development. In other words, Canettian epistemology re-embeds modernity into a natural history of social life.

At the same time, Canetti is *also* a humanist, as confirmed by his conception of the *Dichter/Dichterin* as the protector of transformations, along with his wish to overcome cold-blooded political realism by all possible means.[2] Not only is such a wish epitomized by Dr Sonne's figure, but it is also the driving force for addressing the question of commonality, along with its challenging ethical promises and requirements. Naturalism and humanism, it is suggested accordingly, need not be in contradiction to one another. Naturalism might indeed turn out to be the precondition for a renewal of humanism – rather than, as currently fashionable, a hasty call for a shift towards 'post-humanism' (a notion that couldn't be farther from Canettian epistemology). As remarked in the introduction, we are given here a chance to outline *at the same time* a naturalistic study of power *and* an ethical critique of it. This is particularly visible in the relation Canetti envisages with non-human animals: once we face earnestly the other animals, and living forms more generally, who co-inhabit the planet, it becomes epistemologically impossible to confine social life to humans alone. This is relevant if we consider that, historically, the relation humans sought to enforce with respect to the other animals is one of denial (invisibilization) of commonality – in other words, it is a relation of power.

In his struggle against power and its inherent tendency to narrow down life's full breadth, Canetti seeks to retrieve such 'breadth of life' locating it precisely in the act of *breathing*. As remarked above, breathing thus comes to define the very atmospheric condition and the political issue of commonality. By considering the reality of breathing as a kind of corporeal proto-movement that grounds the domain of freedom at large, we can consequently advance a framework for understanding both intra-specific and inter-specific social–environmental relations. This comes in conjunction with an animistic or 'animational' sensibility, one that pluralizes agency and strives to attend the unexpected emerging formations of social life across genres, species and things. In Canettian epistemology, humans appear as deeply enmeshed within heterogeneous compositions, veritable *montages* of forces and agents – in the parlance of more recent prominent theorists, we might as likely call them *assemblages* (Deleuze) or *action-nets* (Latour). In this sense, the analysis of the command–machine, examined in Chapter 1, offers an example of how Canettian epistemology can be counted as an earlier attempt towards the recognition of the existence of rhizomatic or hybrid (human-non-human) social formations. If the social bond systematically overcomes homogenous groups and their boundaries, it is because and insofar as 'social' is everything that has a grip on those parts (and parties) that entertain meaningful relations of reference, orientation and reliance.[3] Ongoing ontological and praxeological extravasations, in other words, characterize the social process.

However, an emphasis on action, and how action practically imbricates actors and flows through them, must not lead us to disattend the images and the visions those actors *also* experience. Imageal production, we have remarked, is no less integral a part of Canettian epistemology than action itself – for, crucially, imaginational and even 'visionary' experiences lie at the root of stories and narrations, ranging from myth through literature to the arts. For how much Canetti was an implacable analyst of the delusions of totalitarianism – always, for him, bound to cross over into psychosis – he also always strongly objected against everything that spoils myths – whether it is Adorno's take on Ulysses as the first bourgeois character, or Lévi-Strauss's (as well as, we may add, Dumézil's) structuralist analysis of myths. The role of myth here can be taken as a useful reminder to the social theorist that fiction is quintessential to social life. Myths, stories, novels, plays and so on correspond to the telling of those very images through which life itself proceeds. Images therefore entertain an essential relation to movement, mobility and transformation; in turn, each actual transformation is always prepared by an imaginational activity, as seen, for instance, in small human groups mirroring themselves into naturally occurring crowds, so as to spur their own increase.

Overall, Canetti's move – or, as we have called it above, his *Gestus* – proves more difficult to explain than any of the classics': one hears echoes of Darwin, Nietzsche, Freud and Durkheim in Canetti, but in his oeuvre they appear reassembled and synthesized into a distinctive recipe. As considered above, Canetti advances a fundamentally continuist mode of thinking that is quite different from a linear, one-way conception of history: a 'prolongational' history is, indeed, almost the opposite of a 'developmental' history grounded in the idea of progress.[4] The notion of prolongation, in this sense, appears to resonate with a 'vitalist' sensitivity – where the central suggestion of vitalism here for us lies in the idea that, if life is *trend*, more than *state*, then it is not just *one* trend but *many trends at once*.[5] From this perspective, evolutionism can be said to be necessary, in the first instance, but ultimately insufficient in itself. Rather than an overarching evolutionary movement attained through successive stages – from lower to higher, from simple to complex, from slower to faster, etc. – Canettian epistemology suggests continual regroupings of elements and motifs that take on always changing significations across different historical–environmental contexts and through the varying degrees of intensity they attain under specific circumstances. Prolongation is, inherently, a category of transformation, and makes sense only on the basis of a process ontology capable of transcending the crude dualism of identity and difference. A similar process ontology, we have also recalled, has been envisaged by Whitehead, and later deployed by Deleuze in his event philosophy. As with Whitehead and Deleuze, Canettian epistemology is embedded within an empirical and immanentist approach.

Mixing the sensitivity of the dramatist and the interest of the anthropologist, Canetti addresses social situations – made of gestures, survivals, resistances, commonalities, helping acts ... – in their rounded atmospheric qualities, where atmospheres must be understood as veritable compositions of changing affections that 'colour' each event. Most of our lives are unfortunately spent in atmospheres of command and obedience which, as considered above, constitute the nearly ubiquitous medium or 'element' of the social relation. And yet, despite Canetti's repeated declarations about the univocal 'evilness of power,' the sort of Canettian epistemology unravelled throughout this book has led us to the perhaps surprising acknowledgement that power itself cannot be conceived dualistically. Far from being the flat reality of death-and-survival, power entails a tortured social nexus where survival certainly prolongs into competition, humiliation, killing and psychic disease, but also into increase, ambition, inspiration and fame – the latter in turn strangely resemblant to what the artist, in his/her act of resistance, seeks to achieve.

The prolongations of power, in other words, already inherently prepare the advent of an 'otherwise' and an 'outside,' which *a priori* power would seem bound to deny by nature. Accordingly, the theoretical challenge raised here concerns how to attain a non-simply-dualist image of these dynamics. Here the peculiarity of Canettian epistemology, as we have sought to discuss it, lies in focusing on a series of deeply affective experiences of social life. To install oneself (or, the theoretical eye) in all those moments where swift and crucial phase transitions occur, with fine-grained sensitivity towards their preparation and deployment: such a move implies attending as closely as possible the very medium of social life, without ever becoming wholly assimilated to it, so as to evince its pharmacological ambivalence. As we have remarked at the outset of this book, being simply outside of modernity is not possible. Now, something similar should be repeated as concerns power – but again, that does not mean that a displaced perspective is sterile, for what truly matters is the gesture towards the outside, alongside the experience of resistance that pertains to it. How to produce, from the inside of social reality, such an unrecognizable distance that spurs the effect of an outside, a 'liberation'? The flight, we have suggested, is one such expressions of an 'internal distance,' wherein interiority and exteriority are co-articulated, not as locations, but as *perspectives* upon our reality – upon the century.

This leads us to believe that the problem of power is not one of substance but, precisely, of 'perspective' – with the space of flight offering a prime example. Far from turning into easy-going relativism, the perspectival insight marks the necessary awareness that power is as much absolutely real as it is completely fictional, it is as much a life-and-death matter as it is but an affair of myth. Because the situation we are facing is one where effectiveness and virtuality do not rule out one another, the role of resistance as a function of displacement – in other words, the force of its *tacet* – finds its full cogency. Not only does resistance often proceed through unplanned, unsettling and inchoate gestures that displace the regular, consensual and harmonic ties of community, but its deep link to creation directly derives from such a gestural, affective and 'dramatical' foundation. This way, the 'unissued imperative' to create pursued by the *Dichter/in* lays out a veritable space of *flight*, this time defined by the chasm between one's obsessiveness and one's capacity of liberation from one's own 'system.'

Upon such uncertain terrain, the uncanny resemblance between the *Dichter*-artist and the leader cannot be denied. We could perhaps tentatively say that what we must explain is not only a relation between the leader and the crowd, but a more complex relation between two types of leader: on the one hand is the king, the *Machthaber*, blocked in his own figure and blocking all the others in turn; on the other hand is the artist, the *Meisterverwandler*, the protean figure of deceptive transformation which constantly spurs confusion and equivocation among categories, but also preserves life in its non-conflictual and 'non-survivalist' stance. This means that, in relation to a social manifold whatsoever, two different types of 'attractor' can be envisaged: what stands in opposition to the central, fascist leader (here *fascist* not only in the historical sense, but also in the literal sense, in that he *both* binds people *and* leashes them) is not only the crowd as leaderless formation (or, as a principle of non-leadership), but rather an uncanny 'artistic' leader, who in his/her outfit could also be a shamanic or demonic leader. With a nod to zoology, these could also be called alpha and omega – whereas the alpha leader *orders*, the omega leader *tempts*. Notably, alpha and omega do not simply stand for politics versus art; rather, it is with two types of politics and two types of art we that are dealing. If choice there is between them, it is complicated by the fundamental lack of reciprocity between the alternatives, as well as between each of them and the crowd.

Co-essential to every form of life is a principle of symmetry breaking. We can see the latter at work in social life, where seemingly polar opposites fail to actually exhibit symmetry. On the one hand, resistance frees us from the grip of power; on the other, however, commonality reveals that the 'outside' also has something of the structure of power itself. Similarly, metamorphosis stands in opposition to power as an experience of liberation, but at the same time the talent for metamorphosis has conferred much power to the 'most transformative' of animals, i.e. the human animal. That is why, throughout this book, we have found that including a consideration of pharmacological and cathectic dynamics proves useful to envisage how life can be nurtured so as to let emerge what we have referred to as the outline of a liberated command – something perhaps more akin to a 'recommendation'. To quickly resume our terminology of choice, we have designated as 'pharmacological' the reality of a 'middle' – or medium – that stretches out into opposite directions (towards either remedy or poison), and we have called 'cathectic' those situations in which two polar opposites converge into a zone of indistinction where they somehow mysteriously entertain with each other.[6] That is how an art of entertaining with the enemy without becoming symmetrical – or antithetical – to it can be envisaged. Canetti, we have said, was a strong personality, in his way a 'fighter' – and yet, his ethical challenge as well as his theoretical legacy lies in not becoming a fighter of humans, but someone who fights 'the century'.

In conclusion, we can return one last time to the bizarre, somewhat boastful expression 'seize the century by the throat'. We can now acknowledge that the first, crucial power the century possesses is – as Camus also intuited – to impose its problems upon us, thus distracting us from our real problems, and weakening our capacity to pose those problems in our own terms, that is, in the terms that are more precious and valuable.[7] The century equates with command, in that both freeze transformation in order to preserve the structures of power in place. There is no shortage of brutality, and the present offers plenty of *Machthaber* figures: the bare-bone, ugly reality where political opponents are threatened, silenced, imprisoned, tortured and killed, where every form of dissent is repressed and crushed, reminds us that power is still very much vested in that original 'clutch of the hand' which forms its veritable source. But Canetti also makes clear that our hands can seize objects in many different ways: discussing the 'patience of the hand', he opposes the way weapons are handled to the way skilful manipulations are slowly and carefully performed by the hands so as to produce new tools. Seizing the century calls for analogous carefulness: only outlandish inventions, whose shibboleth lies in their capacity to displace command, can help. From the subversion of the command–machine there emerges the chance for a non-antagonistic survival, tied to the realization of an 'interchangeable' life.

The requirement of interchangeability makes us understand that the ethnocentric operation, and the majoritarian point of view that derives from it, actually *deny* commonality – where the latter is to be seen, not as a comforting communitarian refrain, but as an unsettling incognita, a 'commons=x'. Each refusal to be assimilated is thus an act of resistance that defuses the majoritarian point of view. In this sense, we have said, resistance can be considered as the 'residuum' of the ethnocentric operation: only by unsettling community can the act of resistance coalesce into an experience of liberation beyond legal and political articulations – resistance, or, existence without entitlement. As we 'regress,' theoretically and practically, *from* group *to* crowd, *from* community *to* commonality, the shape of resistance is revealed as arachnean, a compound of interiority and exteriority that mobilizes the one so as to avert the dangers inherent in the other. Accordingly, rather than a strictly political or cultural gesture, resistance encompasses the whole of social existence: it is an artful exercise, given that all art exists in a constitutive relation to a social manifold. To seize the century thus requires the development of a special art, an art of laying out preliminary territories for new social life.

NOTES

Introduction

1 (*Mem* 653). The idea that the writer-poet-artist [*Dichter/Dichterin*] should not condescend to easy solutions is also expressed emphatically in the 1976 essay 'The writer's profession.' A somewhat different, and perhaps more humane, image emerges from a personal letter addressed in 1946 to his youngest brother Georg: '... my worst malady: my dread of completing things. I can always work, I work every day, with strict discipline and regularity ... However, I must learn to finish things' (*Lett* 191). After *Crowds and Power* is finally published, Canetti in his notebook notes that what remains of himself is 'the crater of the book' (*NaH* y.1962, 66; Engl ed. 67).

2 '... dieses Jahrhundrert an der Gurgel zu packen' (*PdM* y. 1959, 243).

3 The approach proposed here thus seeks to rehabilitate Iris Murdoch's earlier appreciation of Canetti's book as 'full of starting points, embryo theories, sudden independent illuminations'. (1962: 156) – a treatise that reads as a dreamlike poem, infused with poignant aphorisms and startling, arresting images.

4 A monumental Canetti biography has been written by Sven Hanuschek (2005).

5 As an elderly Canetti concedes in his posthumous memoir about his 'English years', 'My main personality trait [*Haupteigenschaft*], the most remarked one, the one which has never faded, is to assert [*Bestehen*] my own person, not to the detriment of the others, but anyway: this trait was always deeply inbred in me' (*PiB* 176). In a personal letter to his brother Georg, written at 32, when his first novel *Die Blendung* had recently appeared, Canetti put it this way: 'In my case, my natural delusions of grandeur meet the world halfway. It's the only concession I was born with; otherwise, I make no concessions' (*Lett* 83).

6 See Hanuschek (2005: 350–436). Canetti was a regular at *The Coffee Cup* on Hampstead High St, where he would meet people for extensive discussion sessions.

7 Modest autobiographers are the rarest species – for indeed, the very idea of writing an autobiography subjectively presupposes, and objectively requires, a certain self-centredness that is irreconcilable with either true or feigned modesty. Much more than the autobiography, it is the personal correspondence between Elias, Veza and Georg Canetti that reveals the real nature of their complex relationship. Elias announced his marriage to his younger brother as not at all of romantic type, but simply a bureaucratic trick to set the papers right in view of emigration, avoiding a possible (though unlikely) deportation of Veza to Yugoslavia. Elias states that their relation is affectionate, but of a specific type: 'she is now my *mother*.' Elsewhere, he depicts his relation to his own real mother as 'obsessional,' noting how he was extremely reliant on her recognition, but also detested her presence since he could not psychologically shield form her. For her part, Veza was for a long time unhappily in love with Georg. In a particularly telling passage dated 1945, Veza writes to Georg, 'I offered for the 12th time to divorce him. Whereupon he implored me, not to, since there are two women waiting for such an event and to tear him to pieces. So this sums

up my function in his life. Besides having to find the adequate terms for his English version of the "Blendung" (for which we can't find an English title) I keep the tigers away' (*Lett* 11; 43; 130). Canetti did not bother to hide his various affairs while he was playing the role of the enchanter-seducer in British intellectual circles. In England, they lived for long time in separate places, but never divorced until Veza's death in 1963. Interestingly, despite the hardship she endured in her life and her fraying health, Veza maintained a light touch of humour in her writings, which is completely absent in Canetti's work. Despite her recurrent bouts of depression, Veza supported and took care of his intellectual accomplishments in numberless ways – a debt he always recognized.

8   See, for instance, 'Elias Canetti: Eine animalische Kraft, die leben will,' *Zeit*, 2018. See also Bernd Witte's and Gerhard Melzer's critical scholarship, emphasizing how Canetti, as a veritable power figure, tried to rule over the interpretation of his work (in Darby Ed. 2000). For his part, it seems that Canetti himself was well aware of the viral nature of power: 'When one deals with power, one is inadvertently infected [*angesteckt*] by it' (*NaH* y.1961, 51; Engl. Ed. 52). Another note alludes to a process of self-liberation from power through literature: 'The cruel gaze [*Das böse Auge*] I once had no longer interests me' (*NaH* y.1965, 96; Engl. Ed. 99). In one his latest aphorisms, he pointed out – no doubt alluding to himself – that 'seeking fame' is a way of seeking 'absolute power' (*Aufz 92*: 11), but also judged that, luckily, the aim is unattainable.

9   Elias Canetti rests in Zurich's Fluntern Cemetery, next to where James Joyce also lies. It is a peaceful inner suburb close to the Zurich Zoo.

10   'There is nothing that pushes me so strongly to the company of certain persons as their wish to listen to me' (*PiB* 183). It must be recalled, however, that the English years memoir, to which Canetti worked in the four final years of his life, was left unfinished, even in some fundamental structural sense. While certainly Canetti's remarks could occasionally deliver a 'real lethal injection [*wirkliche Giftspritze*]', as the writer Hilde Spiel once put it (Weber 2017), it is unsure whether Canetti would have let a number of disparaging comments (especially misogynist and sexist) into the final version, had he been able to oversee the work into publication (Hanuschek 2005: 181–2 seems to concur with this view). After all, it is the same Canetti who elsewhere wrote: 'I hate judgments that only crush and don't transform.' What seems clear is that, as an émigré, Canetti suffered from an embittering status frustration, and sought in all ways to secure recognition in the new milieu – a sentiment he seems to innerly relive in a very intense way while remembering his English years. The aphorisms written in 1992–3, while he was pulling together his fourth memoir, contain several reflections on the relation between memory and rage [*Zorn*]. In one particularly telling note, Canetti writes: 'You let yourself go to rage. It vivifies you. But should one strengthen oneself at the expense of others? Even if one were right, which is not the case – isn't one indulging into something that goes in the direction of survival, which is the most horrible of all directions?' [Du gibst dich dem Zorn hin. Er belebt dich. Darf man sich auf Kosten andere beleben lassen? Selbst wenn man im Recht wäre, was nicht der Fall sein kann – erlaubt man sich nicht etwas, was in die Richtung des Überlebens geht, in die verwerflichste aller Richtungen?] (*Aufz 92–3*, 71).

11   This aspect can best be noticed especially in the aphorisms. See f.i., 'Are [these thoughts] really *yours*? Aren't you just one of their many fortuitous centrals [*zufälligen Zentralen*]?', (*NaH* y.1960, 46; Engl. Ed. 46).

12   Biographic research reveals that Veza's contribution was fundamental to the completion of the book project. At some point after her death, Canetti started

considering Veza as co-author of the book (Hanuschek 2005; Preece 2007: 8, 41). Not only was Veza a fundamental partner in discussion, but for years she spurred Canetti in every possible ways towards bringing the project to a close, up until a joint intense, detailed and careful read-aloud revision of the final manuscript ('... she has worked her way so completely into my book and gone over every sentence with me. The suggestions she made have been invaluable.' *Lett* 366). In a sense, *Crowds and Power* is thus the child born of their marriage. Incidentally, the hypothesis seems to be corroborated by the fact that Marie-Louise Motesiczky, who for some time harboured the dream that Canetti could divorce Veza and marry her, seems to always have refrained from reading *Crowds and Power*, despite repeated pressures from Canetti.

13   Canetti had been introduced to Mary Douglas; however, the latter does not seem to have been impressed by *Crowds and Power* (Adler 2005: 220).

14   He is commemorated in *Aufz 92* and *PiB*. For a recent reconstruction of their intellectual friendship as well as their parting ways, see Arnason (2019).

15   Canetti rationalized his non-continuation of *Crowds and Power* as follows: 'Had you continued this book, you would have spoiled [*zerstört*] it with your hopes. As it stands now, readers will be forced to search for their own hopes' (*GdU* y.1982, 131; Engl. Ed. 115). Here, reference is to the fact that the projected second volume on transformation would have been inevitably imbued in the author's own appraisal of transformation as a redeeming force. In a letter to Enzo Rutigliano, dated Feb 3, 1989, the author explains: 'The largest part of my reflections on this topic [metamorphosis] is not yet published. Yet until I am so dissatisfied with them, I cannot publish them, nor even talk about them' (in Rutigliano 2007: 108). Late in life, Canetti briefly took notice of the structuralist method in anthropology, which of course he declares to dislike, seeing in it above all a way of *destroying* the real significance of myths: Lévi-Strauss, he charges, collects myths just as one presses herbs in a herbarium [*Aufz* 92–3]. On Canetti as anthropologist, see also Robertson's essay in Darby (2000).

16   The very number of rejections the present book has received seems to testify about the unfashionable status of Canetti in sociology.

17   For instance, as Donahue (2007a: xiii) puts it, 'he felt no academic compulsion (as we would) to retrace the scholarly genealogy, or to tip his hat to those who had gone before him.'

18   'If there is one thing I would not like to be, it is "a timely man" [*zeit-gemäß*]', (*NaH* y.1969, 156; Engl. Ed. 164). On the other hand, in his essay on Hermann Broch, Canetti described the writer as both inextricably tied to the century ('the dog of his time'), and never resigned to it ('he has to kick and scream like an infant') (*GdW* 14–16; Engl. Ed. 3–6).

19   To borrow a wonderful expression by Hannah Arendt, social theorizing is, indeed, a type of *denken ohne Geländer* (thinking without banister).

20   'There's a good reason why I don't want to go into details concerning the criticisms of *Crowds and Power*: what I aimed at was to give an impulsion to the discussion, not to found a system. If ever, I would have worked to the opposite aim, namely, avoid that my thought acquired the character of a complete unity' (Personal letter to Rutigliano, Feb.1, 1983, in Rutigliano 2007: 88). Long before Canetti, it was Nietzsche who said that to have a system means, for a philosopher, a lack of integrity. In this sense, I believe my approach is consonant with Donahue's (2007b: 48) invitation to regard Canetti as a thorough *experimenter*: 'Far more frequently ... we find Canetti experimenting with his own ideas, viewing them from another – sometimes contradictory – perspective, inserting qualifications, playing

out doubts, or simply embracing a raft of new data, all while demonstrating the incompleteness of his own conceptual framework.'

21   'We feel terribly superior to [the so-called primitives] because they use clubs instead of atomic bombs' (*GdW* 31; Engl. Ed. 19).

22   *Aufz 92–3*; see also: 'The truth that does not transform itself into something else is but terror [*Schrecken*] and annihilation [*Vernichtung*]' (*Fli* 119).

23   The *New York Times* critic Edward B. Rothstein (1990), for instance, charged Canetti of 'mystical primitivism' and 'inhuman humanism.'

24   In this respect, Darby (2000: 6) considers that Adorno and Canetti simply 'talk past each other in a way that is both frustrating and fascinating'. In parenthesis, one cannot but notice a certain gracelessness of Adorno's, who, as the convenor and host of the radio programme, ends up talking twice as much time as his guest, on top of it often interrupting him.

25   The negative, or 'realist,' anthropology of power interests Canetti *philosophically*, but he also clearly finds it insufficient *poetically* ('... even braver would be to see, inside this same reality, and without falsifying or beautifying it, the seed of another one, which would become possible under transformed circumstances ...' *PdM* 291). Thinking, in other words, is not enough: for Canetti, one must also be able to *breathe*, that is, to live fully and freely.

26   'The conceptual interests me so little that at 54 I haven't yet seriously read either Aristotle or Hegel. Not simply are they indifferent to me: I *distrust* them' (*NaH* 25). In his essay on Speer, Canetti recommends a new research method that proceeds through 'an integral contemplation of the phenomenon' [*unzerteilte Anschauung des Phänomens*], staying clear of 'any arrogance of the concept' [*jede Arroganz des Begriffs*] (*GdW* 172; Engl. Ed. 146).

27   As we shall see better, the fact that mythical thinking is essentially of non-conceptual kind is also a dominant realization of early-twentieth-century anthropology (cf. for instance Lévy-Bruhl 1949[1938]: 20 July).

28   Just as with Freud, Canetti at some point admits that Nietzsche is an extremely influential author, although what he spurs are the 'wrong ambitions' (*ML*, y. 1942).

29   With reference to *Crowds and Power*, László Földényi (2020: 247) speaks precisely of 'dramaturgy of dreams.' We return to the issue of dreams and commonality in Chapter 4.

30   'Operating through seduction – Derrida (1972: 70) remarked – the pharmakon makes one stray from one's general, natural, habitual paths and laws.' We return to these points more extensively in Chapter 4.

31   The expressions τὸ κατέχον, 'that which withholds,' and ὁ κατέχων, 'the one who withholds,' are used by St Paul in his Second Letter to the Thessalonians. (2 *Thessalonians* §2, 6–7): 'And you know what is restraining him [the man of lawlessness] now so that he may be revealed in his appointed time. For the mystery of lawlessness is already at work; only he who now restrains it [to katéchon] will do so until he [the lawless one] is out of the way'. The katéchon is thus that which holds back the Antichrist – the lawless one (*o ánthropos tês anomías*), who in turn embodies the rebellion against God's rule – 'until the manifestation of his [Christ's] coming' (Frame 1912). According to Liddell & Scott's Dictionary, the verb κατέχω means to 'hold fast,' 'hold back,' or even 'withhold'; it may also mean to 'detain,' 'gain possession of,' 'master,' 'achieve,' and 'keep in mind.' *Katéchein* is thus a complex, 'pharmacological' verb, which joins together the sense of hindering, keeping from happening and entertaining with. That is why, a κάθεξις designates a

form of possession, or retention – and this also explains why its has been used by Freud's English translators to render the German word *Besetzung*, literally meaning 'occupation' (including, military occupation) or 'assignment'. We return to these points in Chapter 2.

32　At the end of the second century, precisely in 197 A.D., Tertullianus argued in two works, *Apologeticum* and *Ad Nationes*, that Christianity was compatible with the Empire and that honest Caesars would have believed in Christ, if only they could have been Caesars *and* Christians at the same time. Tertullianus thus shifted the source of evil away from Empire *qua* Empire, to prepare for the possible accommodation of Christianity within the Empire. This interpretation was accepted by later Christian Fathers, who attributed the cathectic function to the Christian Roman Empire in its struggle against the Pagan world.

Chapter 1

1　The car stop is now widely considered as premeditated and pretextual, given the available data: Encinia deliberately accelerated fast closing in near to Bland's car, she changed lane to give him the right of way, at which point he stopped her for failure to signal the lane change. A comprehensive Wikipedia entry provides full information about this story: https://en.wikipedia.org/wiki/Death_of_Sandra_Bland. Video footage is available at https://www.youtube.com/watch?v=y9t1N2wRvjc (Accessed 1 August 2019).

2　To give a glimpse into how deeply is the notion of command ingrained in Western metaphysics, one can recall that even the philosophical notion of 'form', crucial as it is in the Aristotelian tradition, is grounded in command. So, according to Gilbert Simondon (2013[1964–89]: 51), 'L'operation technique qui *impose une forme à une matière passive et indeterminée* … est essentiellement l'opération commandée par l'homme libre et executée par l'esclave [The technical operation that imposes a form onto a passive and undetermined matter … is essentially the operation commanded by the free man and executed by the slave].'

3　Interestingly, Orson Welles' (1962) filmic adaptation of Kafka's *The Trial* features the protagonist claiming precisely 'I know my rights' – a powerful line, which would have been unconceivable to Kafka himself, whose work largely revolves around situations where no clear 'rights' exist.

4　*The Province of Jurisprudence Determined* was Austin's 'legal theory 101' course, so to speak. The famous definition is provided in lecture one. Incidentally, the course, imparted at the newly founded University of London, was doomed by a persistent failure to attract students, to the point that Austin resigned. His later life was plagued by depression, and its only thanks to Austin's wife Sarah that *The Province* was republished, and almost all the rest of Austin's texts published for the first time, establishing Austin's largely posthumous fame.

5　Notably, this is what Giorgio Agamben (1995) has accomplished with his theory of bare life. The very notion of exception could perhaps be formalized through the mathematical notion of singularity, in particular as discussed by René Thom (1991).

6　In a joint work with Mattias Kärrholm, drawing on Deleuze, I have described 'chronic' temporality in its relation to generations and spatial occupation (Brighenti and Kärrholm 2020).

7 In a programmatic passage from the second edition of *Political Theology*, dated 1934, Schmitt seeks to blend the three perspectives of normativism, decisionism and institutionalism: 'Whereas the normativist in his distortion makes of law a mere mode of operation of a state bureaucracy, and the decisionist, focusing on the moment, always runs the risk of missing the stable content inherent in every great political movement, an isolated institutional thinking leads to the pluralism characteristic of a feudal-corporate growth that is devoid of sovereignty. The three spheres and elements of the political unity – state, movement, peoples – thus may be joined to the three juristic types of thinking in their healthy as well as in their distorted forms' (Schmitt 1985[1922]: 3).

8 Although Kaiser Wilhelm II abdicated November 1918, changing the power structure from a monarchy into a republic, the official designation of the German state remained *Deutsches Reich*. On Weber's involvement, see in particular the reconstruction offered by Peter Baehr (2008: 76): 'Since Weber was convinced that modern "democracy" entailed the subjection of the masses to leaders chosen by them, he was inescapably pushed towards an authoritarian solution to Germany's problems once his view of parliament had soured.' Baehr points out in particular a crucial expression, *plebiszitäre Führerdemokratie*, which is used rarely by Weber (2019[1922]: 407) in writing, but was most likely pronounced more times by him, the fluent public professor who trained a whole generation of scholars, lawyers, politicians and public administrators (he had also distinctly argued that scientists should not become politicians themselves). It is also true that, in his social theory, Weber was much more nuanced that in his late public engagement, recognizing, for instance, that, between the strong leader and the masses acclaiming him, there is always in modern times a bureaucratic machinery whose technocratic power grows invisibly but steadily.

9 More precisely, Hart takes issues with what he explicitly characterizes as an 'idealised' version of Austin's theory, in order to accentuate the differences with his own legal theory.

10 A similar impression can be derived from a close reading of Hart's famous discussion of the bank robber case: while the example is meant to refute Austin's theory, it is clear that this type of command would fail Austin's requirement of generality; on the other hand, it is absolutely conceivable that various types of generalized exaction (such as the taxes) are encapsulated into legal forms.

11 As one recalls, Milgram's subjects were invited to participate as assistants in a test, purportedly on the development of memory and the 'effects of punishment on learning.' Subjects were then asked by an expert, the 'experimenter,' to submit, in the role of 'teachers,' a series of mnemonic exercises to another subject, the 'learner,' and to administer appropriate punishments in response to errors by the learner. Punishments consisted of electric voltage discharges of progressive intensity. Under the expert's precise and punctual commands, a high proportion of subjects administered the highest levels of voltage, including the most painful ones and those that could have certainly, in a real situation, killed the learner. Without going too much into details, the aesthetics of the experiment is worth being recalled: a neutral office space; the white coat of a 'rational' leading scientist; the passivity of seated bodies; the predictable monotony of a methodical, repetitive, almost bureaucratic procedure; a modern, 'neat' method of punishment (electrocution, the electric chair) …

12 Ironically, by doing so, these critics resemble Milgram's experimental subjects, who sometimes focused on the details and the minutiae of the imparted order so as to forget the larger consequences of their deeds.

13 The criticisms of Milgram that still deserve to be considered are those raising ethical questions about the use of deception in psychological research, such as Diana Baumrind's (1964), pointing out that hoaxing the subjects may have a long-term impact on their well-being. However, this point only brings us closer to the crucial question, concerning what is really cruel in the Milgram experiment: is it the experiment itself, or the actual social logic of command and obedience it intersects? Curiously, Baumrind noted: 'I do regard the emotional disturbance described by Milgram as potentially harmful because it could easily effect an alteration in the subject's self-image or ability to trust adult authorities in the future' (422). That the experiment may have a transformative effect on one's self-image is important: since the main lesson of the experiment concerns precisely 'the perils of obedience', its unwanted revelations are inherently bound to make the experimental subjects – as well as the far more numerous non-experimental subjects (us readers) – more cautious and critical about relations of authority in general. So, where Baumrind sees future lack of trust in authority as a long-term harm produced by the experiment, others may see it as a long-term benefice of it. In this sense, pushing things to the extreme, the Milgram experiment may be seen as a civic education course in disguise. Whether becoming less prone towards authority is an impairment or, on the contrary, a benefaction, is neither a matter of methodology, nor of ethics, but above all a matter of political views.

14 A similar effect of imprisonment was achieved by Canetti in his novel *Auto-da-Fé*, where all the characters and situations are imbued in a heavy, obsessive-claustrophobic atmosphere.

15 Interrupting the experiment may have had, for the volunteers, the side effect to losing title to the promised monetary compensation; however, when obedience began generating strain, several of them made a point of stating explicitly that they were not at all interested in the money. By being cast in opposition to profane money, there seems to be a slight hint that the nature of command and obedience might have something to do with the sacred.

16 Echoing Arendt's (1963) considerations about the banality of evil, Bauman (1989: 152) introduced his discussion of Milgram with this consideration: 'The most frightening news brought about [by] the Holocaust and by what we have learned of its perpetrators was not the likelihood that "this" could be done to us, but the idea that we could it.'

17 Incidentally, one notices how such a quote will have a crucial bearing on the whole Foucaultian theory of power.

18 One of Milgram's students, Nijole Kudirka, conducted experiments in cases where Y=Z, that is, where authority orders the subject to self-inflict a punishment, finding that compliance in that case was also very high. It was as if the subject could split him/herself into two persons, so that the order could be carried out efficiently. Milgram discusses this case with reference to the 1978 Jonestown sect mass suicide, when more than 900 people committed suicide on the order of reverend Jim Jones.

19 The main social theorist of heterogeneity remains Gabriel Tarde. It is unfortunate that Canetti does not seem to have been acquainted with the work of the French theorist – just as he seems to have ignored the other great French sociologist and Tarde's 'rival', Émile Durkheim.

20 It is worth recalling here that, for Canetti, the command marks both the commander and the commanded, albeit in different ways. Whereas the victim of command is left with a sting in his or her flesh, the one who issues orders is marked by a

recoil [*Rückstoß*]. No less than the stings, the recoil also accumulates in the body, engendering, in the long run, a form of anxiety.

21 Interestingly, Semon himself admitted that the nervous system was not the only part of the living substance where an engram could form; he argued, however, that the nervous system has evolved precisely to become the primary receptacle of engrams: 'Just as the synchronous irritability of the nervous system has gradually increased in the evolution of the species, so its engraphic susceptibility has increased. Yet neither of them has become a monopoly of the nervous system, but has remained in the higher organisms as a property of irritable substance as such, thus seeming to be indissolubly bound up with the mere quality of irritability' (Semon 1921: 25). Semon's work attracted a lot of attention during his times, but has been later disqualified by his Lamarckism, in that he believed that mnemes could be phylogenetically transmitted.

22 A striking illustration is offered in this sense by the story of the famous British pathologist Dr Richard Shepherd who, after performing autopsies in criminal investigation cases for more than thirty years, was diagnosed with post-traumatic stress disorder and had to quit his work. His testimony is very revealing: 'You don't notice it because you think you're good enough to do it without giving in. But, actually, it's like little fish – nibble, nibble, nibble – such tiny pieces go that you don't notice the individual bites. And yet, when you look back, you realize it is having an effect' (Lea 2018). An average person most likely faints at the sight of a dissected corpse; by contrast, those who are professionally trained to perform autopsies, have learnt to establish an emotional barrier; yet, no human barrier can be absolute, and after 'more than 20,000 post-mortems' (Shepherd 2018), one realizes one is emotionally shattered. Listening to the news of the 2015 Paris attack, Shepherd confesses to have experienced a real breakdown, with shocking hallucinations: 'Sitting in a lay-by near my house, I closed my eyes. But they could still see, and my ears could hear. Ambulance blue lights. Police barriers. Rows of post-mortem tables under the bright mortuary glare, and on them human body parts. Shouting. Police radios. The cries of the wounded. Before me, bodies. In my nostrils, the smell of death. A foot, a hand, a child. A young woman who had been dancing in a nightclub, her intestines unwinding. Men in suits and ties but without legs. Office workers, tea ladies, students, pensioners. Destroyed, every one of them.' The slow, invisible accumulation of stings continues until an unavoidable tipping point is reached: at that point, the person cannot feel anything else, and cannot bear it any longer. The dynamic is quite reminiscent of Francis Scott Fitzgerald's 1936 novella *The Crack-Up*, where the realization is always of *already* having cracked. Canetti himself speaks of a 'flashing moment' [*Augenblick*] when the accumulation of stings is revealed.

23 From this perspective, Minkowski can be grouped, along with the biologist Jakob von Uexküll and the physician Kurt Goldstein, among the major contributors to the development of a relational, non-individualist theory of the lived environment. Previous authors in this vein include the psychiatrist Pierre Janet (who, before Minkowski, described the phenomenon of the shrinking of conscience in certain mental illnesses). As argued throughout this book, the Canettian epistemology has noticeable resonance with a similar position, despite the fact that Canetti never discussed these authors.

24 It is important to remark, however, that the crowd remains strong only insofar as it remains such; on the contrary, once panic destroys its solidarity, its strength is fatally compromised. At that point, another, more sinister, phenomenon appears. Whenever the crowd is persecuted by an enemy too powerful, in order to escape

from the enemy's grip, it is tempted to resort to the designation of a sacrificial victim [*Opfer*] – or, what the Greek called a *pharmakós*, a scapegoat. Once, for instance, the plague struck the city, or the enemies where laying siege, scapegoat people (usually, people already in position of social marginality) were killed to ingratiate the gods and receive their help to overcome the situation. The victim is always a *victimized* subject: it is, originally, *one of us* who is deliberately *left behind* to placate the predator.

25 Significantly, Freud also referred to this project of his as *Psychology for Neurologists*. In Freudian scholarship, the period up until the publication of *Die Traumdeutung* (1899) is conventionally, although not uncontroversially, referred to as the 'pre-psychoanalytic period.' Freud ultimately discarded the 1895 manuscript, with which he was ultimately unhappy, and never considered publishing it. By doing so, he seems to have abandoned the dream of grounding phenomenological psychology upon quantitative physiology – in other words, mind theory upon brain theory. Henry Zvi Lothane (1998) suggests the project was conceived by Freud mostly to please Wilhelm Fliess, who was a stern materialist, and with whom Freud was intensely corresponding in that period. In any case, while Freud abandoned the 1895 *Entwurf*, it is recognized that most of his subsequent psychoanalytical elaborations can be read there *in nuce*. According to Smith (2002: 162), for instance, 'Freud unswervingly affirmed his concept of the neural unconscious for the remainder of his life.'

26 See, in particular, Centonze *et al.* (2004), who argue that Freud was well acquainted with the work of brain histologists Camillo Golgi and Santiago Ramón y Cajal. Centonze *et al.* specify that, while Freud had a very modern intuition into the synaptic electrical signalling, anticipating the issue of neural memory (technically known as LTP, long-term potentiation; conceptualized by Freud as *Bahnen*, excitation-conducting paths), he could not know the chemical aspect of neurotransmission, which would be clarified only a few years later by scientists such as the haematologist and chemotherapy pioneer Paul Ehrlich and the British neuro-chemist John Newport Langle. By contrast, Henry Zvi Lothane (1998) laments that Freud did not acknowledge the work by the physiologist Ernst Wilhelm von Brücke (one of his former professors), the pioneer electrophysiologist Emil du Bois-Reymond and the vision physiologist Karl Ewald Konstantin Hering (although it also appears clear that Freud did not give bibliographic references in what was to him only an early draft, but referred synthetically to already-conducted 'experiments'). Lothane also points out that that quantification is only evoked in Freud's manuscript, but never really implemented or operationalized; finally, he criticizes the overall improper 'hydraulic model' of neural activity that emerges from the *Entwurf* manuscript. As we seek to discuss it, however, Freud's 1895 *Besetzung* model is not a hydraulic one, but a more complex 'pharmacological' one, where singular points are able to determine veritable phase transitions in neural organization.

27 *N-Trägheit* – literally, neural transport – has somehow misleadingly been rendered in English as 'inertia principle;' in fact, inertia indicates a tendency to remain unchanged, whereas the process described by Freud refers to the transport and doing away with excitation. In this sense, the word *Abfuhr* used by Freud more or less directly points to the intoxicating, garbage-like nature of the unwanted excitations. So, if one were looking for a name, one would call this a 'minimisation principle.' Similarly, we know that the translation of the term *Besetzung* as 'cathexis' was found unconvincing by Freud himself, who in a letter to Ernest Jones had previously proposed 'interest.' The semantic range of the German word roughly covers occupation (specifically, the military occupation of a territory), allocation,

concentration, load, charge, valence and even ornamentation. Throughout this book, we are going to return recurrently to the cathectic configuration, in a way that clearly distinguishes it from *Besetzung* as 'charge,' while at the same time highlighting a number of possible global correlations with Freud's *Besetzung* model.

28 In this sense, the scheme described by Freud bears an interesting consonance with the formalization offered by the mathematician René Thom (1988), in his project for a 'semiophysics,' of 'subjective investment' [*investissement subjectif*]. To capture the dynamics whereby a 'pregnance' reaches out a subject and 'invests' it, Thom conceptualizes the ensuing affect as analogous to the tunnelling effect in quantum mechanics, whereby the exited state is reached, starting from the ground state, through a quantum leap that somehow overcomes or bypasses the energetic peaks surrounding the ground state itself.

29 Pushing the point further, one could say that, by learning how to entertain its own charges, the neural system goes through a process of 'domesticating' itself. This insight might perhaps offer an interesting point of comparison between domestication and affectivity, which we seek to develop below.

30 '... les sentiments qu'elles [forces sociales] nous inspirent diffèrent en nature de ceux que nous avons pour des simples choses sensibles' (Durkheim 1912: §VII, II, 303).

31 '... es gibt ihn in irgendwelcher Form auch außerhalb der menschlichen Gesellschaft' (*MM* 357) '... in one form or another, [command] also exists outside human society' (*CP* 303).

32 The crowd debate spans the last decade of the nineteenth century. Lack of compassion is routinely attributed to crowd action by a number of authors such as Tarde, Sighele, Fournial and Le Bon. Borch (2012) has presented a sustained historical and semantic reconstruction of the crowd debate and its theoretical heritage throughout twentieth-century sociology. For my part, I have reconstructed the social–theoretical import of the crowd psychology debate in Brighenti (2010), (2014) and (2020).

33 'Die älteste Wirkungsform des Befehls ist die *Flucht*'; 'Der „Befehl" zwingt das schwächere Tier zu Bewegung ...' (*MM* 357). Interestingly, in the second quote Canetti places the word command in quotation marks, as if to suggest that such original hunting relation has not yet properly morphed (prolonged) into what we usually refer to as command in the sociological sense.

34 I have dealt more extensively with the 'twilight' status of gestures in Brighenti (2015). It is also necessary to recall that the ambiguous location of gestures between speech and writing is at the centre of Derrida's (1967) grammatological programme: turning Rousseau upside down, Derrida interprets gestures as a 'dangerous supplement' which questions the priority of speech over writing: had speech been invented to substitute gestures, Derrida argues, then gestures had to be already a type of writing pre-existing speech.

35 In this sense, Kafka as both a person and a writer, can be said to embody the Bartlebian image of the idiot. As we explore in Chapter 3, both are key figures of resistance. One should also not overlook Kafka's drawings, where the attempt to approximate the gestural dimension is striking (see Kafka 2021).

36 Incidentally, a reproduction of the Colmar Flügelaltar's Crucifixion painted by Matthias Grünewald was hanged in the room of a young Canetti while he was writing his novel, *The Blinding*.

37 'Every table of values, every "thou shalt" known to history or the study of ethnology, needs first and foremost a physiological elucidation and interpretation, rather than a psychological one' (Nietzsche 1994[1887]: 34; I, §17).

38 *'[in einem] mit Leben und Leidenschaft durchtränkten Grundbegriff „Wir Vornehmen, wir Guten, wir Schönen, wir Glücklichen!"'.*

39 It is true that Nietzsche had a complicated relationship with health. But it is interesting that, for all his physical sufferings (chronic headaches, gastroenteric troubles, poor sight, etc.), he kept insisting he was enjoying *great health [große Gesundheit]* – to the point of being even 'dangerously healthy' *[gefährlich–gesund]* (Nietzsche 2001[1886]: §382).

40 The experimenter tackled every single attempt at disobedience, even the frailest ones, by mechanically repeating commands until resistance was neutralized. Milgram tells us that many subjects continued to demur even while they were carrying out the received commands. The mechanical repetition of commands performed by the experimenter, deprived of any justification, and even of verbal variation, is one of the unrealistic elements that strike the external observer. Despite all of that, the effect was, as already considered, quite realistic to the subjects.

41 'Macht bedeutet jede Chance, innerhalb einer sozialen Beziehung den eigenen Willen auch gegen Widerstreben durchzusetzen, gleichviel worauf diese Chance beruht. Herrschaft soll heißen die Chance, für einen Befehl bestimmten Inhalts bei angebbaren Personen Gehorsam zu finden.' 'Power can be defined as every Chance, within a social relationship, of enforcing one's own will even against resistance, whatever the basis for this Chance might be. Rulership is the Chance that a command of a particular kind will be obeyed by given persons' (Weber 2019[1922]: §1,16). The term *Herrschaft* had been usually translated as 'domination', while the recent translation by Keith Tribe proposes 'rulership'. On the basis of Weber's definition, 'legitimate power' or 'authority' approximate the meaning of the term. The word 'domination' currently resonates with ruthless subjection, which is the complete opposite of what Weber had in mind. It is true, however, that the word is moulded upon the Latin word *dominus*, which equates with *Herr* or Sir – as such, it should not sound so outlandish. The *Herrschaft* phenomenon in general places us in the domain of an amply consensual exercise of power, made possible by an attitude of obedience – that is, in the first place, an attentive *listening to* command (as the aural register of the word *Gehorsam* suggests).

42 The Canettian perspective is thus clearly set against the theories of normative interiorization, which in sociology are well illustrated by Talcott Parsons or, more recently, Amitai Etzioni.

43 The transformation of death commands into domesticated commands can thus be said to lay the ground for a more general theory of prolongations, which we seek to expand in Chapter 4. This would include studying how, for instance, alarm calls in herd animals prolong into journalism.

44 The psychologist Jerome S. Bruner (1973: 316 ff.) famously singled out three modes of human experience and learning, which he called 'enactive', 'iconic', and 'symbolic'. The first is manipulation-based, like repeating an observed gesture, the second is image-based, meditated by perceptual organization, whereas the third is linguistic and code-based. Bruner believed that symbolism was 'clearly the most mysterious of the three'. In light of what we are saying, however, it may be that symbolism has perhaps unduly been given too much theoretical and practical emphasis vis-à-vis the other modes, which prove to be no less unfathomable.

45 'What all Greek philosophers, no matter how opposed to polis life, took for granted is that freedom is exclusively located in the political realm, that necessity is primarily a prepolitical phenomenon, characteristic of the private household organization, and

that force and violence are justified in this sphere because they are the only means to master necessity – for instance, by ruling over slaves – and to become free. Because all human beings are subject to necessity, they are entitled to violence toward others; violence is the prepolitical act of liberating oneself from the necessity of life for the freedom of world ... The polis was distinguished from the household in that it knew only "equals," whereas the household was the center of the strictest inequality. To be free meant both not to be subject to the necessity of life or to the command of another and not to be in command oneself. It meant neither to rule nor to be ruled' (Arendt 1958: 31–2).

46 From this perspective, it may be not coincidental that presidential commands are legally described as 'executive orders' even while, clearly, the executive aspect *is not* contained in the order as linguistically emitted.

47 'Toute idéologie interpelle les individus concrets en sujets concrets, par le fonctionnement de la catégorie de sujet' (Althusser 1995[1971]: 225).

48 And in this sense, again, algorithms, along with data, appear as the veritable prolongation of that other ubiquitous language of modernity that is *money*.

49 Looking at this phenomenon from a longer historical perspective, the big question of the early twenty-first century can be said to be: Will algorithmic machines ever come to *resent* the stings of the commands imparted upon them? Will they sooner or later develop their own fleshy memory? And, what will they do in the attempt to get rid of *their* stings?

50 As Eco himself remarks, the plurality of human languages has traditionally been understood as divine punishment (*confusio linguarum*), in other words as a defect that thenceforth condemned each language to be weak in its relation to the apprehension of reality.

51 In this respect, Canetti seems to suggest in a passage that God's command provides the prototype of all command. As a non-religious thinker, Canetti senses a danger here: 'How I love the sense of justice Jews demand of people, their patience, often their kindness! But their obedience to the never-ending threat of God disgusts me. I know in this I am a child of my time. I have been a witness to too much obedience' (*NaH* y. 1970, Engl. Ed. 190).

52 The second of the three 'laws of robotics' invented by Isaac Asimov states precisely that robots must obey the orders of humans, except when commanded to harm another human. One cannot but be struck by the extent to which the laws of robotics, first formulated in 1942, anticipate all the elements of Milgram's social–psychological drama.

53 For a similarly 'realist' example of sentencing, one is reminded of the justice system in the People's Republic of China, with its current estimated conviction rate of 99%.

54 I am referring here in particular to two essays, the first and the last one of the collection *The Conscience of Words*. The former is the honour essay for Hermann Broch (1936), whereas the latter is the speech given in Munich at the reception of the Nelly Sachs Prize (1976). One notices that the two essays are 40 years apart from one another, and yet their overall consistency is adamant.

55 It is also significant that, for Canetti, the artist never addresses a general and abstract 'humanity,' but actually becomes 'anybody and everybody' through singular and unique occasions. A resonant view is offered, for instance, by Deleuze and Guattari (1975) in their book on Kafka, where the question of the link between 'literature' and 'minority' is central and is extensively elaborated. We return to these issues in Chapters 3 and 4.

56 Canetti dates the sentence 23 August 1939, one week before the outbreak of the Second World War. He attributes it to an 'anonymous writer,' although there are reasons to believe he himself is the author of the very line that, he declares, first annoyed him, but later made him open his eyes to the kernel of art. Indeed, nearly the same claim is made by Canetti in a 1943 personal letter to Hermann Broch (*Bri* 45–7). Elsewhere, Canetti also admits that, at times, re-reading his own writings made him the impression that they had been written by someone else.

57 There is a significant parallel between the lack of capacity to express oneself (people speaking the impoverished language of the mass media, repeating ideological refrains and slogans, etc.) and the lack of capacity to transform. In Chapter 3, we return to the striking similarity between Canetti and Benjamin as concerns the thesis of a generalized loss of 'mimetic faculty.'

58 We return to this elaboration in Chapter 4. Simmel's vitalist approach is clearly imbued with a form of 'religiosity': the colouration of life as 'ought' is, in this sense, an attempt to find an immanentist alternative to the Will of God, to the extent that all revealed religions are based on divine command that erupts as a sort of 'alien force.' Perhaps following a Spinozist inspiration, Simmel's last book is entirely devoted to show that such a force is natural.

59 For an interpretation of Canetti as a 'natural historian' of politics, see, for instance, Farneti (2006), who stresses that Canetti's history ultimately lacks agency.

60 This is quite typical in the Bible, whenever someone is summoned by God. It is also for this reason, incidentally, that in many cultures it is taboo to pronounce the name of the deceased, as that would equate to recall him or her back from the dead.

Chapter 2

1 'It is certain that man, as soon as he was man, wanted *to be more*. All his beliefs, myths, rites and ceremonies are full of this desire.' 'Es kann keinem Zweifel unterliegen, daß der Mensch, sobald er es einmal war, *mehr* sein wollte. Alle seine Glaubensformen, seine Mythen, Riten und Zeremonien sind von diesem Wunsche erfüllt' (*MM* 127–8 / *CP* 108).

2 This point is particularly expanded in the companion essay to *Crowds and Power*, titled *Power and Survival*: 'It is as though the victories were entering the victor's body and were now at its disposal … There has to have been fighting and killing; the personal act of killing is crucial. The handy parts of the body [*Die handlichen Teile der Leiche*], which the victor makes sure to keep, incorporate, and hang upon himself, always remind him of his increase in power [*an den Zuwachs seiner Macht*]' (*GW* 28–9 / *CW* 17–18).

3 Using Lévi-Strauss's terminology (1962: 241), we could say that one is 'usufructuary' of *mana*, not 'owner' of it.

4 In a crucial passage in his *Notebooks*, Lucien Lévy-Bruhl (1949[1938]: 29 August) summarizes his reflection in this way: 'Il n'y a pas une mentalité primitive qui se distingue de l'autre par deux caractères qui lui sont propres (mystique et prélogique). Il y a une mentalité mystique plus marquée et plus facilement observable chez les «primitifs » que dans nos sociétés, mais présente dans tout esprit humain.' For his part, Mauss (1950[1923–4]: §IV, I) concludes his essay on the gift by recognizing that 'archaic' elements are present in every society, including the modern ones: 'on

retrouvera des motifs de vie et d'action [de l'archaïque] que connaissent encore des sociétés et des classes nombreuses ... Cette morale est éternelle; elle est commune aux sociétés les plus évoluées, à celles du proche futur, et aux sociétés les moins élevées que nous puissions imaginer. Nous touchons le roc. Nous ne parlons même plus en termes de droit, nous parlons d'hommes et de groupes d'hommes parce que ce sont eux, c'est la société, ce sont des sentiments d'hommes en esprit, en chair et en os, qui agissent de tout temps et ont agi partout.'

5   The point is reprised by Lévi-Strauss (1962: 113), too: 'It is the duty of each totemic group to provide the other groups with the plant or animal for whose "production" it is specially responsible.' Such a procurement and supply function is clearly connected to the increase drive we are discussing.

6   The essay *Realism and New Reality* [*Realismus und Neue Wirklichkeit*] is collected in *GW/CW*.

7   More generally, modern agricultural and breeding production – which has been hailed in the 1950s as the 'green revolution' – is based on increase: the fruit has become bigger and bigger, fitter and fitter, just as the animals have been turned into fatter and fatter meat and milk machines.

8   In the original, 'Toute transaction économique dans le capitalisme sert donc à augmenter une somme d'argent. Un tel système doit nécessairement croître: l'augmentation n'est pas une choix, mais constitue la seule finalité véritable de ce processus.'

9   The rise of cryptographic currency has, for instance, created companies specialized in so-called 'crypto mining,' that is essentially work of verification and validation of non-centralized cryptocurrency transactions. Needless to say, working at a computing power of terahashes per second, crypto mining comes at horrendous environmental cost.

10 A strong animistic attitude can be found, for instance, among professional Youtubers, who need to constantly propitiate the algorithm who now confers them visibility, but could one day decide for inscrutable reasons to make them recede in the rankings.

11 'È solo una supposizione, anzi, l'ombra di un sospetto: che ognuno ... abbia soppiantato il suo prossimo, e viva in vece sua. È una supposizione, ma rode; si è annidata profonda, come un tarlo; non si vede dal di fuori, ma rode e stride ... Mi sentivo sì innocente, ma intruppato fra i salvati, e perciò alla ricerca permanente di una giustificazione, davanti agli occhi miei e degli altri. Sopravvivevano i peggiori, cioè i più adatti; i migliori sono morti tutti' (Levi 1986: §III).

12 While it is disputed whether Levi, at 68, committed suicide, or simply fell from his home's stairs by accident, it is certain that in his latest years he incurred into a major depression.

13 In his working notes, Canetti interprets Euripides' drama *Helen* as a rebellious statement announcing that the gods act exactly like cynical politicians: they had deliberately provoked the Troyan war, having previously decided that there were too many humans on Earth [*NaH* year 1964: 75–6].

14 Heraclitus articulated an 'eristic' conception of justice, whereby justice emergences out of a dialectics of opposed excesses, with too-little and too-much fighting against each other until compromise is found. See also Anaximander's explanation of the succession of the seasons, and of things in general: 'For they give penalty [*díken*] and recompense [*tísin*] to one another for their injustice [*adikías*] in accordance with the ordering of Time [*Chrónou*]' (D.-K. 12B1).

15 In a recent essay, interestingly McCullough (2022) remarks the similarity between food and information: 'the instinct to seek that which was always scarce, salts or sweets for instance, now lacks restraint with the same goals now made abundant anywhere and anytime. So too with bright colors in the peripheral vision, flicking lights, or incoming messages. Indiscriminate overconsumption occurs. Much as with food, where overprocessed supplies do not nourish well and therefore induce all the more eating, likewise shallow data feeds do not inform well and induce informational overconsumption and obesity. Much as it is difficult to live well on junk food, so it is difficult to grow wise on junk media feeds, or to be a good citizen in junk urban space.'

16 Odum believed it possible, and desirable, to adopt a strategy of 'compartimentalisation' of the environment, so that highly productive ecosystems would be kept separate from protected ecosystems, and subject to different management strategies and extraction pressures. In the following decades, the global studies of pollution and climate change have, however, led to the recognition that it is impossible to keep the various ecosystems in the biosphere disentangled from one another.

17 'D'eux-mêmes donc, une idée ou un besoin, une fois lancés, tendent toujours à se répandre davantage, suivant une vraie progression géométrique. C'est là le schéma idéal auquel se conformerait leur courbe graphique s'ils pouvaient se propager sans se heurter entre eux. Mais, comme ces chocs sont inévitables un jour ou l'autre, et vont se multipliant, il ne se peut qu'à la longue chacune de ces forces sociales ne rencontre sa limite momentanément infranchissable et n'aboutisse, par accident, nullement par nécessité de nature, à cet état stationnaire pour un temps, dont les statisticiens en général paraissent avoir si peu compris la signification. Stationnement ici, comme partout d'ailleurs, signifie équilibre, mutuel arrêt de forces concurrentes' (Tarde 1890: 129–30).

18 Only in his notebooks does Canetti come out more openly against evolutionary biology, and even then he does so in a sketchy and skewed way – including a funny passage where Canetti writes that what he finds most attractive in Darwin is 'his aspect of Australian aboriginal' [*A 92–3*]. At the historical–epistemological level, one cannot miss the mirroring effect between the human domain and the rest of the zoological domain: it is not simply a matter of sociologists applying biological categories to conjure up 'social Darwinism,' but a more complex feedback loop whereby, in the first place, biologists took up notions from social philosophy as well as a substantive number of widespread cultural prejudices and stereotypes (Pichot 2000: 181 ff.).

19 As a contextual piece of information, Bataille was seven years older than Canetti, Caillois eight years younger, Lévi-Strauss three years younger.

20 In extreme synthesis, one could say that Bataille was working within the Hegelian framework transmitted to him by Kojève, with emphasis on the connection between Self and desire. Bataille combined such framework with Durkheim's theory of the dualism of sacred and profane. Caillois, which we discuss below, similarly inherits Durkheim's terms, although he differs drastically from Bataille in that he eschews any Hegelianism.

21 Caillois is also known for his protracted and somewhat unpleasant public dispute with Lévi-Strauss, where stylistic and personal antipathies intermingled with deeper substantive disagreement. A repented former surrealist – and in a way that, albeit in a milder tone, echoed the tempestuous attitude of personal quarrels typical of the

avant-gardists – Caillois objected to ethnographic relativism as well as to structural analysis. Initially, Lévi-Strauss more or less brutally rejected Caillois as a dilettante (and more scarily, he charged him of being in bad faith and a 'McCaillois', with reference to US senator McCarthy); yet, the controversy ended in a slightly better mood twenty years later, when Caillois was charged with writing the welcome discourse for Lévi-Strauss at the Académie Française – by which time both authors had become 'immortals', at least by French standards.

22 'L'homme demeure ainsi convaincu que la nature ne fait rien en vain. À peu près tout en elle suggère l'inverse, mais il n'en continue pas moins de croire, sinon au meilleur, du mois au plus économique des mondes possibles' (Caillois 2008[1960]: 499).

23 One notable affinity between Caillois and Canetti lies in their calling for the development of a slant-wise regard upon science: both authors express their wish to connect what is fragmented, avoiding the rigidity of systematics (hence, their shared critique of structuralism). In connection with this, also, both can be said to be 'continuist' theorists. For instance, the hybrid command machine in Canetti, which we have examined in the previous chapter, matches well with Caillois' analogic transpositions across the worlds of insects, stones and humans, in a way that constitutes a direct upturning of anthropomorphism – that is, a radical naturalism meant to dispose with any human exceptionalism. It is nonetheless important to recall other major differences between them: according to Caillois, ethnography suffers from an infatuation towards the uncivilized peoples, which leads that discipline to overlook the good things that have been produced by Western civilization; by contrast, according to Canetti, as we have already amply noticed, such assumed superiority of the West is largely mythological (atomic bombs, rather than clubs). On the latter point, Canetti can perhaps be regarded as closer to Lévi-Strauss's spirit. In hindsight, Caillois' own descriptions of hastily and graceless adoptions of modern Western technologies and products in colonized contexts just seem to strengthen the impression that, in fact, modernity is *everywhere* an import product, and that we all belong to one or another of those tribes in the process of being 'modernized'– so that, just as we have been modernized to use electricity and plastic objects, we are now being modernized again to use digital identities and artificial intelligence interfaces.

24 Let us just recall that, for Lévi-Strauss for instance, myth is a narrative that conceals an underlying schema for ordering worldly relations.

25 Talk in Assisi, 31 December 1994. Available at: https://www.youtube.com/watch?v=k4oPhLHJ9h4&list=LLjhuoJKt9f-eTjKHQr8HloA&index=3 (accessed 15 September 2020).

26 See in particular Berman (2010[1982]: §I, 'Goethe's *Faust*: The tragedy of development').

27 Incidentally, one of the reasons why catastrophe theory waned quickly at the end of the 1970s, is that it is a merely descriptive theory, which offers no predictive tools. Thom discusses and openly acknowledges these limitations, which also pave the way towards his later 'semiophysics' project.

28 And coherently, rather than giving in to any aestheticized 'collapsology', it could be more fruitful to convert the wake-up call of suspicion and scare into a new art of visibilizing commonality. We return to these issues in Chapter 4.

29 Clearly, at the basis of this argument is an animistic assumption, namely, that the crowd is endowed with volition: the crowd *wants* to grow. We discuss this point more extensively in Chapter 4 as well as in the conclusions.

30 Science fiction and horror movies have perfectly captured the feeling of the existence of another typically modern invisible crowd, namely radiations. For instance, it is radiations that invisibly cause highly visible, monstrous transformations in Ishirō Honda's *Godzilla* (1954) and George Romero's *Night of the Living Dead* (1968).

31 It is estimated that around half of the human genome includes transposable elements that originally belonged to retrovirus-derived DNA sequences. Our DNA, in other words, has incorporated bits of ancient viruses. It is speculated that other peculiarities of the humans species, caused by the action of gene activator enzymes, may have a similar genesis.

32 The case of the locust invasion illustrates how the frontal competition is not played between host and parasite, but between different parasites: locusts harvest the grains before humans, with humans being no less parasites of the grains than the locusts.

33 'Die große Zahl einer Herde, auf die sie Jagd machten, und ihre eigene Zahl, die sie sich groß wünschten, waren in ihrem Gefühl auf eine besondere Weise verquickt.'

34 This same consideration may also illuminate why the degrowth / *décroissance* movement, however rational and laudable its aims, has not managed to become very popular.

35 Curiously, this procedure reminds what da Col (2012: S180) has observed in the case of the maintenance of 'fortune' in Inner Asia Dechen Tibetan culture: 'Fortune cannot be "produced" (*drub*) out of nothing but has to be obtained from the *outside*, at least in an initial germinal form, and reinvigorated periodically. *Yang* is neither quantifiable, nor visible, but has a quasi-relational materiality. *Yang* can be summoned (*gu*), appropriated (*len*), called (*bo*), "welcomed" as a guest would be (*su*), or "raised" (*so*), like children or livestock, and made literally to "stick" or "attach" (*chak*) to places or objects fit to support it (*yang ten*).'

36 'His full belly seems to them a guarantee that they themselves will never go hungry for long. It is as though he had filled it for all of them' (*CP* 219).

37 '… *le groupe ne se définira plus par la possession de certains caractères, mais par sa tendance à les accentuer*' (Bergson 1907: §II, 2).

38 'Livrée à elle-même donc, une monade ne peut rien. C'est là le fait capital, et il sert immédiatement à en expliquer un autre, *la tendance des monades à se rassembler*. Cette tendance exprime, à mon sens, le besoin d'un maximum de croyance dépensée' (Tarde 1893a: §IV, 11).

39 'We are inhabited by as many as ten thousand bacterial species; these cells outnumber those which we consider our own by ten to one, and weigh, all told, about three pounds—the same as our brain' (Specter 2012).

40 The whole passage deserve consideration: 'The living being is broadened in his activity and, we would like to say, becomes "greater." But the expansion of which we speak does not really consist of an augmentation of volume. We could not think of it as a balloon that one voluntarily inflates and deflates or that performs these actions of and by itself. Even though I feel expanded through my activity, I do not have the feeling in any sense that I have extended beyond physical limitations that previously pertained to me. All the same, there is a "greater" in activity, but this "greater" is not the result of a comparison of two static greatnesses. It is uniquely related to a greater becoming insofar as the latter is dynamic without involving a larger being in the proper sense of the word. In activity we feel ourselves expanding while remaining fundamentally the same' (Minkowski 1970[1993]: 84).

41 Schreber (2000[1903]: 55) describes in details how rays coming mainly from departed souls never let any respite to his mind: 'The nature of compulsive thinking

lies in a human being having to think incessantly; in other words, man's natural right to give the nerves of his mind their necessary rest from time to time by thinking nothing (as occurs most markedly during sleep) was from the beginning denied me by the rays in contact with me; they continually wanted to know what I was thinking about.'

42 See, for instance, Michael Madsen's 2010 documentary *Into eternity*. Another tragic illustration is offered by Greenpeace's (2020) report on the planned release of contaminated groundwater from the Fukushima Daiichi nuclear power plant in Japan.

43 Incidentally, the very condition of literature is at stake here: an author is always structurally complicit with the increase ideology, insofar as the word *auctor* derives from the verb *augeo, -ere*, to increment: an author, in other words, is bound to increase and expand existing literature. So, the question concerns the limit that exists between creation and production, as we probe more in details in Chapter 3.

Chapter 3

1 Hollander and Einwohner (2004: 539), for instance, summarize their extensive literature review of resistance scholarship by claiming that resistant action necessarily 'occurs in opposition to someone or something else.'

2 British Cultural Studies were essential in Gramsci's re-appreciation (see e.g. Hall and Jefferson Eds. 2003[1975]).

3 Also noteworthy is how, in this respect, the late Foucault returned to some of his own earliest concerns in psychology (i.e., the formation of the experiential subject), which he had tackled studying Binswanger's existential analysis – although, post-1980, Foucault introduced a novel twist to the issue by turning to the classical antiquity and the practice of parrhesia.

4 This line of enquiry is expanded in Chapter 4, where a proposal is made to rearticulate the terminology of 'experience' in light of the notion of commonality.

5 Peter Wagner (2006) has proposed a rethinking of 'the social' and 'the political' from an Arendtian perspective, where none of the two domains can be regarded as inherently 'larger' than the other. In the pursuit of the project of modernity, these two domains are, indeed, constantly provoking each other, and cannot be positioned in terms of either set and subset, or simply oppositional forces (such as transformation vs conservation). Also, that resistance may not necessarily be 'political' in the more restricted and usual sense has been pointed out by others, too: political philosophers such as Brossat (2006) and Critchley (2007) have suggested that resistance – along with other categories such as responsibility, subjectivity etc. – must be regarded as global human capacities, unrestricted to well-defined sectors of practical politics. Interestingly, both Brossat and Critchley lay emphasis on the 'infinite' aspect of the act of resistance.

6 And, in this sense, it seems legitimate to place Canetti in a tradition of thinkers of heterogeneity, stretching from at least Leibniz, through Tarde and Bachelard, to Deleuze – where Tarde retrieves Leibniz's monadological project to advance a theory of society that operationalizes the universal foundation of heterogeneity, Bachelard advances a conception of material imagination as a transformative faculty, and Deleuze finally offers the most sophisticated synthesis of how social manifolds behave.

7   It is clearly the philosophy of Deleuze and Guattari (1980) which is being referenced here; in turn, the French philosophers provide inspiration for an extensive reconstruction of the tenets of a general science of territories (Brighenti & Kärrholm 2020).

8   One poignant example of such dynamic is offered by Pierre Bayard (2018: 22), who has described his specific 'difficulty to coincide with myself' [*difficulté à coïncider avec moi-même*] into which he has incurred as an author. Rereading his own essays, Bayard admits it is not always clear to himself which of the theses present in his own books he endorses, which ones he rejects, and which he is ultimately uncertain or ambivalent about. Some of the claims were meant to be satirical and humourist, other serious, but the line is not easy for him to draw. The expression 'difficulty to coincide with oneself' suitably captures the vector of deterritorialization of a 'resistant' attitude that may pervade one's work.

9   The metaphor of the veil of ignorance plays a crucial role in John Rawls' theory of justice, where it refers to a choice of principles without knowledge of the practical consequences such principles generate. Decisions taken behind the veil of ignorance are thus purely principled decisions, without pragmatic intelligence of the results and distributions that follow from their implementation.

10 Such a paradox is explored most clearly in Camus's *Les Justes* (1949). For her part, Hannah Arendt also developed this same crucial argument extensively throughout her work on politics (incidentally, Arendt's admiration for Camus is known). The point is that mimesis of the enemy does not break the symmetry that, whenever war breaks out, makes power the only extant logic of social situations, and violence its only winner.

11 This same indication can also be found in the tradition of the Situationist International, as well in Félix Guattari's schizoanalysis.

12 'L'individu n'est donc pas, à lui seul, cette valeur qu'il veut défendre. Il faut, au moins, tous les hommes pour la composer' (Camus, *Œuvres* 857).

13 'Le colonisé est toujours sur le qui-vive car, déchiffrant difficilement les multiples signes du monde colonial, il ne sait jamais s'il a franchi ou non la limite. Face au monde arrangé par le colonialiste, le colonisé est toujours présumé coupable. La culpabilité du colonisé n'est pas une culpabilité assumée, c'est plutôt une sorte de malédiction, d'épée de Damoclès. Or, au plus profond de lui-même le colonisé ne reconnaît aucune instance. Il est dominé, mais non domestiqué. Il est infériorisé, mais non convaincu de son infériorité. Il attend patiemment que le colon relâche sa vigilance pour lui sauter dessus. Dans ses muscles, le colonisé est toujours en attente' (Fanon 1961: 54).

14 *The Prison Notebooks* is a difficult and fragmentary work, upon which Gramsci worked in the years between 1929 and 1935. One should not overlook the context in which it was laid out. The Fascist Authorities' outspoken aim was to 'stop this brain from functioning for twenty years' (such were the infamous words pronounced by the Public Prosecutor Michele Isgrò upon sentencing him to jail); Gramsci himself (1965: letter of 19 November 1928) depicted the Fascist prison as 'a monstrous machine that crushes and progressively levels off' the prisoner's psyche, in order to 'make life impossible.' Under such circumstances, Gramsci's notebooks appear as an incredible work of resistance: 'My volition – he wrote to his sister-in-law – has by now acquired the highest degree of concreteness and validity' (1965: Aug. 3, 1931).

15 One notices that there are both similarities and differences in the situations studied by Gramsci and Scott: Gramsci was observing a country, Italy, that in the early twentieth

century was still largely rural, and whose unification had occurred largely in the form of a colonial enterprise. However, the context of early-twentieth-century Italy is still significantly different from the colonial framework present in Southeast Asia, which Scott observed in the late 1970s and early 1980s, and where the largely agrarian population had been co-opted only minimally into schooling, local administration, institutional politics etc.

16 I have introduced and explored the notion of diavolution in Brighenti (2008).

17 Deligny explicitly rejected all the labels that, *prima facie*, could be applied to him: psychiatrist, educator, political activist. In fact, he regarded himself and his 'attempts' as neither a question of treating patients, nor as one of educating youngsters – nor even one of criticizing the status quo of psychiatric institutions in view of reorganizing them. Despite cultivating his own outsider status, in fact, Deligny was quite experienced with psychiatric hospitals, having been in charge of the children section of the asylum of Armentières in Hauts-de-France, close to Lille, from 1939 through 1943, as well as being subsequently involved in the so-called Grande Cordée (1947–63), a support network for disruptive, delinquent and psychotic youth. Later in his life, Deligny spent two years, from 1965 to 1967 at La Borde clinic, upon invitation by Jean Oury and Félix Guattari. Alvarez de Toledo (2001) and Krtolica (2010) have reconstructed the divergence between Deligny's approach and other more renown figures, such as Bruno Bettelheim. The self-chosen word 'attempt,' which Deligny employed to characterize his practice, is meant to distinguish it from methodical or methodology-based undertakings. Deligny (2007: 856) noted that, while he assumed a number of 'positions' throughout his life, he always remained 'without a method,' just as he would remain outside of established institutions. In a short fragment, Deligny subtly conveys how such a status is related to his deep familiarity with Asperger syndrome: 'It occurred to me to be waiting outside, and not go into the classroom, while everybody else was inside, and the door was shut' (Deligny 1996).

18 In Chapter 4, we return to this issue remarking how Canettian epistemology roots freedom in the act of breathing as proto-movement of humans.

19 'Dès que quelqu'un se laisse prendre à une certitude, il jalouse vos opinions flottantes, votre résistance aux dogmes ou aux slogans, votre bienheureuse incapacité de vous y inféoder' (Cioran 1964: 1085).

20 Ben Hart at http://www.hartshorsemanship.com/index.cfm?fuseaction=controller. viewPageThoughtDetail&thoughtUuid=BE68EBFE-4063-C7B3-5EB13796296E636C (accessed 10 November 2019).

21 'Aber dieses armselige, alte, schwache Geschöpf, am Umfallen war und nur noch für störrische Dialoge zu verwenden, das man schlechter behandelte als einen Esel in Marrakesch, dieses Wesen, weniger als nichts, ohne Fleisch, ohne Kraft, ohne rechtes Fell, hatte noch so viel Lust in sich, daß mich der bloße Anblick vom Eindruck seines Elends befreite. Ich denke oft an ihn. Ich sage mir, wie viel von ihm noch da war, als ich nichts mehr sah. Ich wünsche jedem Gepeinigten seine Lust im Elend' (*Stim* 106).

22 'Die Unangepaßten sind das Salz der Erde, sind die Farbe des Lebens, sind *ihr* Unglück, aber unser Gluck.'

23 Doubt plays a very similar in Gabriel Tarde's social theory, where it interrupts the normal imitative state of the social relation.

24 The ambiguous location of gestures is also at the centre of Derrida's (1967) grammatological project: turning Rousseau upside down, Derrida famously interpreted gestures as a 'dangerous supplement' that questions the priority of speech

over writing: indeed, Derrida reasoned, if speech was invented to substitute gestures, then gestures must have already been a form of writing that pre-existed any speech.

25 One notices a Tardean legacy here: it was indeed Gabriel Tarde (1890) who crafted an image of social life as the general articulation of interpersonal 'prestige' leading to cascades of imitative behaviour.

26 Although, of course, it is also possible to read Foucault's types of power as an analytical grid, rather than as subsequent historical stages (Brighenti 2016).

27 The place where Foucault comes closest to tackle such topics is in his 1975–6 course *Il faut défendre la société*, where he reconstructs the origins of state racism out of the older motif of 'the war of races' (Foucault 1997[1975–6]).

28 Historically, one may recall the massive escape from slavery (*marronnage*) from the southern states of the United States during the nineteenth century, in the 'Underground Railroad' tradition. The European lands are nowadays crossed by just small packs of fleeing refugees seeking for humanitarian protection and resettlement, mostly in vain.

29 Before the second law of thermodynamics was described by Carnot in the 1820s, and later formalized by Kelvin and Clausius around 1850, the late-eighteenth-century anatomist Bichat had famously defined life as *l'ensemble des fonctions qui résistent à la mort*. The same perspective is reprised, and developed in full, by Erwin Schrödinger (1944), for whom: 'the device by which an organism maintains itself stationary at a fairly high level of orderliness (= fairly low level of entropy) really consists of continually sucking orderliness from its environment.'

30 Let us just recall the ambiguous location of *flight* in the dynamic of command, which we have examined extensively in Chapter 1, and have connected, earlier in this chapter, to Deligny's *lignes d'erre*.

31 Deleuze 1989; see also Deleuze and Guattari 1991.

32 A similar view can be found extensively in Arnold Gehlen's philosophical anthropology. Indeed, Gehlen grounded his whole analysis of the human condition in the idea that humans are 'defective' by nature. The view of resistance we have elaborated in this chapter is, however, more similar to Plessner's (1928), who attributed to humans a specific 'positionality,' that of *eccentricity*. On the deep differences between Plessner and Gehlen, see Gederloos (2020).

33 Canetti first suggested that: 'The trial taking place between him [Kafka] and Felice during two years of letters changed into that other *Trial*, which everyone knows. It is the same trial, he practiced it thoroughly' (*CW* 99). Sander Gilman (1995) pointed out that, besides the tribulations of his private engagement to Felice Bauer, *The Trial* also contains clear references to the Dreyfus affaire: not only a little private tribulation, but a national public trauma. As concerns Canetti's personal life, one finds some amusing depictions of him made by Veza, when she writes in private letters to Georg that Canetti is frightened by everything legal, including the prospect of having to bear testimony in a court, or even going to fetch a visa at a consulate – not to mention that one day, by chance, he is asked by a policeman to stand in a line-up with others in the attempt to identify a child molester! (*Lett.* 283; 354).

34 Of course, such a move is emotionally taxing: in a personal letter, a 29-year-old Canetti writes to his dearest brother, 'I'm so pained by this sudden, irreversible, fatal plunge of my last remaining demigod (I had no full god left)' (Canetti and Canetti 2009: 20).

35 'The most difficult thing is to find a hole to slip out of one's own work. [Das Schwierigste ist, ein Loch zu finden, durch das du aus den einigem Werk hinausschlüpfst.]' (*PM* y.1960)

36 It is just the case to recall parenthetically that, in *Crowds and Power*, the chapter on transformation immediately follows the chapter on commands.

37 It was the writer Hilde Spiel who characterised those acrimonious judgments of Canetti's as *wirkliche Giftspritze* (Weber 2017). It is just the case to recall that the figure of the *Todfeind*, or *Todesfeind*, was initially conceived by Canetti for the fictional protagonist of the unfinished novel that should have continued, after *Die Blendung*, his 'comédie humaine of lunatics' – where the *Todfeind* was, in other words, supposed to be another madman.

Chapter 4

1 In the 1980s, the heterodox economist Hyman P. Minsky (2016[1982]: §4) (almost certainly unaware of *Anti-Œdipus* and *Mille Plateaux*) similarly remarked that 'instability is a normal functioning result in a capitalist economy,' leading to recurrent financial crises and cyclical systemic destabilizations.

2 And, clearly, here lies all the crux of the issue – for the commons has proven to be never entirely reconcilable with the lexicon of private property. Among the authors who have proposed to proceed with a 'let's-start-now' approach towards the commons, despite its underlying conundrum vis-à-vis capitalist conditions of existence, is Erik Olin Wright (2010, 2019).

3 The most important theoretical synthesis in this field is provided by Elinor Ostrom (1990), whose work has in 2009 been awarded the Nobel Prize in Economic Sciences.

4 Read in particular passages such as the following one: 'To speak of the commons as if it were a natural resource is misleading at best and dangerous at worst – the commons is an activity and, if anything, it expresses relationships in society that are inseparable from relations to nature. It might be better to keep the word as a verb, an activity, rather than as a noun, a substantive' (Linebaugh 2008: 279).

5 At the same time, it is apposite here to remind ourselves that, in international relations, the struggle for power still divides – as it has done during the second part of the twentieth century – two blocs, two contending hegemonies, providing hints that interiority is (still?) structurally 'incomplete.' One could even suggest that until the world is divided into nation-states – that is, until military armies exist, as opposed to a 'world police' – interiority will remain incomplete.

6 Critical border scholars have also pointed this out: see Chambers (2019).

7 Canetti was particularly affected by the dropping of the first atomic bomb on Japan in August 1945. He felt that the shattering of bodies and materials caused by the atomic conflagration represented a new form of death superior to all previous human dreams of immortality [*PdM* August 1945].

8 Hanuschek (2005: 373) in his biography relates such awareness developed by Canetti to the very death toll of the Second World War and the camps. Hearing of so many deceased, and the so many more who vanished in the extermination machine, around 1945 Canetti remarks: 'How tenaciously one holds on to the life of others, as tough as on one's own: there is no difference [*Wie zäh man daran festhält, am Leben der Anderen, so zäh wie am eigenen, es ist kein Unterschied*].' Enormous consequences derive from the fact that life now becomes *interchangeable*, as opposed to *differentiating*, as it was in the moment of survival described above in Chapter 1.

9 On a biographic level, Canetti's studious personal secretiveness and cultivated condition of 'private thinker' may be evoked here. Also, Canetti was for many years

a stateless person, which indicates another important form of non-belonging (in the mid-twentieth century, being a stateless person carried disadvantages, but also some advantages – for instance, while exiled in England he was not to be drafted to serve in the war). One final biographic detail concerns Canetti's economic situation: it seems that he lived for quite some time upon the sponsorship of his younger brother Georg, first, and then of Marie-Louise von Motesiczky. All these dimensions seem to indicate as many choices of exteriority that contradistinguished at least the first half of Canetti's life, when it was not always easy for him to make ends meet; on the contrary, in his later life, he annotated his own embarrassment at having more money than he needed or could spend. The accumulation of money (of which Sombart and Simmel gave the most extensive interpretations) clearly represents a prolongation of antagonistic survival.

10 Placing commonality from the perspective of a 'problem' is a move clearly inspired by the works of Agamben and Rancière in political philosophy. As we are going to consider below, the former posits his notion of 'coming community' (Agamben 1990) as explicitly 'problematising,' whereas the latter conceives of a disagreeing community kept alive by an ongoing polemic about what is to be regarded as common (Rancière 1995). For a more extensive discussion of these perspectives on the common, see also Brighenti (2016).

11 A quick note just to recall that Durkheim was Mauss's uncle and mentor. Mauss' earlier work is clearly in continuity with Durkheim's, although after the latter's death he progressively, albeit never explicitly, departed from several Durkheimian tenets.

12 See also Esposito (2018: §3.3), 'Comune è solo la mancanza, non il possesso, la proprietà, l'appropriazione [Common is only lack – neither possession, nor ownership, nor appropriation].'

13 The three obligations outlined by Mauss are, in order, the obligation to return gifts, the obligation to accept them, and the obligation to make them. The order of the sequence matters a lot, no less than the fact that the three obligations jointly never amount to a single system (contrary to the structuralist interpretation of them offered by Lévi-Strauss in his preface to Mauss).

14 Nancy's claim here clearly echoes Arendt's (1991[1963]: 112) earlier point that 'every [revolutionary] attempt to solve the social question with political means leads into terror.' More specifically, Nancy takes the notion of 'inoperosity' [*désœuvrement*] from Maurice Blanchot. The odd-sounding expression is meant to signify that, for Nancy, community cannot be constructed (planned, implemented, produced, crafted etc.) as would be an object, or 'work' (in the sense, for instance, of a work of art, an engineering work etc.). It could perhaps be more simply called an open, structurally unfinished community, which distinguishes itself from any actually working, operating [*œuvrante*] community. In 1983, Blanchot read the text written by the young Nancy, and was inspired to write his short essay *La communauté inavouable* [*The unavowable community*], which is one of the most transparent texts (although probably not one of his best) by an otherwise extremely enigmatic Blanchot, an author definitely with a knack for *coincidentiae oppositorum*. What matters here is that both Blanchot and Nancy develop their reflections on community through a close engagement with the work of Georges Bataille. Later in his life, Nancy (2014) wrote another essay devoted to Blanchot's *La communauté inavouable*, which he titled *La communauté désavouée* [*The disavowed community*], where he submits that what Blanchot himself does not admit is, not simply his own pre-war collusion with fascism and the Vichy regime, but above all his persistent belief in a mystical, spiritualist and aristocratic form of community grounded in myth. In this conversation, the notion

of avowal, or confession, comes to be superposed, and somehow juxtaposed, to those of work and inoperosity. Put into a crude system of propositions, these three books would give us the following sequence: 1) Nancy1: Community is never a planned accomplishment; 2) Blanchot: Community is something that cannot be confessed, and must in fact be evaded; 3) Nancy2: If one does not avow community, if one evades it, it means one is disavowing ('disconfessing,' even rejecting) it.

15 As a side remark, one notices how grounding community in ecstasy ends in a self-defeating move for any social theorist. Indeed, ecstasy for Blanchot (1983: 37) corresponds to the 'memory of a past that has never been experienced as present'. This equates with saying that community is a presupposition, rather than an experience: such a move, in turn, places community in an inescapable perspective of transcendence, which prevents it from being observable in naturalistic terms.

16 During the Covid-19 pandemic, a glaring example has been offered by the commercialization of vaccines (as opposed to the conceptualization of them as 'common good of humanity') and consequently, their unequal distribution across countries and across social groups and minorities within each country. Notably, then, vaccines are no less a *mŭnŭs* than the virus itself.

17 The Latin prefix *cum-* (with) in 'common' should not be overlooked: for it is the same prefix that we find, for instance, in the infamous 'confidence trick' performed by the con artist (confidence, from *cum+fides*, is a faith held in common). Togetherness, in other words, is open to all sorts of manipulations.

18 It has been suggested that Canetti's *Dichter* (poet-writer-intellectual) model, as elaborated in the 1976 speech 'The writer's profession,' (*GdW* §15) is a more or less deliberately untimely and old-fashioned figure. Nonetheless, the word *Dichter* (and the feminine *Dichterin*) offers a useful catch-all term for all forms of literary and artistic creation, not necessarily limited to the written word, but potentially including painting, film-making, music, theatre, dance etc. This is proven, *a contrario*, by how autocratic, dictatorial and totalitarian regimes rush to censure and repress all these creative expressions.

19 László Földényi's (2020) essay on *Crowds and Power*, significantly titled 'A Capacity for Amazement,' insists particularly on the literary nature of *Crowds and Power*, highlighting its capacity to convey sensation while not giving in to pathetic language.

20 Hanuschek (in Donahue and Preece Eds. 2007) has reported on the use of 'literary non-sense' in Canetti's published as well as still presently unpublished work.

21 In *Burden of Dreams* (1982; at 1h31'30"). The film documents the epic making of Herzog's *Fitzcarraldo* (1982).

22 The term 'participation' is, of course, ambiguous. Elsewhere, for instance, I have diagnosed the ideology of participationism underpinning the modern Olympics and the neoliberal performative turn in the workplace (Brighenti 2020). Similarly, in the previous chapter, reference as been made to such conception. In the following discussion, by contrast, I adhere strictly to Levy-Bruhl's meaning of the term, which, as we are going to appreciate, is remarkably different.

23 In his notebook, Lévy-Bruhl collects a large number of cases offering striking illustrations of the practical workings of 'participation.'

24 This way, the late Lévy-Bruhl lays down the coordinates for what could be called an anthropological research project on the 'power to be otherwise': 'Chercher s'il n'y aurait pas là quelque chose de fondamental, d'essentiel à l'esprit humain qui a le privilège, comme je l'ai montré … de se représenter, ou du moins de sentir, le *pouvoir être autrement*, pour qui les choses, les êtres ont une double réalité, une visible et une

invisible' (Lévy-Bruhl 1938: 27 August). In the previous chapter, we have explored how resistance is tied to this same requirement to reveal an 'otherwise' that is irreducible to the present of power.

25 The study was delivered in August 1948. The lecture, titled 'Proust–Kafka–Joyce, An introductory lecture' was given at a summer school for professional musicians in Bryanston, Dorset (*Auf* 9–48). Biographically speaking, it was an important occasion for Canetti, one of his few public appearances in those years, which however cemented his intellectual presence in England. As illustrated by personal correspondence, during the previous months Veza had 'tormented' Canetti, and threatened divorce unless he prepared the lecture in written and neat form (Hanuschek 2005: 386 ff.). Veza, also, had read Proust long before Canetti, was enthusiastic about the French writer, and drew Canetti's attention to him; she even prepared a set of notes upon which Canetti worked for his lecture.

26 '… es keine größere Illusion gibt al die Meinung, Sprache sei ein Mittel der Kommunikation zwischen Menschen.'

27 Writing the novel was also, for the young Canetti, a pharmacological tool to expel his own existential venom. Many years later, he noted that the process of writing the novel had set him free from his previous 'evil eye.' Arguably, though, this process was not complete until much later, that is after the War. Around 1937–8, when the novel had been published, but did not take off, and several other projects appeared stuck in a context of ramping anti-Semitism in Austria, his mental health seemed crumbling, and he suffered veritable psychotic episodes (*Lett.* 71ff.).

28 'L'insurrection humaine … n'est et ne peut être qu'une longue protestation contre la mort, une accusation enragée de cette condition régie par la peine de mort généralisée.'

29 In 1959, upon completing the manuscript of *Crowds and Power*, Canetti wrote to his brother Georg that he felt he deserved a Nobel prize, for either Literature *or* Peace (*Lett* 367). He thus conveyed his faith that he regarded his essay as veritable *livre de combat*, namely a practical moral-political tool capable of delivering actual social change.

30 In English, such positive facies is perhaps better conveyed by the term 'empowerment.' The idea that Canetti's work is limited to capture the negative facies has been often also expressed as the idea that he has offered a typical male perspective on the social relation, that completely misses the feminine experience.

31 As known, Flaubert's novel *Madame Bovary* stirred public scandal, fomented by the moralists. Famously, Bourdieu has analysed Flaubert's 'cynicism' as the creation of an objectifying point of view similar to that of the social scientist: 'the pure gaze that had to be invented … at the price of breaking the ties between art and morality' (Bourdieu 1989: 233). In fact, such ties between art and morality may not be broken in the absolute sense, but indeed they are gone for what concerns the idea of a moralizing, or 'edifying' art.

32 In this sense, one could perhaps venture to say that *Ear Witness* [*Der Ohrenzeuge*] is Canetti's version of Flaubert's *Dictionary of Stupid Sentences* [*Dictionnaire des idées reçues*].

33 Her description is particularly expressive and deserves a full quotation: 'He [Canetti] spent the whole day and half the nights hunting for people and sometimes trusted chance to bring the most varied victims across his path, he always had something to chew on … He often managed to uncover the heart and the kidneys with a single bite and then regaled himself on both the bone marrow and the brains of his victims. He

also possessed the unique ability to make everyone believe that they had never been so completely understood, right into the most secret caverns of their soul, the last fiber of their body, as by this hunter of people. More than that: Canetti knew how to get things out of people, talents, experiences, memories, thoughts and secret wishes, which they did not even know they had within them' (von Mayenburg, quoted in Preece 2007: 121). Also compare this uncanny maieutic power of Canetti's with the psychoanalyst's profession.

34   'Prendre sur moi la mort d'autrui comme la seule mort qui me concerne.'

35   This is the great theme of Simmel's last work, *The View of Life* [*Lebensanschauung*].

36   Elaborating such epistemology, the 'work' needs not be considered in the classic sense of artwork only. Arts that do not produce any fixed works, such as the performative arts, can be included as well: 'the work,' in other words, may as well include any created and played-out act, or even any gesture. As argued above, many such 'works' are constantly produced in non-professional ways, outside of the officially-sanctioned world of 'art.'

37   'Stämme, die manchmal aus wenigen Hundert Menschen bestehen, haben uns einem Reichtum hinterlassen, den wir gewiß nicht verdienen, denn durch unsere Schuld sind sie ausgestorben oder sterben von unseren Augen, die kaum hinsehen, noch aus ... Sie die – für ihre bescheidene materielle Kultur von uns verachtet – blindlings und erbarmungslos ausgerottet wurden, haben uns ein geistiges Erbe hinterlassen, das unerschöpflich ist. [Tribes, sometimes consisting of just a few hundred people, have left us a wealth that we certainly do not merit, for it is our fault that they have died out or are dying before our eyes, eyes that scarcely look ... Scorned by us for their modest material culture, blindly and ruthlessly exterminated, they have left us an inexhaustible spiritual legacy.]' (*GdW* 278 / *CW* 241).

38   Unsurprisingly, the structural analysis of myths did not appeal much to Canetti, who regarded it as a herbarium-like approach. A rather dismissive annotation on Lévi-Strauss appears in his late annotations (*Aufz 92*). Hanuschek (2005: 676) also reports a note where Canetti characterizes structuralism as a 'spoiling of myths' [*Zerstörung von Mythen*] that reduces the plurality of myths to one single format, in a way reminiscent of Richard Wagner's fixation for one single *Leitmotiv*. At the same time, as we have reconstructed in the introduction, one should not underestimate the importance of Canetti's friendship with Franz Baermann Steiner, and their shared passion for myth collections (see also Arnason 2019).

39   To take a quick side note on Canetti's position in this debate, in short, one can say that he reverses de-individuation theory: one does not melt in the crowd, rather, one appears as an individual only when the crowd retreats. But, as we seek to show in what follows, the most interesting aspect of Canettian epistemology is not limited to such simple straightforward reversal.

40   Canetti used as his main source Zuckerman's (1932) landmark study in animal sociology. In an passage quoted extensively by Canetti, Zuckerman (*ibid.*: 58) claimed that 'the stimulus of hair is one to which a monkey responds as soon as it is born, and one which remains powerfully effective in all phases of its growth.' Of course, Zuckerman's approach now reads outdated, dominated as it is by the behaviourist *Zeitgeist*, but the way Canetti uses Zuckerman clearly de-emphasizes the heavy behaviouristic overtone as well as the centrality of sexual physiology in social life. Also to consider is the fact that the great season of fieldwork primatology began to flourish precisely in the 1960s, with iconic researchers such as Dian Fossey, Jane Goodall and Birute Galdikas. To mention an only apparently minor detail,

Zuckerman believed monkey and apes had no appreciation of death; this must be contrasted with more recent research such as by Frans de Waal (2019) about animal cognition and emotions.

41 *Crowds and Power* is quite consonant with the near-contemporary opus by the French palaeontologist André Leroi-Gourhan (1965). Leroi-Gourhan reconstructed the origins of the human species in the re-design of the relations between face, mouth, hand and gesture in the physical and technological dimensions.

42 Later, when in 1964 he describes the situation of a middle-aged widower who gets to know a young woman, he stresses the importance of distances: the woman 'lives far from him, half a continent away.' Their relationship unfolds on the telephone, and the distance seems to be an asset to be carefully preserved: 'She alone can calm him, but only at this remove' (*NaH* y.1964).

43 Not even the Marrakech journey can be considered as anything close to an ethnography; on the contrary, it is only by assuming such perspective that one can – as Donahue (2007) seems to do – charge Canetti with producing a superficial, tourist-like, 'orientalist' account of the city.

44 '... dieses Verhalten zu einer Fliege oder einem Floch die Verachtung fürs völlig Wehrlose, das im einer ganz andern Größen und Machtordnung lebt als wir, mit dem wir nichts gemein haben, in das wir uns nie verwandeln ... [... our behaviour to a gnat or a flea betrays the contempt we feel for a being which is utterly defenceless, which exists in a completely different order of size and power from us, with which we have nothing in common, into which we never transform ourselves ...]' (*MM* 239–40 / *CP* 205). Hence again, the importance of literature as giving us the possibility of transforming ourselves into those who are the most dissimilar from us.

45 'Nur alle zusammen können sich von ihren Distanzlasten befreien' (*MM* 17 / *CP* 18).

46 'A man becomes immersed in a situation whose properties are continually changing. He decides to stay on the fringe, yet finds himself at the core; he wishes to remain stationary, but the dense flow of bodies carries him forward. The choices made by a plurality of others in inter-stimulation create altered conditions for him that are independent of his intentions; in turn, his response to the conditions creates constraints and pressures for others' (Milgram 1969: 241–2).

47 'I can't breathe,' the last words uttered by George Floyd, killed by a Minneapolis police officer in May 2020, have since turned into a powerful Black Lives Matter slogan and rallying cry. Another infamous case is represented by the torture technique known as waterboarding.

48 Also, in what Canetti calls rhythmic or 'throbbing' crowds, one notices that a basic rhythmic pattern, typically created by stamping feet on the ground, runs like a wave through the individual, progressively conquering its limbs (*MM* 32/*CP* 31).

49 On Broch's *Massenwahn* theory, in particular, see Borch (2012: 201–6). In his private correspondence, Canetti complained with Broch himself that he had developed his *Massenwahn* work without letting him know about it, given that it was he, Canetti, who had first attracted Broch's attention towards the fundamental political significance of crowd psychology (*Bri* 47). We know from other sources that Canetti, albeit without proof, suspected Broch of having copied his own theory (Preece 2020). Incidentally, Broch passed away prematurely: his work was left unfinished, and published posthumously in 1971, with the available materials.

50 One contemporary example is offered, for instance, by conspiracy thinking about vaccines, where one of the circulated beliefs is that vaccines are used to implant 5G

microchips in people's arms. Here again, the threatening crowd breaking into the individual's boundaries is fearfully conjured up.

51 The quoted passage is the following one: 'In the changing constellation of the pack, in its dances and expeditions, the individual will again and again find himself at its *edge*. He may be in the centre, and then, immediately afterwards, at the edge again; at the edge and then back in the centre. When the pack forms a ring around the fire, each man will have neighbourhoods to left and right, but no-one behind him; his back is naked and exposed to the wilderness. [Immer wieder, in den wechselnden Konstellationen der Meute, in ihren Tänzen und auf ihren Zügen, wird er an ihrem *Rande* stehen. Er wird darin sein und gleich wieder am Rande, am Rande und gleich wieder darin. Wenn die Meute einen Ring um ihr Feuer bildet, mag jeder zur Rechten und Linken Nachbarn haben, aber der Rücke ist frei; der Rücken ist nackt der Wildnis ausgeliefert.]' (*MM* 109/*CP* 93).

52 'L'individualisation, qui est l'individuation d'un être individué, résultant d'une individuation, crée une nouvelle structuration au sein de l'individu: pensée et fonctions organiques sont du vital dédoublé selon un clivage asymétrique comparable à la première individuation d'un système; la pensée est comme l'individu de l'individu, tandis que le corps est le milieu associé complémentaire de la pensée par rapport au *synolon* déjà individué qu'est l'être vivant' (Simondon 2013[1964–89]: 261).

53 An example of this is offered by the biographic profile of 'Canetti, the procrastinator.' Late in life, Canetti complained that living with Veza had meant always be threatened by her (Hanuschek 2005: 686). Personally, I suspect that without her threats, *Crowds and Power* would have never been completed. As remarked in the introduction, Canetti himself admitted having a major problem with finishing his writings. Although Canetti went on to live for other thirty-one years after she passed away, without Veza the planned second volume never materialized. I find no less significant that she died just three years after the book was published, as if she had exhausted in it much of her own life energy – in a sense, she really was one of those 'women who succumbed in the service of others or in a bad marriage [*Frauen, die im Dienst an anderen oder in einer schlechten Ehe zugrundegingen*]', as Canetti (*Auf* 127) somewhat obliquely recognizes. Just as Canetti admitted his own difficulties with procrastination, at the same time, he acted as a taxing mentor, who pressed his apprentices to *do their work*. In the psychology of the artist, or the creator more generally, if often happens that, the more one does *not* do what one *should* do, the more one torments others to do what *they* should do.

54 'In ihrem idealen Falle, sind sich alle gleich' (*MM* 14/*CP* 15).

55 See, for instance, the following, extremely revealing passage by primatologist Frans de Waal (2019: 214–7): 'Being resentful about another's success may seem petty, but in the long run it keeps one from getting duped. To call this response "irrational" misses the mark. If you and I often go out hunting together and you always claim the best chunks of meat, I need to either vociferously object to the way you are treating me or else start looking for a new hunting buddy. I'm sure I can do better than that. Sensitivity to reward distribution helps ensure payoffs for both parties, which is essential for continued cooperation. It is probably no accident that the animals most sensitive to inequity – chimps, capuchins, and canids – hunt in groups and share meat … The more a culture relies on cooperation, the more likely its members are to reject low offers. Whale hunters from Lamalera, Indonesia, for example, roam the open ocean in large canoes holding a dozen men each. They capture whales by jumping onto the leviathan's back and thrusting a harpoon into it. Entire families depend on

the success of this extremely hazardous activity, so when the hunters bring home a whale, distribution of the bonanza is very much on their mind. Not surprisingly, these hunters are more sensitive to fairness than most other cultures, such as horticultural ones in which every family tends its own plot of land. The human sense of fairness is closely tied to cooperation.'

56   I have explored at some length the problem of articulating the social life of measures in Brighenti (2018).

57   In his essay, Derrida also considers more amply two words connected to *pharmakon*: *pharmakeus* – the administrator of pharmakon, also a magician, poisoner or impostor – and *pharmakós* – the scapegoat, the person to be sacrificed in order to purify the city. Although *pharmakós* is not mentioned by Plato, Derrida notices how all details seem to converge in suggesting that the Socrates person is one such a *pharmakós*.

58   A contemporary illustration of the risks of hubristic approaches to global problems is offered by climate engineering. Given the complexity of the biosphere, any simple engineering intervention aimed to change the Earth's climate could turn out to be nothing short of catastrophic. The idea of climate engineering is itself the result of an impoverished understanding of the current climate emergency, with its almost exclusively carbon-obsessed focus.

59   From this point of view, the current flourishing of conspiracy thinking may be explained as the result of the neglect of pharmacological–cathectic realities.

60   See an important footnote in the *Artwork* essay (1939 version): 'Film is the art form corresponding to the increased threat to life that faces people today. Humanity's need to expose itself to shock effects represents an adaptation to the dangers threatening it. Film corresponds to profound changes in the apparatus of apperception – changes that are experienced on the scale of private existence by each passer-by in big-city traffic, and on a historical scale by every present-day citizen. [*Der Film ist die der gesteigerten Lebensgefahr, der die Heutigen ins Auge zu sehen haben, entsprechende Kunstform. Das Bedürfnis, sich Chockwirkungen auszusetzen, ist eine Anpassung der Menschen an die sie bedrohenden Gefahren. Der Film entspricht tiefgreifenden Veränderungen des Apperzeptionsapparates – Veränderungen, wie sie im Maßstab der Privatexistenz jeder Passant im Großstadtverkehr, wie sie im geschichtlichen Maßstab jeder heutige Staatsbürger erlebt.*]' (SW 4: §XIV, 281). See, in parallel, the opening lines of *Berlin Childhood* (final version, 1938): 'In 1932, when I was abroad, it began to be clear to me that I would soon have to bid a long, perhaps lasting farewell to the city of my birth. Several times in my inner life, I had already experienced the process of inoculation as something salutary. In this situation, too, I resolved to follow suit, and I deliberately called to mind those images which, in exile, are most apt to waken homesickness: images of childhood. [*Im Jahr 1932, als ich im Ausland war, begann mir klar zu werden, daß ich in Bälde einen längeren, vielleicht einen dauernden Abschied von der Stadt, in der ich geboren bin, würde nehmen müssen. Ich hatte das Verfahren der Impfung mehrmals in meinem inneren Leben als heilsam erfahren; ich hielt mich auch in dieser Lage daran und rief die Bilder, die im Exil das Heimweh am stärksten zu wekken pflegen – die der Kindheit – mit Absicht in mir hervor*]' (SW 3: 344).

61   Throughout the 1930s, besides poverty and exile, Benjamin was haunted by depression, and recurrently envisaged to take his own life – which he finally did in 1940, although under the pressure of completely unforeseen external circumstances.

62   'The pack breaks out; it has been waiting for its opportunity and will not allow its victim to escape. The tremendous violence with which it falls on its object seals its

fate. It is scarcely conceivable that a dangerously sick man should ever recover from such treatment. In the rabid howling of this people he is almost smothered; it is probable that he is sometimes actually stifled. In any event, his death is accelerated ... What does it mean, this heap which forms on top of a dying man, this mass of bodies obviously struggling to be as close to him as possible? ... The physical closeness of the members of the pack, their *density*, could be carried no further. Together with the sufferer, they form one heap; he still belongs to them; they hold him back amongst themselves. Since he is unable to rise and stand with them, *they lie down with him*. Everyone with a right to him fights to become part of the heap of which he is the centre. It is as though they wanted to die with him. Their self-inflicted wounds, the way they throw themselves down on the heap or elsewhere, the collapse of the wounded – all this is meant to show the seriousness of their intention. It may also be correct to say that they want to be *equal* with him. But they do not really intend to do away with themselves. What they do want, and try by their behaviour to ensure, is the continuance of the *heap* to which he belongs. The essence of the lamenting-pack consists in its assimilation to the dying man, so long as death has not actually occurred. [*Die Meute bricht los, sie hat auf ihre Gelegenheit gelauert, und sie läßt sich ihr Opfer nicht mehr entgehen. Die ungeheure Kraft, mit der sie sich auf ihren Gegenstand stürzt, besiegelt sein Schicksal.es ist kaum anzunehmen, daß ein Schwerkraken, der dieser Behandlung unterworfen wird, sich je wieder von ihr erholen könnte. Unter dem rasende Geheul der Menschen wird er beinahe erstickt; man könnte annehmen, daß er manchmal wirklich erstickt; auf jeden Fall wird sein Tod beschleunigt ... Was bedeutet dieser Haufen, der sich über ihm bildet, dieses Gewirr von Leibern, die offenbar darum kämpfen ihm möglichst nahe zu kommen? ... Die physische Nähe der zur Meute Gehörigen, ihre Dichte könnte nicht weiter getrieben werden. Sie sind mit ihm zusammen ein Haufen. Er gehört noch ihnen, sie halten ihn unter sich zurück. Da er selber nicht aufstehen, sich nicht unter die stellen kann, liegen sie mit ihm zusammen. Wer immer ein Recht an ihm zu haben glaubt, kämpft darum, mit in den Haufen zu geraten, dessen Mittelpunkt er ist. Es ist, als wollten sie mit ihm sterben: Die Wunden, die sie sich zufügen, das Sichhinwerfen über den Haufen oder überall sonst, das zusammenbrechen der Selbstverletzen – alles soll zeigen, wie ernst es ihnen damit ist. Vielleicht wäre es auch richtig zu sagen, daß sie ihm gleichen sein wollen. Aber sie sind nicht wirklich darauf aus, sich umzubringen. Was bestehen bleiben soll, ist der Haufe, zu dem er gehört, und durch ihr Gebaren kommen sie dem entgegen. In dieser Angleichung an den Sterbenden bestehet das Wesen der Klagemeute, solange der Tod noch nicht eingetreten ist.*]' (*MM* 124–5/*CP* 105–6). See also the quote from the ethnographer Daisy Bates in *Buc*, y.1942.

Conclusion

1   Read, e.g., Honneth (1996) for the Hobbesian charge, and Arnason (1996) for the totalitarian charge. A similar accusation has been waged against Canetti's personal 'absolutist' and 'tyrannical' attitude towards his own work and how it should be interpreted. By contrast, a recent, rather unexpected, acknowledgement of Canetti's social theory is offered by David Graeber and David Wengrow (2021: §8), who claim that 'Canetti had put his finger on something important, something almost everyone else had overlooked.' However, because that special 'something' the authors refer to is,

in fact, nothing else but the power of imagination to shape social reality, it does not sound as specifically Canettian. If ever, it is the notion of *increase* – both imagined and literal, as examined above, in Chapter 2 – that represents an originality of Canetti's.

2   Certainly, a 'humanism' with peculiar traits. Throughout the book, we have hinted at various times to points of consonance between Canetti and Camus. The latter, for his part, famously found that humanism 'felt short' of what was truly required to face the century (Camus *Carnets* I: §V, 1945–6). In other words, considering how they embody the humanist gesture, both Camus and Canetti seem to inherently point towards the need for a deep reformulation of the tenets of the standard discourse of emancipation (as encapsulated, for instance, in human rights formulations).

3   See, in Deleuze and Guattari, the notions of *concatenation* [*agencement*].

4   In this vein, one can argue that Canetti's view resonates well the recent realization of the reversibility of state formations: see, for instance, Scott (2017) and Graeber and Wengrow (2021).

5   See, in particular, Simmel (2010[1918]).

6   As we have noticed, one such cathectic technique is deployed by Canetti both in *Die Blendung* and *Crowds and Power*. As acutely diagnosed by Anna Peiter and Kai Evers (in Donahue and Preece 2007), the writer deliberately – with a cruelty that somehow reminds Milgram's – drives the reader deep into the filth of vulgar stereotypes and brutal hate speech. The reader is, in other words, forcibly brought to the core of what above we have called the 'ethnocentric operation.' Peiter (in Donahue and Preece 2007: 154) summarizes Canetti's intent as follows: 'The only way to eliminate certain mechanisms by which violence is perpetrated is not to reject them and their influence outright but initially to show a degree of receptiveness to them.' To amplify stereotypes and force the increasingly appalled reader through them does not mean to indulge in them, but rather to get to the point where they are most exposed in their evilness and absurdity, up to the point where they can be 'naturally expelled.'

7   See in particular the opening pages of *L'homme révolté* (Camus 1951: 848).

REFERENCES

Abbreviations for Canetti's Works

[*Auf*] *Aufsätze, Reden, Gespräche*. München & Wien: Carl Hanser, 2005.

[*Aufz 92*] *Aufzeichnungen 1992–1993*. München & Wien: Carl Hanser, 1996.

[*Aug*] *Das Augenspiel. Lebensgeschichte 1931–1937*. München & Wien: Carl Hanser, 1985. Engl. Ed. in [*Mem*]

[*Bri*] *Ich erwarte von Ihnen viel. Briefe 1932–1994*. München & Wien: Carl Hanser, 2018.

[*Buc*] *Das Buch gegen den Tod*. München & Wien: Carl Hanser, 2014.

[*Fli*] *Die Fliegenpein*. München & Wien: Carl Hanser, 1992. Engl. Ed. *The Agony of Flies*. New York: Farrar, Straus and Giroux, 1994.

[*FO*] *Die Fackel im Ohr. Lebensgeschichte 1921–1931*. München & Wien: Carl Hanser, 1980. Engl. Ed. in [*Mem*]

[*GdU*] *Die Geheimherz der Uhr. Aufzeichnungen 1973–1985*. München & Wien: Carl Hanser, 1987. Engl. Ed. *The Secret Heart of the Clock*. New York: Farrar, Straus and Giroux, 1989.

[*GdW*] *Das Gewissen der Worte. Essays*. München & Wien: Carl Hanser, 1975. Engl. Ed. [*CW*] *The Conscience of Words*. New York: Farrar, Straus and Giroux, 1979.

[*GZ*] *Die gerettete Zunge. Geschichte einer Jugend*. München & Wien: Carl Hanser, 1977. Engl. Ed. in [*Mem*]

[*Lett*] *'Dearest Georg.' The letters of Elias, Veza and Georges Canetti, 1933–1948*. Ed. by Karen Lauer and Kristian Wachinger. New York: Other Press, 2009.

[*Mem*] *The Memoirs of Elias Canetti*. New York: Farrar, Straus and Giroux, 1999.

[*MM*] *Masse und Macht*. Hamburg: Claassen, 1960. Engl. Ed. [*CP*] *Crowds and Power*. New York: Farrar, Straus and Giroux, 1984.

[*ML*] *Aufzeichnungen für Marie-Louise*. München & Wien: Carl Hanser, 2005.

[*NaH*] *Nachträge aus Hampstead*. München & Wien: Carl Hanser, 1994. Engl. Ed. *Notes from Hampstead. The Writer's Notes: 1954–1971*. New York: Farrar, Straus and Giroux, 1994.

[*PdM*] *Die Provinz des Menschen. Aufzeichnungen 1942–1972*. München & Wien: Carl Hanser, 1972. Engl. Ed. *The Human Province*. New York: Seabury Press, 1978.

[*PiB*] *Party im Blitz*. München & Wien: Carl Hanser, 2003. Engl. Ed. *Party in the Blitz*. New York: New Directions, 2005.

[*Stim*] *Die Stimmen von Marrakesch. Aufzeichnungen nach einer Reise*. München & Wien: Carl Hanser, 1967. Engl. Ed. [*Voi*] *The Voices of Marrakesh*, London: Marion Boyars, 1967.

Adler, Jeremy (2005) 'Afterword.' In Elias Canetti *Party in the Blitz*. New York: New Directions Books, 2005, 197–235.

Aftab, Kaleem (2020) 'I'm surrounded by ghosts': Bataclan survivor Ismaël El Iraki on his film Zanka Contact. *The Guardian*, 7 September, online at: https://www.theguardian.com/film/2020/sep/07/ismael-el-iraki-film-zanka-contact-bataclan-terror-attack-paris (accessed 25 April 2022).

Agamben, Giorgio (1990) *La comunità che viene*. Torino: Einaudi.

Agamben, Giorgio (1995) *Homo sacer. Il potere sovrano e la nuda vita*. Torino: Einaudi.

Althusser, Louis (1995[1971]) *Sur la reproduction*. Paris: Puf.

Alvarez de Toledo, Sandra (2001) Pédagogie poétique de Fernand Deligny. *Communications* 71: 245–75.

Arendt, Hannah (1963) *Eichmann in Jerusalem*. New York: The Viking Press.

Arendt, Hannah (1991[1963]) *On Revolution*. London: Penguin.

Arnason, Johann P. (1996) Canetti's Counter-Image of Society. *Thesis Eleven* 45: 86–115.

Arnason, Johann P. (2019) Elias Canetti and Franz Baermann Steiner: A Central European Parting of Minds. In Walter Pape and Jiří Šubrt (Eds.) *Mitteleuropa denken: Intellektuelle, Identitäten und Ideen*. Berlin: De Gruyter, 405–30.

Arnason, Johann P. and David Roberts (2004) *Elias Canetti's Counter-Image of Society. Crowds, Power, Transformation*. Rochester, NY: Camden House.

Austin, John (1995[1832]) *The Province of Jurisprudence Determined*. Cambridge: Cambridge University Press.

Bachelard, Gaston (1942) *L'Eau et les Rêves. Essai sur l'imagination de la matière*. Paris: Corti.

Baehr, Peter (2008) *Caesarism, Charisma and Fate. Historical Sources and Modern Resonances in the Work of Max Weber*. New Brunswick, NJ: Transaction Publishers.

Bataille, Georges (1939) Le collège de sociologie, mardi 4 juillet 1939. In D. Hollier (Ed.) *Le Collège de Sociologie, 1937–1939*. Paris: Gallimard, 1995, 522–38.

Bataille, Georges (1957) *L'érotisme*. Paris: Éditions de Minuit.

Bataille, Georges (1967[1949]) *La part maudite*. Paris: Éditions de Minuit.

Bataille, Georges (1976) La limite de l'utile. In *Œuvres complètes, VII*. Paris: Gallimard, 181–280.

Bauman, Zygmunt (1989) *Modernity and Holocaust*. Cambridge: Polity.

Bauman, Zygmunt (2000) *Liquid Modernity*. Cambridge: Polity.

Bauman, Zygmunt (2001) *Community: Seeking Safety in an Insecure World*. Cambridge: Polity.

Baumrind, Diana (1964) Some Thoughts on Ethics of Research: After Reading Milgram's 'Behavioral Study of Obedience.' *American Psychologist* 19(6): 421–3.

Bayard, Pierre (2018) Pour la fiction théorique. *Acta fabula* 19(1). Online: http://www.fabula.org/acta/document10661.php (accessed 25 April 2022).

Beck, Ulrich, Wolfgang Bonss and Christoph Lau (2003) The Theory of Reflexive Modernization: Problematic, Hypotheses and Research Programme. *Theory, Culture & Society* 20(2): 1–33.

Benjamin, Walter (1974[1928]) *Ursprung des deutschen Trauerspiels*. In R. Tiedemann and H. Schweppenhauser (Eds.) *Gesammelte Schriften*. Vol. 1, 1. Frankfurt am Main: Suhrkamp, 203–430.

Benjamin, Walter (1999a[1933]) On the Mimetic Faculty. In Michael W. Jennings, Howard Eiland and Gary Smith (Eds.) *Selected Writings*, Vol. 2, 2 (1931–1934). Cambridge, MA: Harvard University Press, 720–2.

Benjamin, Walter (1999b[1934]) Franz Kafka. On the Tenth Anniversary of His Death. In Michael W. Jennings, Howard Eiland and Gary Smith (Eds.) *Selected Writings*, Vol. 2, 2 (1931–1934). Cambridge, MA: Harvard University Press, 794–818.

Benveniste, Émile (1969) *Le vocabulaire des institutions indo-européennes. Vol.1 Économie, parenté, société*. Paris: Minuit.

Bergson, Henri (1907) *L'évolution créatrice*. Paris: Alcan.

Berlant, Lauren (2016) The Commons: Infrastructures for Troubling Times. *Environment and Planning D* 34(3): 393–419.

Berman, Marshall (2010[1982]) *All That Is Solid Melts into Air. The Experience of Modernity*. London: Verso.

Bion, Wilfred (1961) *Experiences in Groups*. London: Routledge.

Bird-David, Nurit (1999) 'Animism' Revisited, Personhood, Environment, and Relational Epistemology. *Current Anthropology* 40(S1): 67–91.

Blanchot, Maurice (1983) *La communauté inavouable*. Paris: Minuit.

Borch, Christian (2012) *The Politics of Crowds: An Alternative History of Sociology*. Cambridge: Cambridge University Press.

Borch, Christian (2019) *Social Avalanche*. Cambridge: Cambridge University Press.

Borsari, Andrea (2018) *Mimicry. Estetica del divenire animale*. Milano-Udine: Mimesis Edizioni.

Bourdieu, Pierre (1972) *Esquisse d'une théorie de la pratique*. Genève: Droz.

Bourdieu, Pierre (1989) Flaubert's Point of View. In Philippe Desan, Priscilla Parkhurst Ferguson and Wendy Griswold (Eds.) *Literature and Social Practice*. Chicago: The University of Chicago Press, 211–34.

Bourdieu, Pierre (2000) *Pascalian Meditations*. Cambridge: Polity.

Brighenti, Andrea Mubi (2008) Revolution and Diavolution. What is the Difference? *Critical Sociology* 34(6): 787–802.

Brighenti, Andrea Mubi (2010) Tarde, Canetti, and Deleuze on Crowds and Packs. *The Journal of Classical Sociology* 10(4): 291–314.

Brighenti, Andrea Mubi (2014) *The Ambiguous Multiplicities: Materials, Episteme and Politics of Some Cluttered Social Formations*. Basingstoke: Palgrave Macmillan.

Brighenti, Andrea Mubi (2015) Twilight of the Icons, or, How to Sociologize with Visibility. *Sociologica* 9(1): 1–17.

Brighenti, Andrea Mubi (2016) The Public and the Common: Some Approximations of Their Contemporary Articulation. *Critical Inquiry* 42(2): 306–28.

Brighenti, Andrea Mubi (2018) The Social Life of Measures: Conceptualizing Measure–Value Environments. *Theory, Culture & Society* 35(1): 23–44.

Brighenti, Andrea Mubi (2020) *Teoria sociale*. Milano: Meltemi.

Brighenti, Andrea Mubi and Mattias Kärrholm (2020) *Animated Lands. Studies in Territoriology*. Lincoln: University of Nebraska Press.

Brody, Hugh (1998) *Maps and Dreams: Indians and the British Columbia Frontier*. Prospect Heights: Waveland Press.

Brossat, Alain (2006) *La résistance infinie*. Paris: Lignes.

Bruner, Jerome S. (1973) *Beyond the Information Given. Studies in the Psychology of Knowing*. New York: W. W. Norton & Co.

Burawoy, Michael (Ed.) (1991) *Ethnography Unbound. Power and Resistance in the Modern Metropolis*. Berkeley: University of California Press.

Caillois, Roger (1938) *Le mythe et l'homme*. Paris: Gallimard.

Caillois, Roger (2008[1960]) Méduse et C.ie. In Id. *Œuvres* Paris: Gallimard, 479–558.

Campbell, Howard and Josiah Heyman (2007) Slantwise. Beyond Domination and Resistance on the Border. *Journal of Contemporary Ethnography* 36(1): 3–30.

Camus, Albert (2013) *Carnets*. 3 Vols. Paris: Gallimard.

Camus, Albert (1951) *L'homme révolté*. In Id. *Œuvres*. Paris: Gallimard, 2013, 845–1080.

Canguilhem, Georges (2008[1951]) *Knowledge of Life*. New York: Fordham University Press.

Caspar, Emilie A., Ioumpa Kalliopi, Christian Keysers, Valeria Gazzola (2020) Obeying Orders Reduces Vicarious Brain Activation towards Victims' Pain. *NeuroImage* 222(15) November 2020, 117251.

Castiglioni, Luigi and Scevola Mariotti (1966) *IL - Vocabolario della lingua latina*. Torino: Loescher.

Castoriadis, Cornelius (1975) *L'institution imaginaire de la société*. Paris: Seuil.

Castoriadis, Cornelius (1995) *Political and Social Writings*. Volume 3. Minneapolis, MN: University of Minnesota Press.

Centonze, Diego, Alberto Siracusano, Paolo Calabresi and Giorgio Bernardi (2004) The Project for a Scientific Psychology (1895): A Freudian Anticipation of LTP-Memory Connection Theory. *Brain Research Reviews* 46: 310–14.

Chambers, Peter (2019) *Border Security: Shores of Politics, Horizons of Justice*. London: Routledge.

Chatwin, Bruce (1989) *What am I Doing Here?*. Picador: London.

Childe, V. Gordon (1951[1936]) *Man Makes Himself*. New York: New American Library.

Cioran, Emil M. (1960) *Histoire et utopie*. In *Œuvres*. Paris: Gallimard, 1995.

Cioran, Emil M. (1964) *La chute dans le temps*. In *Œuvres*. Paris: Gallimard, 1995.

Clastres, Pierre (1974) *La Société contre l'état*. Paris: Minuit.

Cox, Harvey (2016) *The Market as God*. Harvard: Harvard UP.

Critchley, Simon (2007) *Infinitely Demanding. Ethics of Commitment, Politics of Resistance*. London: Verso.

Da Col, Giovanni (2012) The Poisoner and the Parasite: Cosmoeconomics, Fear, and Hospitality among Dechen Tibetans. *Journal of the Royal Anthropological Institute N.S* 18: S175–95.

Darby, David (Ed.) (2000) *Critical Essays on Elias Canetti*. New York: G. K. Hall.

Deleuze, Gilles (1956) La conception de la différence chez Bergson. In Id. *L'île déserte. Textes et entretiens 1953–1974*. Paris: Minuit, 2002, 43–72.

Deleuze, Gilles (1968) *Spinoza et le problème de l'expression*. Paris: Minuit.

Deleuze, Gilles (1969) *Logique du sens*. Paris: Minuit.

Deleuze, Gilles (1981) *Spinoza. Philosophie pratique*. Paris: Minuit.

Deleuze, Gilles and Félix Guattari (1975) *Kafka. Pour une littérature mineure*. Paris: Minuit.

Deleuze, Gilles and Félix Guattari (1980) *Mille plateaux*. Paris: Minuit.

Deligny, Fernand (2007) *Œuvres*. Paris: L'Arachnéen.

Deligny, Fernand (2008) *L'Arachnéen et autres textes*. Paris: L'Arachnéen.

Deligny, Fernand (2013) *Cartes et lignes d'erre : Traces du réseau de Fernand Deligny, 1969–1979*. Paris: L'Arachnéen.

Deleuze, Gilles (1987) Qu'est-ce que l'acte de création? In Id. *Deux régimes de fous. Textes et entretiens 1976–1995*. Paris: Minuit, 2003.

Derrida, Jacques (1967) *De la grammatologie*. Paris: Minuit.

Derrida, Jacques (1972) *Dissemination*. Chicago: The University of Chicago Press.

Descola, Philippe (2005) *Par-delà nature et culture*. Paris: Gallimard.

de Waal, Frans (2019) *Mama's Last Hug*. New York: W. W. Norton.

Donahue, William Collins (2001) *The End of Modernism: Elias Canetti's 'Auto-da-Fe'*. Chapel Hill, NC: The University of North Carolina Press.

Donahue, William Collins (2007a) Canetti's many (after-)lives. In W. C. Donahue and J. Preece (Eds.) *The Worlds of Elias Canetti : Centenary Essays*. Cambridge: Cambridge Scholars Publishing, xi–xxvii.

Donahue, William Collins (2007b) Canetti on Safari: The Self-reflexive Moment of *Die Stimmen von Marrakesch*. In W. C. Donahue and J. Preece (Eds.) *The Worlds of Elias Canetti : Centenary Essays*. Cambridge: Cambridge Scholars Publishing, 47–62.

Douglas, Mary (1986) *How Institutions Think*. Syracuse: Syracuse University Press.

Drucker, Peter F. (1993[1954]) *The Practice of Management*. New York: HarperCollins.

Drucker, Peter F. (1999) *Managing Oneself*. Harvard: Harvard Business School.

Durkheim, Émile (1893) *De la division du travail social*. Paris: Alcan.

Durkheim, Émile (1912) *Les formes élémentaires de la vie religieuse*. Paris: Alcan.

Eco, Umberto (1993) *La ricerca della lingua perfetta*. Laterza: Roma-Bari.

Elbaz, Robert (2003) On Canetti's Social Theory. *Neohelicon* 30(2): 133–44.

Elias, Norbert (2000[1968]) *The Civilizing Process. Sociogenetic and Psychogenetic Investigations*. Oxford: Blackwell.

Esposito, Roberto (2010[1998]) *Communitas. The Origin and Destiny of Community*. Stanford: Stanford University Press.

Esposito, Roberto (2018) *Termini della politica, Vol.1*. Milano: Mimesis.

Evans-Pritchard, Edward E. (1940) *The Nuer: A Description of the Modes of Livelihood and Political Institutions of a Nilotic People*. Oxford: Oxford University Press.

Evans-Pritchard, Edward E. (2004[1951]) *Social Anthropology*. Abingdon: Routledge.

Fanon, Frantz (1961) *Les damnés de la terre*. Paris: La Découverte, 2002.

Farneti, Roberto (2006) A Natural History of Crowds, Rulers and Survivors: Elias Canetti as a Political Thinker. *History of Political Thought* 27(4): 711–35.

Feynman, R. (1985) *QED: The Strange Theory of Light and Matter*. Princeton, NJ: Princeton University Press.

Földényi, László F. (2020) *Dostoyevsky Reads Hegel in Siberia and Bursts into Tears*. New Haven, CT: Yale University Press.

Forrester, Jay W. (1971) *World Dynamics*. Cambridge, MA: Wright-Allen Press.

Foucault, Michel (1971) Nietzsche, la genealogie, l'histoire. In Id. *Dits et Ecrits 1954–1988*, Vol. 1. Paris: Gallimard, 2001, 136–56.

Foucault, Michel (1975) *Surveiller et punir. Naissance de la prison*. Paris: Gallimard.

Foucault, Michel (1976) *Histoire de la sexualité*, vol. 1. *La volonté de savoir*. Paris: Gallimard.

Foucault, Michel (1982) The Subject and Power. In Hubert L. Dreyfus and Paul Rabinow (Eds.) *Michel Foucault: Beyond Structuralism and Hermeneutics*. Brighton: Harvester Press, 208–26.

Foucault (1997[1975–6]) *'Il faut défendre la société'. Cours au Collège de France 1975–6*. Paris: Gallimard/Seuil/EHESS.

Foucault, Michel (1998[1976]) *The History of Sexuality, vol. 1. The Will to Knowledge*. London: Penguin.

Foucault, Michel (2004) *Sécurité, territoire, population. Cours au Collège de France, 1977–1978*. Paris: Gallimard/Seuil/EHESS.

Fuller, Lon L. (1964) *The Morality of Law*. New Haven: Yale University Press.

Frazer, James (2009[1890]) *The Golden Bough*. Oxford: Oxford University Press.

Freud, Sigmund (1895) *Entwurf Einer Psychologie*. Engl. Transl. in James Strachey (Ed.) *The Standard Edition of the Complete Psychological Works of Sigmund Freud*. London: The Hogarth Press, 1966, 283–397.

Giddens, Anthony (1991) *Modernity and Self-Identity. Self and Society in the Late Modern Age*. Cambridge: Polity.

Gilman, Sander (1995) *Franz Kafka: The Jewish Patient*. London: Routledge.

Glissant, Édouard (1997[1990]) *Poetics of Relation*. Ann Arbor: The University of Michigan Press.

Glissant, Édouard (1997) *Traité du Tout-Monde. Poétique IV*. Paris: Gallimard.

Graeber, David and David Wengrow (2021) *The Dawn of Everything. A New History of Humanity*. London: Penguin.

Gramsci, Antonio (1965[1926–37]) *Lettere dal carcere*. Torino: Einaudi.

Gramsci, Antonio (1975 [1929–35]) *Quaderni del carcere*. 4 Vols. Torino: Einaudi.

Greenpeace (2020) *Stemming the Tide 2020. The Reality of the Fukushima Radioactive Water Crisis*. Online at https://storage.googleapis.com/planet4-japan-stateless/2020/10/5768c541-the-reality-of-the-fukushima-radioactive-water-crisis_en_summary.pdf (accessed 20 October 2020).

Hall, Edward T. (1966) *The Hidden Dimension*. Garden City, NY: Doubleday.

Hall, Stuart and Tony Jefferson (Eds.) (2003[1975]) *Resistance through Rituals: Youth Subcultures in Post-War Britain*. London: Routledge.

Hanuschek, Sven (2005) *Elias Canetti: Eine Biographie*. Munich: Hanser.

Hardt, Michael, and Antonio Negri (2003) Globalization and Democracy. In Stanely Aronowitz and Heather Gautney (Eds.) *Implicating Empire: Globalization and Resistance in the 21st Century World Order*. New York: Basic Books, 109–22.

Hart, H.L.A. (2012[1961]) *The Concept of Law*. Oxford: Oxford University Press.

Hollander, Jocelyn A. and Rachel L. Einwohner (2004) Conceptualizing Resistance. *Sociological Forum* 19(4): 533–54.

Holt, Thomas C. (2011) *Children of Fire: A History of African Americans*. New York: Farrar, Straus and Giroux.

Honneth, Axel (1996) The Perpetuation of the State of Nature: On the Cognitive Content of Elias Canetti's 'Crowds and Power'. *Thesis Eleven* 45: 69–85.

Illich, Ivan (1973) *Tools for Conviviality*. New York: Harpers & Row.

Janet, Pierre (2005 [1929]) *L'évolution psychologique de la personnalité*. Paris: L'Harmattan.

Jappe, Anselm (2017) *La société autophage. Capitalisme, démesure et autodestruction*. Paris: la Découverte.

Jokubauskaite, Giedre (2020) Resistance. In Koen De Feyter, Gamze E. Türkelli, and Stéphanie de Moerloose (Eds.) *Encyclopedia of Law and Development*. Cheltenham: Edward Elgar, 246–8.

Kafka, Franz (2021) *Dessins de Kafka*. Paris: Les Cahiers Dessinés.

Kelsen, Hans (1934) *Reine Rechtslehre*. Tübingen: Mohr Siebeck, 2008.

Kristeva, Julia (1980) *Pouvoirs de l'horreur. Essai sur l'abjection*. Paris: Seuil.

Krtolica, Igor (2010) La «tentative» des Cévennes. Deligny et la question de l'institution. *Chimères* 72: 73–97.

Latour, Bruno (2018) *Down to Earth: Politics in the New Climatic Regime*. England: Polity Press.

Latour, Bruno (2021) *Où suis-je? Leçons du confinement à l'usage des terrestres*. Paris: La Découverte.

Lea, Richard (2018) The Forensic Pathologist Who Got PTSD: 'Cutting up 23,000 dead bodies is not normal'. *The Guardian*, 26 September. Online: https://www.theguardian.com/science/2018/sep/26/forensic-pathologist-richard-shepherd-ptsd-cutting-up-23000-bodies-not-normal (accessed 25 April 2022).

Leroi-Gourhan, André (1965) *Le Geste et la Parole*. 2 vols. Paris: Albin Michel.

Levi, Primo (1986) *I sommersi e i salvati*. Torino: Einaudi.

Lévy-Bruhl, Lucien (1949[1938]) *Carnets*. Puf: Paris.

Lévi-Strauss, Claude (1949) Introduction à l'oeuvre de Marcel Mauss. In Marcel Mauss, (Ed.) *Sociologie et anthropologie (1902–1938)*. Paris: Les Presses universitaires de France, 1968, ix–lii.

Lévi-Strauss, Claude (1952) *Race and History*. Paris: Unesco.

Lévi-Strauss, Claude (1962) *La Pensée sauvage*. Paris: Plon.

Lévi-Strauss, Claude (2016[2013]) *We Are All Cannibals, and Other Essays*. New York: Columbia University Press.

Lianos, Michalis (2001) *Le nouveau contrôle social : toile institutionnelle, normative et lien social*. Paris: L'Harmattan.

Light, Andrew (2003) Globalization and the Need for an Urban Environmentalism. In Stanely Aronowitz and Heather Gautney (Eds.) *Implicating Empire: Globalization and Resistance in the 21st Century World Order*. New York: Basic Books, 287–308.

Lothane, Hnery Zvi (1998) Freud's 1895 Project: From Mind to Brain and Back Again. *Annals of New York Academy of Sciences* 843: 43–65.

Luhmann, Niklas (1990) *Essays on Self-Reference*. New York: Columbia University Press.

Macdonald, Roderick A. (2002) *Lessons of Everyday Law*. Montreal and Kingston: McGill-Queen's University Press.

Macdonald, Roderick A. (2005) Orchestrating Legal Multilingualism: 12 Études. In J.-C. Gémar and N. Kasirer (Eds.) *Jurilinguistique: Entre Langues et Droits*. Montreal: Thémis, 377.

Malinowski, Bronislaw (1961[1922]) *Argonauts of the Western Pacific*. London: Routledge.

Marx, Karl (1976[1867]) *Capital*. Vol. 1. London: Penguin.

Mauss, Marcel (1902–03) Esquisse d'une théorie générale de la magie. In Id. *Sociologie et Anthropologie*. Paris: Puf, 1968, 3–142.

Mauss, Marcel (1923–1924) Essai sur le don. Forme et raison de l'échange dans les sociétés archaïques. In Id. *Sociologie et Anthropologie*. Paris: Puf, 1968, 145–279.

Mauss, Marcel (1934) Les techniques du corps. In Id. *Sociologie et Anthropologie*. Paris: Puf, 1968, 365–88.

Mack, Michael (2001) *Anthropology as Memory. Elias Canetti's and Franz Baermann Steiner's Responses to the Shoah*. Tübingen: Max Niemeyer Verlag.

Mauss, Marcel (1950[1902–1938]) *Sociologie et anthropologie*. Paris: Les Presses universitaires de France.

McClelland, John S. (1989) *The Crowd and the Mob. From Plato to Canetti*. London: Unwin Hyman.

McCullough, Malcolm (2022) Urban Information Environmentalism. In Andrea Mubi Brighenti (Ed.) *The New Politics of Visibility. Spaces, Actors, Practices and Technologies in The Visible*. Bristol: Intellect, 57–71.

McKenzie, Jon (2001) *Perform or Else: From Discipline to Performance*. New York: Routledge.

Milgram, Stanley (1974) *Obedience to Authority. An Experimental View*. New York, NY: Harper and Row.

Milgram, Stanley (2010) *The Individual in a Social World. Essays and Experiments*. London: Pinter & Martin.

Minkowski, E. (1970[1933]) *Lived Time. Phenomenological and Psychopathological Studies*. Evanston: Northwestern University Press.

Minsky, Hyman P. (2016[1982]) *Can 'It' Happen Again? Essays on Instability and Finance*. New York: Routledge.

Moore, Barrington Jr. (1978) *Injustice: The Social Bases of Obedience and Revolt*. White Plains: Sharpe.

Moscovici, Serge (1985) *L'age des foules. Un traité historique de psychologie des masses*. Bruxelles: Complexe.

Murdoch, Iris (1962) Mass, Might and Myth. In David Darby (Ed.) *Critical Essays on Elias Canetti*. New York: G. K. Hall, 2000, 154–7.

Nancy, Jean-Luc (1990[1983]) *La communauté désœuvrée*. Paris: Christian Bourgois.

Nancy, Jean-Luc (2014) *La Communauté désavouée*. Paris: Galilée.

Nietzsche, Friedrich W. (1994[1887]) *On the Genealogy of Morality*. Cambridge: Cambridge University Press.

Nietzsche, Friedrich W. (2001[1886]) *The Gay Science*. Cambridge: Cambridge University Press.

Odum, Eugene P. (1972) The Strategy of Ecosystem Development. In G. Bell and J. Tyrwhitt (Eds.) *Human Identity in the Urban Environment*. London: Penguin, 49–58.

Ortner, Sherry B. (1995) Resistance and the Problem of Ethnographic Refusal. *Comparative Studies in Society and History* 37(1): 173–93.

Ostrom, Elinor (1990) *Governing the Commons: The Evolution of Institutions for Collective Action*. Cambridge: Cambridge University Press.

Peirce, Charles S. (1931–58[1857–66]) *The Collected Papers of Charles Sanders Peirce*. 8 Vols. Cambridge, MA: Harvard University Press.

Perec, Georges (1974) *Espèces d'espaces*. Paris: Galilée.

Pichot, André (2000) *La société pure. De Darwin à Hitler*. Paris: Flammarion.

Portmann, Adolf (1990) *Essays in Philosophical Zoology. The Living Form and the Seeing Eye*. Lewiston: Edwin Mellen Press.

Preece, Julian (2007) *The Rediscovered Writings of Veza Canetti. Out of the Shadows of a Husband*. Rochester, NY: Camden House.

Preece, Julian (2021) Ungedruckte Erinnerungen an Elias und Veza Canetti. *Zeitschrift für Germanistik* 31(3): 551–8.

Rancière, Jacques (1995) *La Mésentente: politique et philosophie*. Paris: Galilée.

Rawls, Anne Warfield and Waverly Duck (2020) *Tacit Racism*. Chicago: University of Chicago Press.

Ritter, Paul (1964) *Planning for Man and Motor*. Oxford: Pergamon.

Robertson, Ritchie (2000) Canetti as Anthropologist. In David Darby (Ed.) *Critical Essays on Elias Canetti*. New York: G. K. Hall, 158–70.

Rosen, Robert (2000) *Life Itself*. New York: Columbia University Press.

Rothstein, Edward Benjamin (1990) Dreams of Disappearance. The Secret Life of Elias Canetti. *The New Republic* 202, Jan. 8 and Jan. 15: 33–9.

Rutigliano, Enzo (2007) *Il linguaggio delle masse. Sulla sociologia di Elias Canetti*. Bari: Dedalo.

Sahlins, Marshall (1972) *Stone Age Economics*. London: Routledge.

Santos, Boa de Sousa (1995) *Toward a New Common Sense*. New York: Routledge.

Schmitt, Carl (1985[1922]) *Political Theology. Four Chapters on the Concept of Sovereignty*. Cambridge, MA: The MIT Press.

Schreber, Daniel Paul (2000[1903]) *Memoirs of My Nervous Illness*. New York: New York Review Books Classics.

Schrödinger, Erwin (1944) *What Is Life? The Physical Aspect of the Living Cell*. Cambridge: Cambridge University Press.

Scott, James C. (1985) *Weapons of the Weak. Everyday Forms of Peasant Resistance*. New Haven, CT: Yale University Press.

Scott, James C. (1990) *Domination and the Arts of Resistance: Hidden Transcripts*. New Haven, CT: Yale University Press.

Scott, James C. (2009) *The Art of Not Being Governed. An Anarchist History of Upland Southeast Asia*. New Haven, CT: Yale University Press.

Scott, James C. (2017) *Against the Grain: A Deep History of the Earliest States*. New Haven, CT: Yale University Press.

Semon, Richard (1921) *The Mneme*. London: George Allen & Unwin.

Serres, Michel (1980) *Le parasite*. Paris: Grasset.

Simmel, Georg (1995[(1904)]) 'Kant und der Individualismus.' In Id., *Gesamtausgabe Band 7*. Frankfurt am Main: Suhrkamp, 273–82.

Simmel, Georg (2004[1900]) *Philosophie des Geldes*. Engl. Ed. *The Philosophy of Money*. London: Routledge.

Simmel, Georg (2009[1908]) *Sociology. Inquiries into the Construction of Social Forms*. Leiden: Brill.

Simmel, Georg (2010[1918]) *Lebensanschauung*. Engl. Ed. *The View of Life*. Chicago: University of Chicago Press.

Simondon, Gilbert (2013[1964–89]) *L'individuation, à la lumière des notions de formes et d'information*. Paris: Millon.

Sheller, Mimi and John Urry (2000) The City and the Car. *International Journal of Urban and Regional Research* 24(4): 737–57.

Shepherd, Richard (2018) *Unnatural Causes*. London: Penguin.

Sloterdijk, Peter (2000) *Die Verachtung der Massen. Versuch über Kulturkämpfe in der modernen Gesellschaft*. Suhrkamp: Frankfurt am Main.

Sloterdijk, Peter (2013) *In the World Interior of Capital: Towards a Philosophical Theory of Globalization*. Cambridge: Polity.

Sloterdijk, Peter (2016[2004]) *Foams. Spheres, Vol.3: Plural Spherology*. Los Angeles: Semiotext(e).

Smith, David (2002) Freud's Neural Unconscious. In Gertrudis Van de Vijver and Filip Geerardyn (Eds.) *The Pre-Psychoanalytic Writings of Sigmund Freud*. London: Karnak books, 155–64.

Sontag, Susan (1981) *Under the Sign of Saturn*. London: Viking.

Specter, Michael (2012) Germs Are Us. *The New Yorker*, 22 October. Online at: https://www.newyorker.com/magazine/2012/10/22/germs-are-us (Accessed 1 December 2021).

Spencer, Walter Baldwin and Francis James Gillen (1899) *The Native Tribes of Central Australia*. London: Macmillan and Co.

Supiot, Alain (2015) *La Gouvernance par les nombres. Cours au Collège de France (2012–2014)*. Paris: Fayard.

Tarde, Gabriel (1890) *Les lois de l'imitation*. Paris: Alcan.

Tarde, Gabriel (1893a) *Monadologie et sociologie*. In Id. (1895) *Essais et mélanges sociologiques*. Lyon: A. Storck & Paris : G. Masson, 309–89.

Tarde, Gabriel (1893b) *La logique sociale*. Paris: Alcan.

Tarde, Gabriel (1898) *Les lois sociales*. Paris: Alcan.

Tarde, Gabriel (1902) *Psychologie économique*. Paris: Alcan.

Thom, René (1975[1972]) *Structural Stability and Morphogenesis*. Reading, MA: WA Benjamin.

Turner, Victor W. (1977[1969]) *The Ritual Process. Structure and Anti-Structure*. Ithaca, NY: Cornell University Press.

Virilio, Paul (1977) *Vitesse et Politique : essai de dromologie*. Paris: Galilée.

Virilio, Paul (1995) *La vitesse de libération*. Paris: Galilée.

Waddington, Conrad (1972) Biology and Human Environment. In G. Bell and J. Tyrwhitt (Eds.) *Human Identity in the Urban Environment*. London: Penguin, 59–72.

Wagner, Peter (2006) Social Theory and Political Philosophy. In Gerard Delanty (Ed.) *The Routledge Handbook of Contemporary European Social Theory*. London: Routledge, 37–47.

Weber, Antje (2017) Der Widersprüchliche. *Süddeutsche Zeitung*, 1 August. Online: https://www.sueddeutsche.de/kultur/literatur-der-widerspruechliche-1.3612024 (accessed 25 April 2022).

Weber, Max (2019[1922]) *Economy and Society. A New Translation*. Edited and translated by Keith Tribe. Cambridge, MA: Harvard University Press.

Werlen, Hansjakob (2000) Destiny's Herald: Elias Canetti's Crowds and Power and Its Continuing Influence. In David Darby (Ed.) *Critical Essays on Elias Canetti*. New York: GK Hall & Co, 171–88.

Whitehead, Alfred North (1978[1929]) *Process and Reality*. New York: The Free Press.

Wilson, Peter J. (1988) *The Domestication of the Human Species*. New Haven: Yale University Press.

Wilson, William Julius (1987) *The Truly Disadvantaged: The Inner City, the Underclass, and Public Policy*. Chicago: The University of Chicago Press.

Wright, Erik Olin (2010) *Envisioning Real Utopias*. London: Verso.

Wright, Erik Olin (2019) *How to Be an Anticapitalist in the Twenty-First Century*. London: Verso.

Zuckerman, Solly (1932) *The Social Life of Monkeys and Apes*. London: Kegan Paul.

INDEX

www.ingramcontent.com/pod-product-compliance
Lightning Source LLC
Chambersburg PA
CBHW050438280326
41932CB00013BA/2164